Understanding Socialism

Understanding Socialism

Vanessa Turner

MURPHY & MOORE
www.murphy-moorepublishing.com

Understanding Socialism
Vanessa Turner
ISBN: 978-1-63987-558-0 (Hardback)

MURPHY & MOORE
Published by Murphy & Moore Publishing,
1 Rockefeller Plaza,
New York City, NY 10020, USA

Cataloging-in-Publication Data

Understanding socialism / Vanessa Turner.
p. cm.
Includes bibliographical references and index.
ISBN 978-1-63987-558-0
1. Socialism. 2. Communism. 3. Political science. I. Turner, Vanessa.
HX73 .U53 2022
320.531--dc23

For more information regarding Murphy & Moore Publishing and its products, please visit the publisher's website www.murphy-moorepublishing.com

TABLE OF CONTENTS

PREFACE

This book aims to help a broader range of students by exploring a wide variety of significant topics related to this discipline. It will help students in achieving a higher level of understanding of the subject and excel in their respective fields. This book would not have been possible without the unwavered support of my senior professors who took out the time to provide me feedback and help me with the process. I would also like to thank my family for their patience and support.

The social, political and economic philosophy that includes a wide range of economic and social systems which are characterized by public ownership is known as socialism. It refers to the social ownership of property and natural resources. This social ownership can be categorized as public, equity, cooperative and collective. The discipline deals with a wide range of theoretical and socioeconomic systems. These systems are of two types-market and non-market socialism. Market socialism uses monetary prices in relation to the operations of socially owned enterprises and for allocation of capital goods. Non-market socialism involves changing factor markets with technical and engineering criteria thereby producing a different mechanism from that of capitalism. This book presents the complex subject of socialism in the most comprehensible and easy to understand language. It also elucidates the concepts and innovative models around prospective developments with respect to this field. In this book, constant effort has been made to make the understanding of the difficult concepts of this discipline as easy and informative as possible, for the readers.

A brief overview of the book contents is provided below:

Chapter - What is Socialism?

Socialism refers to a political and economic theory of social organization that focuses on the means of production, distribution, and exchange to be regulated by the community. Social ownership includes public, collective, citizen and cooperative ownership of equity. This chapter has been carefully written to provide an easy understanding of socialism.

Chapter - Types of Socialism

Socialism is branched into various types such as religious socialism, revolutionary socialism, state socialism, eco-socialism, neosocialism, yellow socialism, etc. This chapter closely examines the different types of socialism to provide an extensive understanding of the subject.

Chapter - Theories of Socialism

There are many theories that are studied under the domain of socialism. Some of them are Marx's concept of socialism, Marxism-Leninism, mutualism, scientific socialism theory, etc. The topics elaborated in this chapter will help in gaining a better perspective of these theories studied under socialism.

Chapter - Diverse Aspects of Socialism

Anarchism, reformism, blanquism, socialist state, social dividend, social ownership, socialist economics, Lange model, socialist law and realism, etc. are a few of the aspects within socialism. This chapter sheds light on these diverse aspects of socialism for a thorough understanding of the subject.

Chapter - Socialist Calculation

The debate of socialist calculation revolves around the question of how the socialist economy would evaluate economic calculation in the absence of values, money, financial assets and private ownership. A few of the elements within it are decentralized planning, labor-time calculation, participatory economics, etc. All the concepts related to socialist calculation have been carefully analyzed in this chapter.

Vanessa Turner

What is Socialism? 1

- **Principles of Socialism**
- **Institutional Models of Socialism**

Socialism refers to a political and economic theory of social organization that focuses on the means of production, distribution, and exchange to be regulated by the community. Social ownership includes public, collective, citizen and cooperative ownership of equity. This chapter has been carefully written to provide an easy understanding of socialism.

Socialism is a rich tradition of political thought and practice, the history of which contains a vast number of views and theories, often differing in many of their conceptual, empirical, and normative commitments. In his 1924 *Dictionary of Socialism*, Angelo Rappoport canvassed no fewer than forty definitions of socialism, telling his readers in the book's preface that "there are many mansions in the House of Socialism". To take even a relatively restricted subset of socialist thought, Leszek Kołakowski could fill over 1,300 pages in his magisterial survey of Main Currents of Marxism. Both socialism and capitalism grant workers legal control of their labor power, but socialism, unlike capitalism, requires that the bulk of the means of production workers use to yield goods and services be under the effective control of workers themselves, rather than in the hands of the members of a different, capitalist class under whose direction they must toil. As we will explain below, this contrast has been articulated further in different ways, and socialists have not only made distinctive claims regarding economic organization but also regarding the processes of transformation fulfilling them and the principles and ideals orienting their justification.

Socialism and Capitalism

Socialism is best defined in contrast with capitalism, as socialism has arisen both as a critical challenge to capitalism, and as a proposal for overcoming and replacing it. In the classical, Marxist definition, capitalism involves certain *relations of production*. These comprise certain forms of control over the *productive forces*—the *labor power* that workers deploy in production and the *means of production* such as natural resources, tools, and spaces they employ to yield goods and services—and certain social patterns of economic interaction that typically correlate with that control. Capitalism displays the following constitutive features:

- The bulk of the means of production is privately owned and controlled.
- People legally own their labor power. (Here capitalism differs from slavery and feudalism, under which systems some individuals are entitled to control, whether completely or partially, the labor power of others).
- Markets are the main mechanism allocating inputs and outputs of production and determining how societies' productive surplus is used, including whether and how it is consumed or invested.

An additional feature that is typically present is that:

- There is a class division between capitalists and workers, involving specific relations (e.g., whether of bargaining, conflict, or subordination) between those classes, and shaping the labor market, the firm, and the broader political process.

The existence of wage labor is often seen by socialists as a necessary condition for a society to be counted as capitalist. Typically, workers (unlike capitalists) must sell their labor power to make a living. They sell it to capitalists, who (unlike the workers) control the means of production. Capitalists typically subordinate workers in the production process, as capitalists have asymmetric decision-making power over what gets produced and how it gets produced. Capitalists also own the output of production and sell it in the market, and they control the predominant bulk of the flow of investment within the economy. The relation between capitalists and workers can involve cooperation, but also relations of conflict (e.g., regarding wages and working conditions). This more-or-less antagonistic power relationship between capitalists and workers plays out in a number of areas, within production itself, and in the broader political process, as in both the economic and political domains decisions are made about who does what, and who gets what.

Examples here are a society of independent commodity producers or a property-owning democracy (in which individuals or groups of workers own firms). There is debate, however, as to how feasible—accessible and stable—these are in a modern economic environment.

Another feature that is also typically seen as arising is this:

- Production is primarily oriented to *capital accumulation* (i.e., economic production is primarily oriented to profit rather than to the satisfaction of human needs).

In contrast to capitalism, socialism can be defined as a type of society in which, at a minimum, is turned into:

- The bulk of the means of production is under social, democratic control.

Changes with regard to features are hotly debated amongst socialists. Regarding socialists retain the view that workers should control their labor power, but many do not affirm the kind of absolute, libertarian property rights in labor power that would, e.g., prevent taxation or other forms of mandatory contribution to cater for the basic needs of others. Regarding there is a recent burgeoning literature on "market socialism", where proposals are advanced to create an economy that is socialist but nevertheless features extensive markets. Finally, regarding although most socialists agree that, due to competitive pressures, capitalists are bound to seek profit maximization, some puzzle over whether when they do this, it is "greed and fear" and not the generation of resources to make others besides themselves better-off that is the dominant, more basic drive and hence the degree to which profit-maximization should be seen as a normatively troubling phenomenon. Furthermore, some socialists argue that the search for profits in a market socialist economy is not inherently suspicious. Most socialists, however, tend to find the profit motive problematic.

An important point about this definition of socialism is that socialism is not equivalent to, and is arguably in conflict with, statism. involves expansion of social power—power based on the capacity to mobilize voluntary cooperation and collective action—as distinct from state power—power based on the control of rule-making and rule enforcing over a territory—as well of economic power—power based on the control of material resources. If a state controls the economy but is not in turn democratically controlled by the individuals engaged in economic life, what we have is some form of statism, not socialism.

Three Dimensions of Socialist Views

When characterizing socialist views, it is useful to distinguish between three dimensions of a conception of a social justice. We identify these three dimensions as:

- (DI) the core ideals and principles animating that conception of justice.
- (DII) the social institutions and practices implementing the ideals specified at DI.
- (DIII) the processes of transformation leading agents and their society from where they are currently, to the social outcome specified in DII.

The characterization of capitalism and socialism focuses on the social institutions and practices constituting each form of society (i.e., on DII). The central normative commitments of socialism (DI) and to survey their deployment in the socialist critique of capitalism.

Socialist Critiques of Capitalism and their Grounds (Dimension DI)

Socialists have condemned capitalism by alleging that it typically features exploitation, domination, alienation, and inefficiency. Before surveying these criticisms, it is important to note that they rely on various ideals and principles at DI. We set aside the debate, conducted mostly during the 1980s and largely centered on the interpretation of Marx's writings, as to whether the condemnation of capitalism and the advocacy for socialism relies (or should rely), on moral grounds. Whereas some Marxist socialists take the view that criticism of capitalism can be conducted without making use—either explicitly or implicitly—of arguments with a moral foundation, our focus is on arguments that do rely on such grounds.

Socialist Principles

Socialists have deployed ideals and principles of equality, democracy, individual freedom, self-realization, and community or solidarity. Regarding *equality*, they have proposed strong versions of the principle of equality of opportunity according to which everyone should have "broadly equal access to the necessary material and social means to live flourishing lives". Some, but by no means all, socialists construe equality of opportunity in a luck-egalitarian way, as requiring the neutralization of inequalities of access to advantage that result from people's circumstances rather than their choices. Socialists also embrace the ideal of *democracy*, requiring that people have "broadly equal access to the necessary means to participate meaningfully in decisions" affecting their lives. Many socialists say that democratic participation should be available not only at the level of governmental institutions, but also in various economic arenas (such as within the firm). Third, socialists are committed to the importance of *individual freedom*. This commitment includes versions of the standard ideas of negative liberty and non-domination (requiring security from inappropriate interference by others). But it also typically includes a more demanding, positive form of self-determination, as the "real freedom" of being able to develop one's own projects and bring them to. An ideal of *self-realization* through autonomously chosen activities featuring people's development and exercise of their creative and productive capacities in cooperation with others sometimes informs socialists' positive views of freedom and equality—as in the view that there should be a requirement of access to the conditions of self-realization at work. Finally, and relatedly, socialists often affirm an idea of *community* or *solidarity*, according to which people should organize their economic life so that they treat the freedom and well-being of others as intrinsically significant. People should recognize positive duties to support other people, or, as Einstein put it, a "sense of responsibility for their fellow men".Or, as Cohen put it, people should "care about, and, where necessary and possible, care for, one another, and, too, care that they care about one another". Community is sometimes presented as a moral ideal which is not itself a demand of justice but can be used to temper problematic results permitted by some demands of justice (such as the inequalities of outcome permitted by a luck-egalitarian principle of equality of opportunity). However, community is sometimes presented within socialist views as a demand of justice itself. Some socialists also take solidarity as partly shaping a desirable form of "social freedom" in which people are able not only to advance their own good but also to act with and for others.

Given the diversity of fundamental principles to which socialists commonly appeal, it is perhaps unsurprising that few attempts have been made to link these principles under a unified framework. A suggested strategy has been to articulate some aspects of them as requirements flowing from what we might call the *Abilities / Needs Principle,* following Marx's famous dictum, in *The Critique of the Gotha Program*, that a communist society should be organized so as to realize the goals of producing and distributing "From each according to their abilities, to each according to their needs". This principle, presented with brevity and in the absence of much elaboration by Marx has been interpreted in different ways. One, descriptive interpretation simply takes it to be a prediction of how people will feel motivated to act in a socialist society. Another, straightforwardly normative interpretation construes the Marxian dictum as stating duties to contribute to, and claims to benefit from, the social product—addressing the allocation of both the burdens and benefits of social cooperation. Its fulfillment would, in an egalitarian and solidaristic fashion, empower people to live flourishing lives. The normative principle itself has also been interpreted as an articulation of the broader, and more basic, idea of human dignity. Aiming at solidaristic empowerment, this idea could be understood as requiring that we support people in the pursuit of a flourishing life by not blocking, and by enabling, the development and exercise of their valuable capacities, which are at the basis of their moral status as agents with dignity.

Socialist Charges against Capitalism

Exploitation

The first typical charge leveled by socialists is that capitalism features the exploitation of wage workers by their capitalist employers. Exploitation has been characterized in two ways. First, in the so-called "technical" Marxist characterization, workers are exploited by capitalists when the value embodied in the goods they can purchase with their wages is inferior to the value embodied in the goods they produce—with the capitalists appropriating the difference. To maximize the profit resulting from the sale of what the workers produce, capitalists have an incentive to keep wages low. This descriptive characterization, which focuses on the flow of surplus labor from workers to capitalists, differs from another common, normative characterization of exploitation, according to which exploitation involves taking unfair, wrongful, or unjust advantage of the productive efforts of others. An obvious question is when, if ever, incidents of exploitation in the technical sense involve exploitation in the normative sense. When is the transfer of surplus labor from workers to capitalists such that it involves wrongful advantage taking of the former by the latter? Socialists have provided at least four answers to this question.

The first answer is offered by the unequal exchange account, according to which A exploits B if and only if in their exchange A gets more than B does. This account effectively collapses the normative sense of exploitation into the technical one. But critics have argued that this account fails to provide sufficient conditions for exploitation in the normative sense. Not every unequal exchange is wrongful: it would not be wrong to transfer resources from workers to people who (perhaps through no choice or fault of their own) are unable to work.

A second proposal is to say that A exploits B if and only if A gets surplus labor from B in a way that is coerced or forced. This labor entitlement account relies on the view that workers are entitled to the product of their labor, and that capitalists wrongly deprive them of it. In a capitalist economy, workers are compelled to transfer surplus labor to capitalists on pain of severe poverty. This is a result of the coercively enforced system of private property rights in the means of production. Since they do not control means of production to secure their own subsistence, workers have no reasonable alternative to selling their labor power to capitalists and to toil on the terms favored by the latter. Critics of this approach have argued that it, like the previous account, fails to provide sufficient conditions for wrongful exploitation because it would (counterintuitively) have to condemn transfers from workers to destitute people unable to work. Furthermore, it has been argued that the account fails to provide necessary conditions for the occurrence of exploitation. Problematic transfers of surplus labor can occur without coercion. For example, A may have sophisticated means of production, not obtained from others through coercion, and hire B to work on them at a perhaps unfairly low wage, which B voluntarily accepts despite having acceptable, although less advantageous, alternatives.

The third, unfair distribution of productive endowments account suggests that the core problem with capitalist exploitation (and with other forms of exploitation in class-divided social systems) is that it proceeds against a background distribution of initial access to productive assets that is inegalitarian. A is an exploiter, and B is exploited, if and only if A gains from B's labor and A would be worse off, and B better off, in an alternative hypothetical economic environment in which the initial distribution of assets was equal (with everything else remaining constant). This account relies on a luck-egalitarian principle of equality of opportunity. (According to luck-egalitarianism, no one should be made worse-off than others due to circumstances beyond their control.) Critics have argued that, because of that, it fails to provide necessary conditions for wrongful exploitation. If A finds B stuck in a pit, it would be wrong for A to offer B rescue only if B signs a sweatshop contract with A—even if B happened to have fallen into the pit after voluntarily taking the risk to go hiking in an area well known to be dotted with such perilous obstacles. Other critics worry that this account neglects the centrality of relations of power or dominance between exploiters and exploited.

A fourth approach directly focuses on the fact that exploitation typically arises when there is a significant power asymmetry between the parties involved. The more powerful instrumentalize and take advantage of the vulnerability of the less powerful to benefit from this asymmetry in positions. A specific version of this view, the domination for self-enrichment account, says that A exploits B if A benefits from a transaction in which *A* dominates *B*. (On this account, domination involves a disrespectful use of *A*'s power over *B*.) Capitalist property rights, with the resulting unequal access to the means of production, put propertyless workers at the mercy of capitalists, who use their superior power over them to extract surplus labor. A worry about this approach is that it does not explain when the more powerful party is taking too much from the less powerful party. For example, take a situation where *A* and *B* start with equal assets, but *A* chooses to work hard while *B* chooses to spend more time at leisure, so that at a later time *A* controls the means of production, while *B* has only their own labor power. We imagine that *A* offers *B* employment, and then ask, in light of their *ex ante* equal position, at what level of wage for *B* and profit for *A* would the transaction involve wrongful exploitation? To come to a settled view on this question, it might be necessary to combine reliance on a principle of freedom as non-domination with appeal to additional socialist principles addressing just distribution.

Interference and Domination

Capitalism is often defended by saying that it maximally extends people's freedom, understood as the absence of interference. Socialism would allegedly depress that freedom by prohibiting or limiting capitalist activities such as setting up a private firm, hiring wage workers, and keeping, investing, or spending profits. Socialists generally acknowledge that a socialist economy would severely constrain some such freedoms. But they point out that capitalist property rights also involve interference. They remind us that "private property by one person presupposes non-ownership on the part of other persons" and warn that often, although liberals and libertarians see the freedom which is intrinsic to capitalism, they overlook the unfreedom which necessarily accompanies capitalist freedom.

Workers could and would be coercively interfered with if they tried to use means of production possessed by capitalists, to walk away with the products of their labor in capitalist firms, or to access consumption goods they do not have enough money to buy. In fact, every economic system opens some zones of non-interference while closing others. Hence the appropriate question is not whether capitalism or socialism involve interference—they both do—but whether either of them involves more net interference, or more troubling forms of interference, than the other. And the answer to that question is far from obvious. It could very well be that most agents in a socialist society face less (troublesome) interference as they pursue their projects of production and consumption than agents in a capitalist society.

Capitalist economic relations are often defended by saying that they are the result of free choices by consenting adults. Wage workers are not slaves or serfs—they have the legal right to refuse to work for capitalists. But socialists reply that the relationship between capitalists and workers actually involves domination. Workers are inappropriately subject to the will of capitalists in the shaping of the terms on which they work (both in the spheres of exchange and production, and within the broader political process). Workers' consent to their exploitation is given in circumstances of deep vulnerability and asymmetry of power. According to Marx, two conditions help explain workers' apparently free choice to enter into a nevertheless exploitative contract: (1) in capitalism (unlike in feudalism or slave societies) workers own their labor power, *but* (2) they do not own means of production. Because of their deprivation (2), workers have no reasonable alternative to using their entitlement (1) to sell their labor power to the capitalists—who do own the means of production. Through labor-saving technical innovations spurred by competition, capitalism also constantly produces unemployment, which weakens the bargaining power of individual workers further. Thus, Marx says that although workers voluntarily enter into exploitative contracts, they are "compelled to do so by social conditions".

> The silent compulsion of economic relations sets the seal on the domination of the capitalist over the worker. The worker's dependence on capital springs from the conditions of production themselves, and is guaranteed in perpetuity by them.

Because of the deep background inequality of power resulting from their structural position within a capitalist economy, workers accept a pattern of economic transaction in which they submit to the direction of capitalists during the activities of production, and surrender to those same capitalists a disproportional share of the fruits of their labor. Although some individual workers might be able to escape their vulnerable condition by saving and starting a firm of their own, most would find this extremely difficult, and they could not all do it simultaneously within capitalism.

Socialists sometimes say that capitalism flouts an ideal of non-domination as freedom from being subject to rules one has systematically less power to shape than others. Capitalist relations of production involve domination and the dependence of workers on the discretion of capitalists' choices at three critical junctures. The first concerns the labor contract. Due to their lack of control of the means of production, workers must largely submit, on pain of starvation or severe poverty, to the terms capitalists offer them. The second concerns interactions in the workplace. Capitalists and their managers rule the activities of workers by unilaterally deciding what and how the latter produce. Although in the sphere of circulation workers and capitalists might look (misleadingly, given the first point) like equally free contractors striking fair deals, once we enter the "hidden abode" of production it is clear to all sides that what exists is relationships of intense subjection of some to the will of others. Workers effectively spend many of their waking hours doing what others dictate them to do. Third, and finally, capitalists have a disproportionate impact on the legal and political process shaping the institutional structure of the society in which they exploit workers, with capitalist interests dominating the political processes which in turn set the contours of property and labor law. Even if workers manage to obtain the legal right to vote and create their own trade unions and parties (which labor movements achieved in some countries after much struggle), capitalists exert disproportionate influence via greater access to mass media, the funding of political parties, the threat of disinvestment and capital flight if governments reduce their profit margin, and the past and prospective recruitment of state officials in lucrative jobs in their firms and lobbying agencies. At the spheres of exchange, production, and in the broader political process, workers and capitalist have asymmetric structural power. Consequently, the former are significantly subject to the will of the latter in the shaping of the terms on which they work. This inequality of structural power, some socialists claim, is an affront to workers' dignity as self-determining, self-mastering agents.

The third point about domination mentioned above is also deployed by socialists to say that capitalism conflicts with democracy. Democracy requires that people have roughly equal power to affect the political process that structures their social life—or at least that inequalities do not reflect morally irrelevant features such as race, gender, and class. Socialists have made three points regarding the conflict between capitalism and democracy. The first concerns political democracy of the kind that is familiar today. Even in the presence of multi-party electoral systems, members of the capitalist class—despite being a minority of the population—have significantly more influence than members of the working class. Governments have a tendency to adapt their agendas to the wishes of capitalists because they depend on their investment decisions to raise the taxes to fund public policies, as well as for the variety of other reasons outlined above. Even if socialist parties win elections, as long as they do not change the fundamentals of the economic system, they must be congenial to the wishes of capitalists. Thus, socialists have argued that deep changes in the economic structure of society are needed to make electoral democracy fulfill its promise. Political power cannot be insulated from economic power. They also, secondly, think that such changes may be directly significant. Indeed, as radical democrats, socialists have argued that reducing inequality of decision-making power within the economic sphere itself is not only instrumentally significant (to reduce inequality within the governmental sphere), but also intrinsically significant to increase people's self-determination in their daily lives as economic agents. Therefore, most democratic socialists call for a solution to the problem of the conflict between democracy and capitalism by extending democratic principles into the economy. Exploring the parallel between the political and economic systems, socialists have argued that democratic principles should apply in the economic arena as they do in the political domain, as economic decisions, like political decisions, have dramatic consequences for the freedom and well-being of people. Returning to the issue of the relations between the two arenas, socialists have also argued that fostering workers' self-determination in the economy (notably in the workplace) enhances democratic participation at the political level.

Alienation

Socialists have included, in their affirmation of individual freedom, a specific concern with *real* or *effective* freedom to lead flourishing lives. This freedom is often linked with a positive ideal of *self-realization*, which in turn motivates a critique of capitalism as generating alienation. This perspective informs Marx's views on the strong contrast between productive activity under socialism and under capitalism. In socialism, the "realm of necessity" and the correspondingly necessary, but typically unsavory, labor required to secure basic subsistence would be reduced so that people also access a "realm of freedom" in which a desirable form of work involving creativity, cultivation of talents, and meaningful cooperation with others is available. This realm of freedom would unleash "the development of human energy which is an end in itself". This work, allowing for and facilitating individuals' self-realization, would enable the "all-round development of the individual", and would in fact become a "prime want". The socialist society would feature "the development of the rich individuality which is all-sided in its production as in its consumption"; it would constitute a "higher form of society in which the full and free development of every individual forms the ruling principle". By contrast, capitalism denies the majority of the population access to self-realization at work. Workers typically toil in tasks which are uninteresting and even stunting. They do not control how production unfolds or what is done with the outputs of production. And their relations with others is not one of fellowship, but rather of domination (under their bosses) and of competition (against their fellow workers). When alienated, labor is external to the worker, i.e., it does not belong to his essential being; in his work, therefore, he does not affirm himself but denies himself, does not feel content but unhappy, does not develop freely his physical and mental energy but mortifies his body and ruins his mind. It is therefore not the satisfaction of a need; it is merely a means to satisfy needs external to it.

Recent scholarship has developed these ideas further. Elster has provided the most detailed discussion and development of the Marxian ideal of self-realization. The idea is defined as "the full and free actualization and externalization of the powers and the abilities of the individual". Self-actualization involves a two-step process in which individuals develop their powers (e.g., learn the principles and techniques of civil engineering) and then actualize those powers (e.g., design and participate in the construction of a bridge). Self-externalization, in turn, features a process in which individuals' powers become visible to others with the potential beneficial outcome of social recognition and the accompanying boost in self-respect and self-esteem. However, Elster says that this Marxian ideal must be reformulated to make it more realistic. No one can develop all their powers fully, and no feasible economy would enable everyone always to get exactly their first-choice jobs and conduct them only in the ways they would most like. Furthermore, self-realization for and with others (and thus also the combination of self-realization with community) may not always work smoothly, as producers entangled in large and complex societies may not feel strongly moved by the needs of distant others, and significant forms of division of labor will likely persist. Still, Elster thinks the socialist ideal of self-realization remains worth pursuing, for example through the generation of opportunities to produce in worker cooperatives. Others have construed the demand for real options to produce in ways that involve self-realization and solidarity as significant for the implementation of the Abilities Needs Principle, and defended a right to opportunities for meaningful work against the charge that it violates a liberal constraint of neutrality about conceptions of the good.

Further scholarship explores recent changes in the organization of production. Boltanski and Chiapello argue that since the 1980s capitalism has partly absorbed (what they dub) the "artistic critique" against de-skilled and heteronomous work by generating schemes of economic activity in which workers operate in teams and have significant decision-making powers. However, these new forms of work, although common especially in certain knowledge-intensive sectors, are not available to all workers, and they still operate under the ultimate control of capital owners and their profit maximizing strategies. They also operate in tandem with the elimination of the social security policies typical of the (increasingly eroded) welfare state. Thus, the "artistic" strand in the socialist critique of capitalism as hampering people's authenticity, creativity, and autonomy has not been fully absorbed and should be renewed. It should also be combined with the other, "social critique" strand which challenges inequality, insecurity, and selfishness. Other authors find in these new forms of work the seeds of future forms of economic organization—arguing that they provide evidence that workers can plan and control sophisticated processes of production on their own and that capitalists and their managers are largely redundant.

The critique of alienation has also been recently developed further by Forst by exploring the relation between alienation and domination. On this account, the central problem with alienation is that it involves the denial of people's autonomy—their ability and right to shape their social life on terms they could justify to themselves and to each other as free and equal co-legislators.

Inefficiency

A traditional criticism of capitalism (especially amongst Marxists) is that it is inefficient. Capitalism is prone to cyclic crises in which wealth and human potential is destroyed and squandered. For example, to cut costs and maximize profits, firms choose work-saving technologies and lay off workers. But at the aggregate level, this erodes the demand for their products, which forces firms to cut costs further (by laying off even more workers or halting production). Socialism would, it has been argued, not be so prone to crises, as the rationale for production would not be profit maximization but need satisfaction. Although important, this line of criticism is less widespread amongst contemporary socialists. Historically, capitalism has proved quite resilient, resurrecting itself after crises and expanding its productivity dramatically over time. In might very well be that capitalism is the best feasible regime if the only standard of assessment were productivity.

Still, socialists point out that capitalism involves some significant inefficiencies. Examples are the underproduction of public goods (such as public transportation and education), the underpricing and overconsumption of natural resources (such as fossil fuels and fishing stocks), negative externalities (such as pollution), the costs of monitoring and enforcing market contracts and private property (given that the exploited may not be so keen to work as hard as their profit-maximizing bosses require, and that the marginalized may be moved by desperation to steal), and certain defects of intellectual property rights (such as blocking the diffusion of innovation, and alienating those who engage in creative activities because of their intrinsic appeal and because of the will to serve the public rather than maximize monetary reward). Really existing capitalist societies have introduced regulations to counter some of these problems, at least to some extent. Examples are taxes and constraints to limit economic activities with negative externalities, and public funding and subsidies to sustain activities with positive externalities which are not sufficiently supported by the market. But, socialists insist, such mechanisms are external to capitalism, as they limit property rights and the scope for profit maximization as the primary orientation in the organization of the economy. The regulations involve the hybridization of the economic system by introducing some non-capitalist, and even socialist elements.

There is also an important issue of whether efficiency should only be understood in terms of maximizing production of material consumption goods. If the metric, or the utility space, that is taken into account when engaging in maximization assessments includes more than these goods, then capitalism can also be criticized as inefficient on account of its tendency to depress the availability of leisure time (as well as to distribute it quite unequally). This carries limitation of people's access to the various goods that leisure enables—such as the cultivation of friendships, family, and community or political participation. Technological innovations create the opportunity to choose between retaining the previous level of production while using fewer inputs (such as labor time) or maintaining the level of inputs while producing more. John Maynard Keynes famously held that it would be reasonable to tend towards the prior option, and expected societies to take this path as the technological frontier advanced. Nevertheless, in large part because of the profit maximization motive, capitalism displays an inherent bias in favor of the second, arguably inferior, option. Capitalism thereby narrows the realistic options of its constituent economic agents—both firms and individuals. Firms would lose their competitive edge and risk bankruptcy if they did not pursue profits ahead of the broader interests of their workers (as their products would likely be more expensive). And it is typically hard for workers to find jobs that pay reasonable salaries for fewer hours of work. Socialists concerned with expanding leisure time—and also with environmental risks—find this bias quite alarming. If a conflict between further increase in the production of material objects for consumption and the expansion of leisure time (and environmental protection) is unavoidable, then it is not clear, all things considered, that the former should be prioritized, especially when an economy has already reached a high level of material productivity.

Liberal Egalitarianism and Inequality in Capitalism

Capitalism has also been challenged on liberal egalitarian grounds, and in ways that lend themselves to support for socialism.While many of John Rawls's readers long took him to be a proponent of an egalitarian form of a capitalist welfare state, or as one might put it "a slightly imaginary Sweden", in fact Rawls rejected such institutional arrangements as inadequate to the task of realizing principles of political liberty or equality of opportunity, or of keeping material inequalities within sufficiently tight bounds. His own avowed view of the institutions that would be needed to realize liberal egalitarian principles of justice was officially neutral as between a form of "property-owning democracy", which would combine private property in the means of production with its egalitarian distribution, and hence the abolition of the separate classes of capitalists and workers; and a form of liberal democratic socialism that would see public ownership of the preponderance of the means of production, with devolved control of particular firms. While Rawls's version of liberal democratic socialism was insufficiently developed in his own writings, he stands as an interesting case of a theorist whose defense of a form of democratic socialism is based on normative foundations that are not themselves distinctively socialist, but concerned with the core liberal democratic values of justice and equality.

In a similar vein to Rawls, another instance of a theorist who defends at least partially socialist institutional arrangements on liberal egalitarian grounds was the Nobel Prize winning economist James Meade. Giving a central place to decidedly liberal values of freedom, security and independence, Meade argued that the likely levels of socioeconomic inequality under capitalism were such that a capitalist economy would need to be extensively tempered by socialist elements, such as the development of a citizens' sovereign wealth fund, if the economic system were to be justifiable to those living under it and arguing for a range of measures to create a more egalitarian economy, including making the case for a steady-state rather than a growth-oriented economy, arguing for workers' collective ownership and self-management of firms in preference to the hierarchical structures characteristic of most firms under capitalism, and endorsing steep taxation of inheritance and unearned income. More recently, the argument has been advanced that as capitalist economies tend towards higher levels of inequality, and in particular with the rapid velocity at which the incomes and wealth of the very rich in society is increasing, many of those who had seen their normative commitments as requiring only the mild reform of capitalist economies might need to come to see the need to endorse more radical socialist institutional proposals.

Socialist Institutional Designs (Dimension DII)

The foregoing discussion focused on socialist critiques of capitalism. These critiques make the case that capitalism fails to fulfill principles, or to realize values, to which socialists are committed. But what would an alternative economic system look like which would fulfill those principles, or realize those values—or at least honor them to a larger extent? This brings us to dimension DII of socialism.

Central and Participatory Planning

Would socialism do better than capitalism regarding the ideals of equality, democracy, individual freedom, self-realization, and solidarity? This depends on the availability of workable versions of socialism that fulfill these ideals (or do so at least to a greater extent than workable forms of capitalism). A first set of proposals envision an economic system that does away with both private property in the means of production and with markets. The first version of this model is *central planning*. This can be understood within a top-down, hierarchical model. A central authority gathers information about the technical potential in the economy and about consumers' needs and formulates a set of production objectives which seek an optimal match between the former and the latter. These objectives are articulated into a plan that is passed down to intermediate agencies and eventually to local firms, which must produce according to the plan handed down. If it works, this proposal would secure the highest feasible levels of equal access to consumption goods for everyone. However, critics have argued that the model faces serious feasibility hurdles. It is very hard for a central authority to gather the relevant information from producers and consumers. Second, even if it could gather enough information, the computation of an optimal plan would require enormously complex calculations which may be beyond the capacity of planners (even with access to the most sophisticated technological assistance). Finally, there may be significant incentive deficits. For example, firms might tend to exaggerate the resources they need to produce and mislead about how much they can produce. Without facing strong sticks and carrots (such as the prospects for either bankruptcy and profit offered by a competitive market), firms might well display low levels of innovation. As a result, a planned economy would likely lag behind surrounding capitalist economies, and their members would tend to lose faith in it. High levels of cooperation (and willingness to innovate) could still exist if sufficiently many individuals in this society possessed a strong sense of duty. But critics find this unlikely to materialize, warning that "a system that only works with exceptional individuals only works in exceptional cases".

Actual experiments in centrally planned economies have only partially approximated the best version of it. Thus, in addition to the problems mentioned above (which affect even that best version), they have displayed additional defects. For example, the system introduced in the Soviet Union featured intense concentration of political and economic power in the hands of an elite controlling a single party which, in turn, controlled a non-democratic state apparatus. Despite its successes in industrializing the country (making it capable of mobilizing in a war effort to defeat Nazi Germany), the model failed to generate sufficient technical innovation and intensive growth to deliver differentiated consumer goods of the kind available within advanced capitalist economies. Furthermore, it trampled upon civil and political liberties that many socialists would themselves hold dear.

Responding to such widespread disempowerment, a second model for socialist planning has recommended that planning be done in a different, more democratic way. Thus, the participatory planning (or participatory economy, "Parecon") model proposes the following institutional features. First, the means of production would be socially owned. Second, production would take place in firms controlled by workers (thus fostering democracy within the workplace). Third, balanced "job complexes" are put in place in which workers can both engage in intellectual and manual labor (thus fostering and generalizing self-realization). Fourth, in a solidaristic fashion, remuneration of workers would track their effort, sacrifice, and special needs (and not their relative power or output—which would likely reflect differences in native abilities for which they are not morally responsible). Finally, and crucially, economic coordination would be based on comprehensive participatory planning. This would involve a complex system of nested worker councils, consumer councils, and an Iteration Facilitation Board. Various rounds of deliberation within, and between, worker and consumer councils, facilitated by this board, would be undertaken until matches between supply and demands schedules are found—with recourse to voting procedures only when no full agreement exists but several promising arrangements arise. This would turn the economy into an arena of deliberative democracy.

Importantly, it overcomes the deficits regarding freedom displayed by central planning. Critics have warned, however, that Parecon faces serious feasibility obstacles. In particular, the iterative planning constituting the fifth institutional dimension of the Parecon proposal would require immense information complexity. It is unlikely that participants in the operations of this board, even with the help of sophisticated computers, would manage it sufficiently well to generate a production plan that satisfactorily caters to the diversity of individuals' needs. A defense of Parecon would retort that beyond initial stages, the process of economic decision-making would not be too cumbersome. Furthermore, it might turn out to involve no more paperwork and time devoted to planning and to assessment behind computer terminals than is found in existing capitalist societies (with their myriad individual and corporate budgeting exercises, and their various accounting and legal epicycles). And, in any case, even if it is more cumbersome and less efficient in terms of productivity, Parecon might still be preferable overall as an economic system, given its superior performance regarding the values of freedom, equality, self-realization, solidarity, and democracy.

Market Socialism

Some of the above-mentioned problems of central planning, regarding inefficiency and concentration of power, have motivated some socialists to explore alternative economic systems in which markets are given a central role. Markets generate problems of their own (especially when they involve monopolies, negative externalities, and asymmetric information). But if regulations are introduced to counter these "market failures", markets can be the best feasible mechanism for generating matches between demand and supply in large, complex societies (as higher prices signal high demand, with supply rushing to cover it, while lower prices signal low demand, leading supply to concentrate on other products). *Market socialism* affirms the traditional socialist desideratum of preventing a division of society between a class of capitalists who do not need to work to make a living and a class of laborers having to work for them, but it retains from capitalism the utilization of markets to guide production. There has been a lively debate on this approach, with several specific systems being proposed.

One version is the *economic democracy* model. It has three basic features. First, production is undertaken in firms managed by workers. Worker self-managed enterprises would gain temporary control of some means of production (which would be leased out by the state). Workers determine what gets produced and how it is produced, and determine compensation schemes. Second, there is a market for goods and services. The profit motive persists and some inequalities within and between firms are possible, but likely much smaller than in capitalism (as there would be no separate capitalist class, and workers will not democratically select income schemes that involve significant inequality within their firms). Finally, investment flows are socially controlled through democratically accountable public investment banks, which determine funding for enterprises on the basis of socially relevant criteria. The revenues for these banks come from a capital assets tax. This system would (through its second feature) mobilize the efficiency of markets while also (through its other features) attending to socialist ideals of self-determination, self-realization, and equal opportunity. To address some potential difficulties, the model has been extended to include further features, such as a commitment of the government as an employer of last resort, the creation of socialist savings and loans associations, the accommodation of an entrepreneurial-capitalist sector for particularly innovative small firms, and some forms of protectionism regarding foreign trade.

Self-management market socialism has been defended as feasible by pointing at the experience of cooperatives (such as the Mondragón Corporation in the Basque Country in Spain, which has over 70,000 worker-owners participating in a network of cooperative businesses). But it has also been criticized on five counts. First, it would generate unfair distributions, as workers doing the same work in different enterprises would end up with unequal income if the enterprises are not equally successful in the market. Second, workers would face high levels of financial risk, as their resources would be concentrated in their firm rather than spread more widely. Third, it could generate inefficient responses to market prices, as self-managed enterprises reduce hiring if prices for their products are high—so that members keep more of the profit—and hire more if the prices are low—to cover for fixed costs of production, the system could also generate high unemployment. Having the government require firms to hire more would lead to lower productivity. However, the further features in the model discussed above might address this problem by allowing for small private enterprises to be formed, and by having in the background the government play a role as an employer of last resort (although this might also limit overall productivity). Finally, although some of the problems of efficiency could be handled through the banks controlling investment, it is not clear that the enormous power of such banks could be made sufficiently accountable to a democratic process so as to avoid the potential problem of cooptation by elites.

Another market socialist model, proposed by Carens, does not impose worker self-management. The Carensian model mirrors the current capitalist system in most respects while introducing two key innovative features. First, there would be direct governmental provision regarding certain individually differentiated needs (via a public health care system, for example). Second, to access other consumption goods, everyone working full time would get the same post tax income. Pre-tax salaries would vary, signaling levels of demand in the market. People would choose jobs not only on the basis of their self-regarding preferences, but also out of a sense of social duty to use their capacities to support others in society. Thus, honoring the Abilities/Needs Principle, they would apply for jobs (within their competencies) in which the pre-tax income is relatively high. If it worked, this model would recruit the efficiency of markets, but it would not involve the selfish motives and inegalitarian outcomes typically linked to them in capitalism.

One worry about the Carensian model is that it might be unrealistic to expect an economic system to work well when it relies so heavily on a sense of duty to motivate people to make cooperative contributions. This worry could be assuaged by presenting this model as the long-term target of a socialist transformation which would progressively develop a social ethos supporting it, by noting empirical findings about the significant traction of non-egoistic motives in economic behavior and the feasibility of "moral incentives", and by exploring strategies to mobilize simultaneously various motivational mechanisms to sustain the proposed scheme. Two other worries are the following. First, the model makes no explicit provision regarding real opportunities for work in self-managed firms. To cater more fully for ideals of self-determination and self-realization, a requirement could be added that the government promote such opportunities for those willing to take them. Second, the model is not sufficiently sensitive to different individual preferences regarding leisure and consumption (requiring simply that everyone work full time and wind up with the same consumption and leisure bundles). More flexible schedules could be introduced so that people who want to consume more could work longer hours and have higher salaries, while people who want to enjoy more free time could work fewer hours and have lower salaries. Considerations of reciprocity and equality could still be honored by equalizing the incomes of those working the same number of hours.

Many forms of market socialism allow for some hierarchy at the point of production. These managerial forms are usually defended on grounds of greater efficiency. But they face the question of how to incentivize managers to behave in ways that foster innovation and productivity. One way to do this is to set up a stock market that would help to measure the performance of the firms they manage and to push them to make optimal decisions. An example of this approach is *coupon market socialism*. In Roemer's version, this economic system operates with two kinds of money: dollars (euros, pesos, etc.) and coupons. Dollars are used to purchase commodities for consumption and production, and coupons are used in a stock market to purchase shares in corporations. The two kinds of money are not convertible. Each person, when reaching adulthood, is provided with an equal set of coupons. They can use them in a state-regulated stock market (directly or through mutual investment funds) to purchase shares in corporations at market price. They receive the dividends from their investments in dollars, but they cannot cash the coupons themselves. When they die, people's coupons and shares go back to the state for distribution to new generations—no inherited wealth is allowed—and coupons cannot be transferred as gifts. Thus, there is no separate class of capital owners in this economy. But there will be income inequality resulting from people's different fortunes with their investments (dividends) as well as from the income they gain in the jobs they take through the labor market (in managerial and non-managerial positions). Coupons can however be converted into dollars by corporations; they can cash their shares to pay for capital investments. The exchange is regulated by a public central bank. Further, public banks or public investment funds, operating with relative independence from the government, would steer enterprises receiving coupons so that they maximize profit in the competitive markets for the goods and services they produce (so that they maximize the returns on the coupons invested). Part of that profit is also taxed for direct welfare provisions by the state.

This model caters for ideals of equality of opportunity (given equal distribution of coupons) and democracy (given the elimination of capitalist dynasties that have the ability to transform massive economic power into political influence). It also gives people freedom to choose how to use their resources and includes solidaristic schemes of public provision to meet needs regarding education and health care. Via the competitive markets in consumption goods and shares, it also promises high levels of innovation and productivity. The model departs from traditional forms of socialism by not exactly instituting *social* property in means of production (but rather the equal dispersal of coupons across individuals in each generation). But defenders of this model say that socialists should not fetishize any property scheme; they should instead see such schemes instrumentally in terms of how well they fare in the implementation of core normative principles (such as equality of opportunity). Critics have worries, however, that the model does not go far enough in honoring socialist principles. For example, they have argued that a managerial (by contrast to a self-management) form of market socialism is deficient in terms of self-determination and self-realization at the workplace, and that the levels of inequalities in income, and the competitive attitudes in the market that it would generate, violate ideals of community. In response, a defender of coupon market socialism can emphasize that the model is meant to be applied in the short-term, and that further institutional and cultural arrangements more fully in line with socialist principles can be introduced later on, as they become more feasible. A worry, however, is that the model may entrench institutional and cultural configurations which may diminish rather than enhance the prospects for deeper changes in the future.

Less Comprehensive and Piecemeal Reforms

The models discussed above envision comprehensive "system change" in which the class division between capitalists and wage laborers disappears. Socialists have also explored piecemeal reforms that stop short of that structural change. An important historical example is the combination of a market economy and the welfare state. In this model, although property in the means of production remains private, and markets allocate most inputs and outputs of production, a robust governmental framework is put in place to limit the power of capitalists over workers and to improve the life-prospects of the latter. Thus, social insurance addresses the risks associated with illness, unemployment, disability, and old age. Tax-funded, state provision of many of those goods that markets typically fail to deliver for all is introduced (such as high-quality education, public transportation, and health care). And collective bargaining gives unions and other instruments of workers' power some sway on the determination of their working conditions, as well as providing an important foundation for the political agency of the working class.

This welfare state model was developed with great success during the three decades after World War II, especially in Northern Europe, but also, in weaker but significant forms, in other countries (including some in the Global South). However, since the 1980s, this model has been in significant retreat, or even in crisis. Wealth and income inequality have been increasing dramatically during this time. The financial sector has become extremely powerful and able largely to escape governmental regulation as globalization allows capital to flow across borders. A "race to the bottom" features states competing with each other to attract investment by lowering tax rates and other regulations, thus undermining states' ability to implement welfare policies. Some socialists have seen this crisis as a reason to abandon the welfare state and pursue more comprehensive changes of the kind discussed above. Others, however, have argued that the model should be defended given that it has been proven to work quite well while the alternatives have uncertain prospects.

One example of the approach of extending or retrenching the mixed economy and welfare state proposes a combination of two moves. The first move is to revamp the welfare state by introducing mechanisms of greater accountability of politicians to citizens (such as regulation of the dealings of politicians with private companies, and more instances of direct democracy in order to empower citizens), an improvement of the quality of public services delivered by the welfare state (introducing exacting audits and evaluations and fostering the training and recruitment of excellent civil servants), and international coordination of tax policies to prevent tax competition and tax evasion. The second move in this proposal is to run controlled experiments of market socialism to present it as a credible threat to the powerful actors seeking to undermine the welfare state. This threat would help stabilize the welfare state as the menace of communist revolution did after 1945. Specifically, welfare states could create new institutions that would be relatively independent from governments and be run by highly competent and democratically accountable civil servants. "Sovereign Wealth Funds" would invest public money in well-functioning enterprises, to yield an equal "social dividend" for citizens. The second institution, a "Federal Shareholder", would go further by using some of these funds to buy 51% of the shares of selected enterprises and take the lead within their boards of directors or supervisory boards. The objective would be to show that these enterprises (which would include significant participation of workers in their management, and ethical guidelines regarding environmental impacts and other concerns) maximize profits and thus offer a desirable and feasible alternative to the standard capitalist enterprise. Effectively, this strategy would run controlled experiments of shareholder market socialism. The working population would learn about the feasibility of market socialism, and capitalist opponents of welfare entitlements would be disciplined by fear of the generalization of such experiments to settle again for the welfare state.

Another strategy is to introduce various experiments seeking to *expand the impact of social power*. A set of mechanisms would target the deepening of democracy. Forms of direct democracy could foster citizens' deliberative engagement in decision-making, as exemplified by the introduction of municipal participatory budgeting in Porto Alegre, Brazil (which features citizens' assemblies identifying priorities for public policy). The quality of representative democracy can be enhanced (and its subservience to the power of capitalists decreased) by introducing egalitarian funding of electoral campaigns (e.g., by giving citizens a sum of money to allocate to the parties they favor, while forcing parties to choose between getting funding from that source and any other source—such as corporations), and by creating random citizen assemblies to generate policy options which can then be subject to society-wide referenda (as in the attempt to change the electoral system in British Columbia in Canada). Finally, forms of associational democracy can be introduced that feature deliberation or bargaining between government, labor, business, and civil society groups when devising national economic policies or when introducing regional or local (e.g., environmental) regulations. A second set of mechanisms would foster social empowerment more directly in the economy. Examples are the promotion of the social economy sector featuring economic activity involving self-management and production oriented to use value, an unconditional basic income strengthening people's ability to engage in economic activities they find intrinsically valuable, and the expansion of the cooperative sector. None of these mechanisms on its own would make a society socialist rather than capitalist. But if we see societies as complex "ecologies" rather than as homogeneous "organisms", we can notice that they are hybrids including diverse institutional logics. An increase in the incidence of social empowerment may significantly extend the socialist aspects of a society, and even eventually make them dominant.

Socialist Transformation (Dimension DIII)

We turn now to the last dimension of socialism (DIII), which concerns the transformation of capitalist societies into socialist ones. The discussion on this dimension is difficult in at least two respects which call for philosophical exploration. The first issue concerns feasibility. The question is whether socialist systems are accessible from where we are now—whether there is a path from here to there. But what does feasibility mean here? It cannot just mean logical or physical possibility, as these would rule out very few social systems. The relevant feasibility parameters seem instead to involve matters of technical development, economic organization, political mobilization, and moral culture.But such parameters are comparatively "soft", in that they indicate probability prospects rather than pose strict limits of possibility, and can be significantly changed over time. When something is not feasible to do right now, we could have dynamic duties to make it feasible to do later by developing our relevant capacities in the meantime. The feasibility judgments must then be scalar rather than binary and allow for diachronic variation. These features make them somewhat murky, and not straightforwardly amenable to the hard-edged use of impossibility claims to debunk normative requirements (via contraposition on the principle that ought implies can).

A second difficulty concerns the articulation of all things considered appropriate strategies that combine feasibility considerations with the normative desiderata provided by socialist principles. The question here is: what is the most reasonable path of transformation to pursue for socialists given their understanding of the principles animating their political project, viewed against the background of what seems more or less feasible to achieve at different moments, and within different historical contexts? Complex judgments have to be formed about the precise social systems at which it would be right to aim at different stages of the sequence of transformation, and about the specific modes of political action to deploy in such processes. These judgments would combine feasibility and desirability to assess short-term and long-term goals, their intrinsic costs and benefits, and the promise of the former to enhance the achievement of the latter. The difficulty of forming such judgments is compounded by the uncertainty about the prospects of large societal changes (but also about the long-term consequences of settling for the status quo).

Marx himself seemed to address some of these issues in his short text "The Critique of the Gotha Program" of 1875. Marx here envisioned the process of socialist transformation as including two phases. The final phase would fully implement the Abilities /Needs Principle. But he did not take that scenario to be immediately accessible. An intermediate step should be pursued, in which the economy would be ruled by a *Contribution Principle* requiring that (after some provisions are put aside to fulfill basic needs regarding health care, education, and support for those unable to work) people gain access to consumption goods in proportion to how much they contribute. This lower phase of socialist transformation would be reasonable because it would enhance the prospects of transitioning away from capitalism and of generating the conditions for the full realization of socialism. The implementation of the Contribution Principle would fulfill the promise systematically broken by capitalism that people would benefit according to their labor input (as in capitalism capitalists get much more, and workers much less, than they give). It would also incentivize people to increase production to the level necessary for the introduction of socialism proper. Once such level of development is in place, the social ethos could move away from the mantra of the "exchange of equivalents" and instead adopt a different outlook in which people produce according to their diverse abilities, and consume according to their diverse needs. This sequential picture of transformation features diachronic judgments about changes in feasibility parameters (such as the expansion of technical capacity and a change in patterns of motivation). Marx also envisioned political dimensions of this process, including a "dictatorship of the proletariat" (which would not, as some popular interpretations hold, involve violation of civil and political rights, but a change in the political constitution and majoritarian policies that secure the elimination of capitalist property rights). In time, the state (understood as an apparatus of class rule rather than, more generally, as an administrative device) would "wither away".

History has not moved smoothly in the direction many socialists predicted. It has not been obvious that the following steps in the expected pattern materialized or are likely to do so: capitalism generating a large, destitute, and homogeneous working class; this class responding to some of the cyclical crises capitalism is prone to by creating a coherent and powerful political movement; this movement gaining control of government and resolutely and successfully implementing a socialist economic system. Given the fact that this process did not materialize, and seems unlikely to do so, it turns out that it would be both self-defeating and irresponsible to fail to address difficult questions about the relative feasibility and moral desirability of different strategies of potential socialist transformation. For example, if the process of transformation involves two or more stages (be they the two mentioned above, or some sequence going, say, from the welfare state to shareholder or coupon market socialism and then to the Carensian model), it might be asked who is to evaluate and decide upon what is to be done at each stage of the process, on what grounds can it be expected that earlier stages will enhance the likelihood of the success of later stages rather than undermine them (e.g., by enshrining institutions or values that will make it hard to move further along the path), what transitional costs can be accepted in earlier stages, and whether the costs expected are outweighed by the desirability and the increased probability of attaining the later stages. Such questions do not want for difficulty.

Addressing questions such as these dilemmas of transitional strategy, socialists have envisaged different approaches to social and political transformation. Four significant examples are articulated by considering two dimensions of analysis regarding (a) the primary goal of the strategy (either (i) transcending the structures of capitalism, or (ii) neutralizing the worst harms of it) and (b) the primary target of the strategy (either (i) the state and other institutions at the macro-level of the system, or (ii) the economic activities of individuals, organizations, and communities).

The first strategy, *smashing capitalism*, picks out the combination of possibilities (a.i) and (b.i). A political organization (e.g., a revolutionary party) takes advantage of some of the crises generated by capitalism to seize state power, proceeding to use that power to counter opposition to the revolution and to build a socialist society. This is the strategy favored by revolutionary socialists and many Marxists, and pursued in the twentieth century in countries such as Russia and China. If we look at the historical evidence, we see that although this strategy succeeded in some cases in transitioning out of previously existing capitalist or proto-capitalist economic systems, it failed in terms of building socialism. It led instead to a form of authoritarian statism. There is debate about the causes of these failures. Some factors may have been the economically backward and politically hostile circumstances in which the strategy was implemented, the leaders' deficits (in terms of their tactics or motives), and the hierarchical frameworks used to suppress opposition after the revolution which remained in place for the long-term to subvert revolutionaries' aims. Large system changes normally have to face a "transitional trough" after their onset, in which the material interests of many people are temporarily set back. A political dilemma arises, in that, if liberal democratic politics is retained (with a free press, liberty of association, and multiparty elections) the revolutionaries may be unseated due to citizens' political response to the "valley of transition", while if liberal democratic politics are supplanted, then authoritarian statism may be the consequence, eradicating the possibility of a socialist outcome to which it would be worthwhile to seek to transition.

A second strategy, picking out the combination of possibilities (a.ii) and (b.i), has been *taming capitalism*. It mobilizes the population (sometimes in sharp political struggles) to elect governments and implement policies that respond to the worst harms generated by capitalism, with the aim of neutralizing them. New policies include social insurance responding to risks faced by the population (e.g., illness and unemployment), tax funded, state provision of public goods which markets tend to fail to provide (e.g., education, public transportation, research and development, etc.), and regulation of negative externalities produced in markets (e.g., regarding pollution, product and workplace hazards, predatory market behavior, etc.). The strategy, implemented by social-democratic parties, worked quite well during the three decades of the "Golden Age" or *Trente Glorieuses* following World War II. However, progress was halted and partly rolled back since the retreat of social democracy and the introduction of neoliberalism in the 1980s. Possible explanatory factors are the financialization of capitalism, and the effects of globalization,. There is a debate as to whether capitalism is really tamable—it may be that the Golden Age was only a historical anomaly, borne out of a very particular set of political and economic circumstances.

The third strategy, *escaping capitalism*, picks out the combination of possibilities (a.ii) and (b.ii). Capitalism might be too strong to destroy. But people could avoid its worst harms by insulating themselves from its dynamics. They could focus on family and friendships, become self-subsistence farmers, create intentional communities, and explore modes of life involving "voluntary simplicity". However, this strategy seems available mostly to relatively well-off people who can fund their escape with wealth they have amassed or received from capitalist activities. The working poor may not be so lucky.

The final strategy, *eroding capitalism*, picks out the combination of (a.i) and (b.ii). Economic systems are here seen as hybrids. People can introduce new, socialist forms of collective activity (such as worker cooperatives) and progressively expand them, eventually turning them from marginal to dominant. Recently this kind of strategy of the erosion of capitalism through institutional transformation rather than piecemeal changes within existing economic structures, has been referred to as "the institutional turn" in leftist political economy. Wright suggests the analogy of a lake ecosystem, with the introduction of a new species of fish that at first thrives in one location, and then spreads out, eventually becoming a dominant species. Historically, the transformation from feudalism to capitalism in some parts of Europe has come about in this way, with pockets of commercial, financial, and manufacturing activity taking place in cities and expanding over time. Some anarchists seem to hold a version of this strategy today. It offers hope for change even when the state seems uncongenial, and likely to remain so. But critics find it far-fetched, as it seems unlikely to go sufficiently far given the enormous economic and political power of large capitalist corporations and the tendency of the state to repress serious threats to its rules. To go further, the power of the state has to be at least partially recruited. The fourth strategy then, according to Wright, is only plausible when combined with the second.

First, it would address some important, problematic junctures to expand state action in ways that even capitalists would have to accept. And second, the solutions to the crises introduced by state action would be selected in such a way that they would enhance long-term prospects for socialist change. One critical juncture is global warming, and the social and political problems of the Anthropocene era. Responding to its effects would require massive generation of state-provided public goods, which could remove neoliberal compunctions about state activism. A second critical juncture concerns the large levels of long-term unemployment, precariousness, and marginalization generated by new trends in automation and information technology. This involves threats to social peace, and insufficient demand for the products corporations need to sell on the consumption market. Such threats could be averted by introducing an unconditional basic income policy, or by the significant expansion of public services, or by some other mechanism that secures for everybody a minimally dignified economic condition independent of their position within the labor market. Now, these state policies could foster the growth of social power and the prospects for socialist change in the future. Workers would have more power in the labor market when they came to be less reliant upon it. They could also be more successful in forming cooperatives. The social economy sector could flourish under such conditions. People could also devote more time to political activism. Together, these trends from below, combined with state activism from above, could expand knowledge about the workability of egalitarian, democratic, and solidaristic forms of economic activity, and strengthen the motivation to extend their scope.

Although some critics find this strategy naïve, proponents think that something like it must be tried if the aim is democratic socialism rather than authoritarian statism.

Other significant issues regarding dimension DIII of socialism are the identification of appropriate political agents of change and their prospects of success in the context of contemporary globalization. On the first point, socialists increasingly explore the significance not only of workers' movements, but also their intersection with the efforts of activists focused on overcoming gender- and race-based oppression. Some argue that the primary addressee of socialist politics should not be any specific class or movement, but the more inclusive, and politically equal group of citizens of a democratic community. For example, Honneth, following in part John Dewey and Juergen Habermas, argues that the primary addressee and agent of change for socialism should be the citizens assembled in the democratic public sphere. Although normatively appealing, this proposal may face serious feasibility difficulties, as existing democratic arenas are intensely contaminated and disabled by the inequalities socialists criticize and seek to overcome. The second issue is also relevant here. There is a traditional question whether socialism is to be pursued in one country or internationally. The tendency to embrace an internationalist horizon of political change is characteristic among socialists as they typically see their ideals of freedom, equality, and solidarity as having global scope, while they also note that, as a matter of feasibility, the increasing porousness of borders for capitalist economic activity make it the case that socialist politics may not go very far in any country without reshaping the broader international context. A difficulty here is that despite the existence of international social movements (including workers' movements, international NGOs, human rights institutions and associations, and other actors), institutional agency beyond borders that can seriously contest capitalist frameworks is not currently very strong. In addressing these difficulties, action and research on socialist justice must interact with ongoing work in the related areas of gender, race, democracy, human rights, and global justice.

Examples of Socialism

Socialism within a country's economic systems, healthcare, education, corporations or other factions exist in these examples:

- The Mondragon Corporation, a federation of co-ops that currently employs 85,066 people. It is in the Basque region.
- A bakery pays all staff the same amount of money based on the profitability of the business. Workers vote to make business decisions.
- The former Soviet Union is an example of a socialist system.
- Cuba is an example of a socialist nation. Its economy is state run and it lacks a stock exchange. Healthcare and education are all completely managed and administered by the government.

- The country of North Korea is a socialist state, lacking a stock exchange, supporting many social programs, and the economy is state-run.
- Vietnam's economy is largely state-run and can therefore be considered to be following socialist policies.
- China has elements of socialism that remain despite having eliminated socialized healthcare. The economy is still state-run.
- Venezuela's government provides myriad social programs and can be considered a socialist state.
- Syria's economy can be considered socialist as their healthcare is a universal program and their economy is run by the state.
- Laos has many ties with other socialist states and runs the majority of the economy.
- Sweden's healthcare is a socialized program. Education in Sweden is also part of a socialist policy which provides government funded and administered education at all levels to citizens.
- Belarus has some remnants of socialism in its state policies with an economy that is still entirely state-run.
- Zambia's media is considered socialist as it is state-run. Zambia's healthcare is also universal and therefore an example of socialism.
- Turkmenistan is a strong example of socialism with energy subsidized by the government, many housing subsidies and an economy that is largely state run.

Many people use the term socialism to describe behavior in which a government takes on a larger role in the economy. For example, many opponents claim that President Barack Obama is a socialist because he takes the position that the government should be involved in many aspects of people's lives and because he believes that people have a shared responsibility to each other.

The term is not always used accurately and it is very helpful for people to have some actual examples of socialism in order to get a clear picture of this economic theory.

Socialism versus Communism

The difference between communism and socialism is not conveniently clear-cut. The two terms are often used interchangeably, but these economic and political theories are not the same. Both communism and socialism arose from protests against the exploitation of the working class during the Industrial Revolution.

While applications of their economic and social policies vary, several modern countries—all ideologically opposed to capitalism—are perceived as either communist or socialist. In order to understand contemporary political debates, it's important to know the similarities and the differences between communism and socialism.

In both communism and socialism, the people own the factors of economic production. The main difference is that under communism, most property and economic resources are owned and controlled by the state (rather than individual citizens); by contrast, under socialism, all citizens share equally in all economic resources as allocated by a democratically-elected government. This difference and others are outlined in the table below:

Communism vs. Socialism		
Attribute	Communism	Socialism
Basic Philosophy	From each according to his ability, to each according to his needs.	From each according to his ability, to each according to his contribution.
Economy Planned By	Central government.	Central government.
Ownership of Economic Resources	All economic resources are publicly owned and controlled by the government. Individuals hold no personal property or assets.	Individuals own personal property but all industrial and production capacity is communally owned and managed by a democratically elected government.
Distribution of Economic Production	Production is intended to meet all basic human needs and is distributed to the people at no charge.	Production is intended to meet individual and societal needs and distributed according to individual ability and contribution.
Class Distinction	Class is abolished. The ability to earn more than other workers is almost nonexistent.	Classes exist but differences are diminished. It is possible for some people to earn more than others.
Religion	Religion is effectively abolished.	Freedom of religion is allowed.

Key Similarities

Communism and socialism both grew out of grass-roots opposition to the exploitation of workers by wealthy businesses during the Industrial Revolution. Both assume that all goods and services will be produced by government-controlled institutions or collective organizations rather than by privately-owned businesses. In addition, the central government is mainly responsible for all aspects of economic planning, including matters of supply and demand.

Key Differences

Under communism, the people are compensated or provided for based on their needs. In a pure communist society, the government provides most or all food, clothing, housing and other necessities based on what it considers the needs of the people. Socialism is based on the premise the people will be compensated based on the level of their individual contribution to the economy. Effort and innovation are thus rewarded under socialism.

Pure Communism Definition

Pure communism is an economic, political, and social system in which most or all property and resources are collectively owned by a class-free society rather than by individual citizens. According to the theory developed by German philosopher, economist, and political theorist Karl Marx in his classic 1848 book, *"The Communist Manifesto,"* pure communism results in a society in which all people are equal and there is no need for money or the accumulation of individual wealth. There is no private ownership of economic resources, with a central government controlling all facets of production. Economic output is distributed according to the needs of the people. Social friction between white and blue-collar workers and between rural and urban cultures will be eliminated, freeing each person to achieve his or her highest human potential.

Under pure communism, the central government provides the people with all basic necessitates, such as food, housing, education, and medical care, thus allowing the people to share equally from the benefits of collective labor. Free access to these necessities depends on constant advances in technology contributing to ever-greater production.

In 1875, Marx coined the phrase used to summarize communism, "From each according to his ability, to each according to his needs."

Socialist Democracy

Democratic socialism is an economic, social, and political ideology holding that while both the society and economy should be run democratically, they should be dedicated to meeting the needs of the people as a whole, rather than encouraging individual prosperity as in capitalism. Democratic socialists advocate the transition of society from capitalism to socialism through existing participatory democratic processes, rather than revolution as characterized by orthodox Marxism. Universally-used services, such as housing, utilities, mass transit, and health care are distributed by the government, while consumer goods are distributed by a capitalistic free market.

The latter half of the 20th century saw the emergence of a more moderate version of socialist democracy advocating a mixture of socialist and capitalist control of all means of economic production supplemented by extensive social welfare programs to help provide the basic needs of the people.

Green Socialism

As a recent outgrowth of the environmental movement and the climate change debate, green socialism or "eco-socialism" places its economic emphasis on the maintenance and utilization of natural resources. This is achieved largely through government ownership of the largest, most resource consumptive corporations. The use of "green" resources, such as renewable energy, public transit, and locally sourced food is emphasized or mandated. Economic production focuses on meeting the basic needs of the people, rather than a wasteful excess of unneeded consumer goods. Green socialism often offers a guaranteed minimum livable income to all citizens regardless of their employment status.

Communist Countries

It is difficult to classify countries as being either communist or socialist. Several countries, while ruled by the Communist Party, declare themselves to be socialist states and employ many aspects of socialist economic and social policy. Three countries typically considered communist states—mainly due to their political structure—are Cuba, China, and North Korea.

The Communist Party of China owns and strictly controls all industry, which operates solely to generate profits for the government through its successful and growing export of consumer goods. Health care and primary through higher education are run by the government and provided free of charge to the people. However, housing and property development operate under a highly competitive capitalist system.

The Communist Party of Cuba owns and operates most industries, and most of the people work for the state. Government-controlled health care and primary through higher education are provided free. Housing is either free or heavily subsidized by the government.

Ruled by the Communist Party until 1946, North Korea now operates under a "Socialist Constitution of the Democratic People's Republic of Korea." However, the government owns and controls all farmland, workers, and food distribution channels. Today, the government provides universal health and education for all citizens. Private ownership of property is forbidden. Instead, the government grants people the right to government-owned and assigned homes.

Socialist Countries

Once again, most modern countries that identify themselves to be socialist may not strictly follow the economic or social systems associated with pure socialism. Instead, most countries generally considered socialist actually employ the policies of democratic socialism.

Norway, Sweden, and Denmark all employ similar predominantly socialist systems. The democratically chosen governments of all three countries provide free health care, education, and lifetime retirement income. As a result, however, their citizens pay some of the world's highest taxes. All three countries also have highly successful capitalist sectors. With most of their needs provided by their governments, the people see little need to accumulate wealth. As a result, about 10% of the people hold more than 65 percent of each nation's wealth.

Pros and Cons of Socialism

Socialism can be defined in two ways. First, it is an economic system which centers on common ownership. In this system, the government mandates production and prices. Also, private ownership of property is not allowed. Equality is significant for socialists that distribution of wealth and production belongs to the community. Moreover, production is done for use unlike capitalism wherein production is for profit. Second, socialism is a political system with a classless society where there are equal power relationships among people.

While some groups are considering the establishment of a socialist world, there are also other groups opposing the socialist idea.

Pros of Socialism

- Every citizen will have access to education and health care: According to proponents, two major problems of nations practicing capitalism are the high costs of health care as well as education. Because of these, there are countries with high rates of illiteracy and many are not able to continue their education. Also, people who cannot afford health care are not given the medical attention they need.
- In a socialist society, education is available for everybody and people will be able to meet their medical needs because health care costs will be more affordable. With the government owning hospitals and health care facilities, medicines and medical services are relatively low in costs if not totally free.
- It results to a classless society: Socialists believe that equality among people is important, including social class. By making people equal to each other, the gap between the rich and the poor will be bridged. Opportunities are handed to members of the community regardless of race, color, age and gender.
- It allows for balance in wealth and earnings: With the government in control and owning most of the industries like housing, utility companies, poor members of society are given access to basic services which they will not be able to if establishments and industries are privately owned. On the other hand, when it comes to taxes, there is progressive taxation in a socialist society. This means that the higher the income, the higher the taxes. With this taxation system, it will be easier for low income employees to budget their earnings and while those who earn more and pay higher taxes will still have enough left to spend.
- It eradicates monopolies in corporations: In a capitalist nation, companies are

owned privately unlike in a socialist country where the government monitors, controls and owns companies that offer services like transportation and medical institutions, where money spent come from taxes. This way, prices are regulated and made affordable for the people unlike in capitalism where private business owners and suppliers can demand high prices for their goods and services.

Cons of Socialism

- It gives the government much if not full control: Critics of socialism argue that allowing the government to run people's lives, including where to live, how much to earn and what health care is given to them is not good. It is unfair to the people since they have no say on these things. With the state on top of things, citizens have lesser options especially on services and commodities.
- It demands higher taxes: Proponents, especially those who with white collar jobs, are complaining about costly tax payments since the government has to impose these taxes be able to subsidize services offered to the public for free or at lower costs.
- The rights of workers might be too much: With unions and workers' councils having more power in businesses, critics are concerned this can give them too much authority that workers will demand over-the-limit wages. If this happens, employers will be reluctant to hire people while unproductive employees will be retained. For opponents, this will result to economic failure and unemployment.
- People have to deal with bureaucracy: Groups who are not in favor of a socialist society claim that with state-run services, there is too much bureaucracy which only makes it difficult for people to get services fast. With standard operating procedures to follow and the long processes people of the community have to go through just to get basic services, the citizens are being deprived of immediate assistance.
- It can result to lack of motivation: People who are against socialism say that by making people's lives comfortable and providing free services, they might not be driven to work harder and dream of improving their lives. Business owners, on the other hand, will not be motivated to open new businesses while innovative people will not be inspired to invent new things because for them, nothing will change and they will remain stuck.
- It can result to unnecessary spending by the government: Some groups point out that since the government in a socialist setting has the power to spend on services for the general public using taxpayer's money, this can result to too much spending which can lead to poor economy. With the state having the authority to subsidize projects it chooses, this can result to irresponsible spending and inflation.

Socialism exists to bring about equality to a nation and to push for a classless society. In some aspects, it has benefits but the fact still remains, not all are happy with the idea. Just like in any form of government, there are good and bad sides.

Principles of Socialism

The Taking of Political Power

Our goal as socialists in the USA must be the capturing of control of the executive and legislative branches of the federal government, as a necessary first step to structural transformations. In all the socialist movements cited above, although their specific strategies differed, they formed an alternative political party or social movement, outside the political establishment, which sought to take political power. In the USA, the process could include the strategy of taking popular control of the Democratic Party, but not necessarily; the key factor is that there must be a politically intelligent plan for the taking of political power. In addition, there must be constant critical reflection with respect to the norms and regulations of the political process itself, so that alternative institutions for the consolidation of popular political power can be developed in the long run.

In the Name of the People

All of the diverse sectors of the people have been present as leaders and participants in the historic socialist revolutions, and therefore, the most politically effective strategy would be to call all the diverse sectors of the people to popular democratic socialist revolution. Here the concept of the 99% that emerged from the Occupy Movement is a good start. One of the historic errors of third parties and social movements of the United States is that they have been overly identified with one sector of the people, be it workers, blacks, women, or ecologists. In the historic socialist revolutions of the world, a vanguard emerged among the people, and its members came from all popular sectors, including male professionals and middle class students from the ethnic majority, who in some cases played a critically important leading role. In calling the people to socialist revolution, the politically intelligent strategy it to call all of the people, without any prejudgment, based on gender, color, or class, concerning one's individual capacity and commitment to contribute to the struggle.

In Defense of the Nation

The successful socialist revolutions in other lands presented themselves as defenders of the dignity of the nation, as representing the best tendencies of the national political culture. They painted the established ruling class as unpatriotic traitors of the nation.

A socialist movement cannot permit right-wing currents to define patriotism. It must draw upon historic popular movements in the United States to formulate an alternative narrative on the meaning and destiny of America. The nation is itself a unifying concept, enabling the movement to develop an integral understanding in calling the diverse sectors of the people.

In Defense of the National Economy

A national plan for economic and social development must be formulated, in which the necessary role of the state as regulator of and major actor in the economy is articulated and explained. The essential, defining characteristic of socialism is not state ownership of the means of production, even though nationalizations in strategic industries occurred in socialist revolutions. In fact, the nations constructing socialism all have evolved to sanction multiple forms of property, including cooperatives, joint ventures, and private property, both domestic and foreign. Observing this process of evolution, we are able to discern that the defining characteristic of socialist economies is that the state formulates a plan for the economic and social development of the nation, and the state itself is a key actor in the economy. Accordingly, a socialist platform must be presented to the people, explaining the logic of a state-directed plan for national economic and social development, standing in contrast to the capitalist logic of giving priority to the profits of corporations.

In Defense of the Social and Economic Rights of the People

Including employment, health care, education, housing, transportation, and physical safety as fundamental human rights and needs; regardless of income, gender, race, ethnicity, religion, political affiliation, or sexual orientation and identity. Socialist projects have an integral vision of human rights, in which not only political and civil rights are affirmed, but also social and economic rights, which constitute the foundation for a decent standard of living. These rights are universal and unconditioned, that is, not conditioned on ability to pay. In socialism, the state has the obligation to mobilize resources to ensure that the social and economic rights of the people are protected.

In Defense of Humanity

Standing against imperialist policies that sanction intervention in the political affairs and economies of other nations. A central socialist message must be that imperialist policies are shortsighted, for they seek economic gain without consideration of the consequences for other nations or for the world-system as a whole. Such an approach to international affairs by the more powerful nations is not sustainable for humanity in the long run. Here a historical and global understanding is indispensable. Socialists must understand and effectively teach to the people that the neocolonial world-system has been constructed on a colonial foundation, and it is no longer sustainable; and that our own nation's spectacular ascent was attained through strategic imperialist insertion into the evolving colonial/neocolonial world-system, an approach to world affairs that is no longer politically, ecologically, or economically viable. Socialists must raise the banner of anti-imperialism and opposition to neocolonialism, calling the people to a genuine and true form of patriotism that is internationalist and that cooperates with other nations, seeking to develop a just and sustainable world-system.

In Defense of Nature

In cooperation with other nations, in order to guarantee the sustainability of the human species and preservation of natural diversity. With respect to this issue, the failure of the capitalist logic of giving priority to profits is demonstrable, and it should be effectively explained to the people.

In Defense of Knowledge

Seeking to expand alternative and public media, and to transform norms for the dissemination of news and knowledge. The forms in which capitalist logic distorts the media of information and the dissemination of scientific knowledge must be well understood by socialists and effectively explained to the people.

Those of us who consider ourselves socialists do so because of a concern for a nation and a world in profound and sustained crisis. Our experiences and study have led us to the conclusion that none of the currents of thought and action that take as their starting points the assumptions, concepts, and structures of capitalism can resolve the problems that the nation and humanity confront.

Institutional Models of Socialism

Central Planning

Throughout the 20th century, the standard socialist answer to the question "if not capitalism, then what?" was centrally-planned socialism.

Under central planning, "production is organized and coordinated within an administrative hierarchy, with decisions being made at the center and passed down through intermediate levels of the hierarchy to the production units". Political authorities at the top of this hierarchy decide on broad economic objectives—build up heavy industry, satisfy consumer preferences, develop a backward region, and so on. Central planners then generate a concrete plan to achieve these objectives. To this end, they first gather a massive amount of information. Tens of thousands of enterprises inform planners of their productive capabilities and input requirements; millions of consumers communicate their consumption preferences. With this information in hand, planners, through a complex, multi-stage, "iterative" process, arrive at an overall plan for the economy that sets specific production targets for each enterprise. (Factory A, produce X shoes; factory B, produce Y amount of steel, and so on.) The center sends these orders to enterprise managers, who then devise more specific labor processes through which their workers produce the ordered goods in the right way at the right time. To the extent that the overall plan is fulfilled, sufficient resources are produced to meet whatever broad objectives political authorities have chosen, and the economy 'works'.

What is to be said in favor of central planning? In theory, quite a bit. Central planning replaces capitalism's anarchic market production for profit with planned production for use. It therefore promises to eliminate all those problems that socialists associate with private property, markets, and the pursuit of profits—problems like economic instability and poverty, class conflict and exploitation, various barriers to "real freedom" and self-realization, such as alienating labor and inadequate free time, lack of community and solidarity, and unjust economic inequalities. Freed of these capitalist pathologies, a centrally planned society would be classless, prosperous, and harmonious; it would be a society in which "the free development of each is the condition of the free development of all".

Or so the story goes. However, critics allege that in practice central planning performs poorly. There are two problems worth pulling apart here.

The first is economic. Although centrally planned economies eliminate the worst forms of poverty, they do not produce generalized affluence. Under central planning, innovation is sluggish. Product quality is low. Shortages and hoarding are common. Work effort is lacking. These defects stem from underlying information, calculation, and incentive problems. Central planners, critics argue, cannot know what people want, or what producers are able to produce, with sufficient accuracy; nor, even if they could, would they be able to use this massive quantity of information to calculate a coherent overall plan; nor, even if they could calculate such a plan, would they be able to incentivize managers and workers to follow it faithfully.

The second problem with central planning is normative. Central planning, critics say, does not lead to an egalitarian, classless utopia, but to an authoritarian, undemocratic society dominated by a "coordinator class" of political elites, planners, and enterprise managers. Indeed, the basic logic of the system guarantees that central planning is a "road to serfdom" (in Hayek's famous phrase) rather than a route to democratic empowerment. As one critic explains, "Central planners gather information, calculate a plan, and issue 'marching orders' to production units. The relationship between the central agency and the production units is authoritative rather than democratic, and exclusive rather than participatory". Information flows up the hierarchy; orders flow down. Central planners decide; everyone else obeys. This seems rather far from the "radical empowerment" envisioned by many socialists.

Indeed, central planning's economic and normative failings are related; the latter compound the former. It is partly *because* central planning alienates and disempowers workers that it performs so poorly *qua* economic system. Workers, so treated, expend little effort at work, ignore orders, under-report their productive capabilities, over-report their output, and so on.

Persuaded by these objections, most socialists today reject central planning, holding that it simply doesn't work sufficiently well and that it comes at too steep a cost to democratic empowerment and freedom. But if they reject central planning, what do they propose to put in its place? There would seem to be only two options: either socialists rehabilitate planning by decentralizing and democratizing it, or they make peace with the market. The first route leads to some form of "participatory planning"; the second, to "market socialism". The next two subsections explore these models in greater detail.

Participatory Planning

Perhaps the problem with central planning has to do with *centralization* rather than *planning*: this is the core thought behind "participatory" or "democratic" planning. Advocates of this approach include Pat Devine, Michael Albert, and Robin Hahnel. Because Albert and Hahnel's model, called "participatory economics," or "parecon" for short, is especially well developed.

Parecon: Basic Features

Parecon rests on five main institutional proposals:

Social ownership of the means of production: Social ownership means simply that nobody in particular owns the means of production; rather, "we all own them equally, so that ownership has no bearing on the distribution of income, wealth or power". What *does* bear on the distribution of income in a parecon is effort and sacrifice. The underlying rationale here is luck egalitarian. People, Albert and Hahnel argue, should be rewarded or penalized only for those things under their control. But the only thing that people control is their level of effort and sacrifice. Therefore, they should be rewarded and penalized only for their level of effort and sacrifice. Those who work harder or longer should enjoy greater consumption opportunities than those who work less hard and less long. There is an exception here: people who are unable to work will be provided with an average income.

Democratic workplaces: Parecon takes as one of its core values the idea of "democratic self-management," which implies that "each actor in the economy should influence economic outcomes in proportion to how those outcomes affect him or her". In other words, "Our say in decisions should reflect how much they affect us". This norm implies that decisions affecting only a given individual should be left entirely to that individual. But other decisions have broader consequences, and are therefore appropriate objects of democratic choice. Many workplace decisions fall into this "other-affecting" category. Albert and Hahnel propose a complex system of nested "councils" for handling such decisions. Some workplace decisions will be entirely up to individual workers; others, assigned to work-teams; still others, to the enterprise as a whole. Indeed, since some workplace decisions affect people beyond the workplace's four walls, such as consumers, some method for granting an appropriate degree of influence to these affected external actors must be found. Albert and Hahnel propose democratic "consumer councils" and "industry councils".

Balanced job complexes: Parecon proposes to radically remake the division of labor by creating "balanced job complexes" in which "the combination of tasks and responsibilities each worker has would accord them the same empowerment and quality of life benefits as the combination every other worker has". This is, of course, very far from how occupations are structured currently. Under capitalism, considerations of profit and class power largely determine the way in which different productive tasks are bundled into jobs. The result is a division of labor that assigns routine, boring, disempowering (but profitable) work to the many, while reserving varied, complex, empowering work for the privileged few.

Parecon rejects this inequitable division. It does so on grounds of fairness: why should interesting and enjoyable work be hoarded by some rather than shared by all? It also objects on democratic grounds: unequal division of empowering work "inexorably destroys participatory potentials and creates class differences". Any workplace with, say, janitors and managers will be a *de facto* hierarchy, even if it is, on paper, democratically organized. In the name of fairness and democracy, then, we must transform the division of labor so that "every individual will be regularly involved in both conception and execution tasks, with comparable empowerment and quality of life circumstances for all".

Allocation in Parecon: Economic Coordination through Councils

This brings us to feature 5:

Economic coordination through councils. Every economy must decide what gets produced and consumed, and in what quantities. This is the problem of allocation. Market systems solve this problem through decentralized, voluntary, self-interested competition and exchange between buyers and sellers. Recall Adam Smith's baker, who makes bread not because someone tells him to, but because by making bread, he can make money through trade. Centrally-planned economies solve the allocative problem by handing it over to a small group of economic elites, who craft a comprehensive plan for the entire economy and issue binding instructions for realizing it. Moscow decides that X amount of shoes will be produced, Y amount of steel, and so on, and enforces these demands on lower levels in the economic hierarchy.

Parecon rejects both approaches. In place of markets and central planning, it proposes a system of nested worker and consumer councils, through which individuals cooperatively generate an overall plan for production and consumption. Albert and Hahnel call this system "decentralized participatory planning."

Simplifying greatly, its basic gist is this. To figure out what people want to consume, we ask them. To figure out what they are willing to produce, we ask them. We then aggregate all these responses and compare proposed supply with proposed demand. If they don't match, we close the gap through democratic negotiation conducted on a footing of equality. Through such negotiation, we eventually reach, say, five feasible plans. We put them to a vote and implement the winner. Decentralized participatory planning thus promises to solve the allocative problem without hierarchy or markets.

The system features several key participants: first, worker councils (and federations thereof—for example, a "software industry council," a "farming council," and so forth.); second, consumer councils (and federations thereof—for example, neighborhood councils, city-level councils, state-level councils, and so on); and third, the "iteration facilitation board," or IFB. The IFB initiates the planning process by announcing provisional prices for all inputs and outputs. Importantly, these prices should reflect the "full social costs and benefits" associated with these inputs and outputs, including opportunity costs and externalities, whether positive or negative. Albert and Hahnel see this as a key difference with market systems. In a parecon, prices will accurately track the true social costs of production. Prices rarely do this in market societies. Think, for instance, of the absurdly low price of gasoline in the United States, despite the ecological and economic costs of its widespread production and use.

With these provisional prices in hand, each economic actor—individuals and councils and federations of councils—proposes both a) a consumption plan and b) a production plan. The former specifies what the actor would like to consume during the period being planned (the upcoming year, say); the latter specifies which outputs the actor proposes to produce, and the inputs they will require to do this. Plans will go to appropriate councils for approval. Thus, a family might submit their consumption plan to the neighborhood consumption council, while a worker might submit her plan to her work-team or to the larger workplace council.

On what basis are proposals approved or rejected? Individual consumption proposals should be approved if the person's income is equal to or greater than the total cost of the goods requested. Income, remember, is a function of one's effort and sacrifice at work. Higher-level consumption proposals (for a neighborhood, say) should be approved if the *group's* income (minus the costs of members' personal consumption) suffices to cover the costs of the requested items. The underlying thought here is that a community's overall consumption should correspond to the amount of effort its members expend producing goods and services for society: the harder the community works, the more it is entitled to consume. Turning to production proposals, these are evaluated by comparing the estimated social benefits of the goods and services produced with the estimated social costs of producing them. If this ratio is positive, then the production proposal should be accepted; if it is negative, then the proposal does not represent a responsible use of societal resources, and it is sent back for revision.

The IFB aggregates all approved proposals and determines whether projected supply matches projected demand. Barring a miracle, it won't, not at this stage. So the IFB recalculates prices in light of the mismatch between supply and demand, raising prices for goods with excess demand, lowering prices for those with excess supply, and sends the plans back to their originators for revision. Using the new prices, consumers and producers tweak their proposals, perhaps shifting demand to lower-priced goods and increasing supply of goods with high prices. They then send these revised proposals to the relevant councils, which evaluate them as before. Eventually, all approved proposals make their way to the IFB, which recalculates overall supply and demand to see if they match. If they do, then the process is over; if they don't, then another round of revisions is required. If the process ends with multiple feasible plans, then society votes to determine the winner.

Evaluating Parecon

This is, to be sure, an incredibly complex procedure, indeed, much more complex than this brief sketch indicates. Even Albert and Hahnel admit that it will take multiple rounds of negotiation, and no small amount of paperwork, to arrive at a feasible plan. But the hope is that "as every individual or collective worker or consumer participant negotiates through successive rounds of back and forth exchange of their proposals with all other participants, they alter their proposals to accord with the messages they receive, and the process converges". And this, notice, *without markets or central planning*:

> " There is no center or top. There is no competition. Each actor fulfills responsibilities that bring them into greater rather than reduced solidarity with other producers and consumers. Everyone is remunerated appropriately for effort and sacrifice. And everyone has proportionate influence on their personal choices as well as those of larger collectives and the whole society ".

The absence of hierarchy is worth emphasizing. Although there is an IFB, and although one's consumption and production proposals must be approved by others, the overall distribution of power is web-like rather than hierarchical. No one occupies any special position of authority. Economic decisions are not dominated by the wealthy (as under capitalism) or the politically connected (as under central planning). Instead, all economic decision-making is radically democratic and open to negotiation: each person has a say over decisions that affect him or her, proportional to the degree to which he or she is affected. Parecon may have important flaws, but inadequate respect for democratic values would not seem to be among them. Indeed, it is hard to imagine a system more faithful to the core socialist commitment to bottom-up, democratic control over the economy. This, surely, is parecon's chief virtue from the socialist perspective.Erik Olin Wright writes:

> "The information complexity of the iterated planning process described in *Parecon* might in the end simply overwhelm the planning process. Albert is confident that with appropriate computers this would not be a problem Perhaps he is right. But he may also be horribly wrong. As described the information process seems hugely burdensome".

Defenders of parecon reply to such worries in several ways. First, they argue that critics overestimate the amount of planning that parecon requires. Setting up one's initial consumption proposal may well take lots of time and energy. But with that initial investment made, planning in subsequent years should be much quicker. One can simply base future plans off of the original one, tweaking here and there as necessary.

Nor need one specify in great detail what one wants to consume. "For planning purposes," writes Albert, "we need only request *types* of goods, even though later everyone will pick an exact size, style, and color to actually consume". One's consumption proposal must "express preferences for socks, but not for colors or type of socks; for soda, books, and bicycles, but not for flavors, titles, or styles of each".

Second reply to the infeasibility worry: we must remember that *other* economic systems require paperwork and planning, too. Under market socialism (and capitalism) consumers must make budgets, do their taxes, pay bills, go shopping, and so on. Enterprises must decide what they will make and in what quantities. They must also make various personnel decisions, deciding who will work with whom, for how long, on which projects, and so on. Added up over the course of the year, the amount of time spent on such activities is far from trivial. Indeed, one might argue that total planning time will be roughly constant across market- and participatory-planning-based systems.

Finally, suppose that parecon *does* require a substantial amount of time and energy, or perhaps, *more* time and energy than alternative systems. Still, these costs must be judged against the potential benefits. Parecon promises a more equal, fraternal, just, democratic society. Is it even remotely reasonable to reject such a society on the grounds that it requires too much paperwork?

In sum, defenders of parecon argue 1) that their proposal won't prove nearly as burdensome in practice as critics fear; indeed, 2) one may reasonably doubt that it is any *more* burdensome than other systems; and 3) even if parecon *does* prove burdensome both absolutely and comparatively, surely the sacrifice is worth the result.

Market Socialism

Suppose one rejects central planning, but also doubts the feasibility (or perhaps even the desirability) of parecon-style participatory planning.

On the traditional view, socialists must, by definition, be opposed not simply to private property, but also to markets. Market socialists disagree. On their view, socialism requires only a certain form of ownership, namely, social rather than private ownership. About markets, socialists should be open-minded. Markets are just tools for communicating information and motivating economic activity. Like any tool, they should be evaluated instrumentally. Do they work better than alternatives? If so, then socialists should embrace them.

And indeed, market socialists characteristically argue that markets *do* work better than the alternatives: just look at the economic record. This is not to say that markets are perfect, nor is it to say that they should be allowed to operate 'freely,' without any constraints. Market regulations are integral to the market socialist vision. Market socialists are no kind of market fundamentalists. Rather, they view themselves as pragmatists. They see the evils of capitalism, but they also see the problems with planning-based socialist alternatives. The way forward, they argue, is to take the good parts of capitalism and combine them with the good parts of socialism. This will displease fundamentalists on both sides, but what alternative is there? Capitalism is a moral disaster. Central planning was worse. Participatory planning is a pipe dream. 21st century leftists must fuse socialism with markets. There is no other way. Or so market socialists argue.

Schweickart's Economic Democracy

Boiled down to essentials, ED has three main features: worker self-management, the market, and social control of investment.

Worker self-management: "Each productive enterprise is controlled by those who work there". Workers together decide all aspects of production: what to make, how to make it, workplace policies, compensation, and so on. This does not preclude the use of managers or experts. In large firms especially, some delegation of authority will almost certainly prove necessary. Schweickart suggests that workers might elect a workers' council which will then appoint executives, managers, and so on.

The market: In stark contrast with planning-based forms of socialism, ED solves the problem of allocation using market competition between profit-seeking enterprises. ED's enterprises start with a sum of money (M). They use this money to buy productive inputs on the market, which they transform into commodities. They then compete with other enterprises to sell these commodities to consumers or other enterprises, thereby ending up with a new amount of money (M'). (Prices are determined mainly by market forces of supply and demand, although price regulations may sometimes be appropriate: again, Schweickart is no market fundamentalist.) In the normal case M' > M, indicating that the enterprise has turned a profit. Indeed, turning a profit is the immediate aim of production in ED: enterprises produce to make money, not (primarily) to satisfy human needs. As Schweickart says, "profit is not a dirty word in this form of socialism".

This may sound rather close to capitalism, but in fact there is an important difference here. Under capitalism, profits go to owners, not workers, who receive wages. Under ED, by contrast, there are no wages; rather, "workers get all that remains once nonlabor costs have been paid" Precisely how workers divvy up the enterprise's surplus is up to them. In theory they could split it equally. But given the need to outcompete other enterprises—hence, to attract and retain skilled labor—some degree of inequality is likely to be chosen. More productive workers, or workers with skills in higher demand, will almost certainly earn more than their fellows. Notice the difference here with parecon, which links income to effort rather than contribution or other "morally arbitrary" factors beyond the agent's control. Empirical evidence suggests that self-managed firms (like those in the Mondragon cooperative in Spain) opt for a 4 or 5:1 ratio between the incomes of the highest- and lowest-paid employees: quite a dramatic difference from the 300:1 spread typical in large capitalist corporations.

Social control over investment: This is the most clearly "socialist" piece of Schweickart's model. In an ED, the means of production belong to all members of society, not to the enterprises that happen to deploy them. To reflect this social rather than sectional or private ownership, all enterprises must pay a capital assets tax. "This tax," writes Schweickart, "may be regarded as a leasing fee paid by the workers of the enterprise for use of social property that belongs to all". Revenues from this tax constitute the national investment fund, which is the sole source of investment money in ED. By tweaking the tax rate, society can determine the size of the national investment fund—hence, the amount of money available for investment, and thus the overall level of economic growth and development.

Note the contrast with capitalism: under capitalism, most investment comes from private rather than public sources. Both the amount and direction of economic development therefore depend on the whims and abilities of private investors. This leads to the boom and bust cycle as well as other pathologies such as excessive growth, ecological devastation, underdeveloped regions alongside overdeveloped ones, unemployment, poverty, and all the rest. Under ED, by contrast, investment is democratically controlled by all members of society. In theory, this should enable "more rational, equitable, and democratic development than can be expected under capitalism".

How, specifically, should social control over investment be institutionalized? There are many options. At one extreme, society might opt for a planning-heavy system in which a democratically accountable planning board draws up a plan for all new investment, which Schweickart estimates would constitute about 15% of GDP, and allocates funds accordingly. For example, the planning board might decide to prioritize renewable energy, or consumer goods, or whatever. At the other extreme, society might prefer a *laissez-faire* model in which funds are channeled through public banks to enterprises using essentially the same criteria that capitalist banks use: namely, profitability. In this version of ED, market forces would largely determine the pattern of investment.

Schweickart himself proposes something in the middle of these two options. Funds should go to regions (for example, Texas) and communities (for example, Fort Worth) on a *per capita* basis. If the Fort Worth region has the same population as Silicon Valley, then it will receive the same amount of investment. In ED, then, there will be no economic backwaters, no regions or communities left behind. Nor will regions or communities be locked into a destructive neoliberal "race to the bottom" to attract investment dollars. Each community receives its "fair share" no matter how business-friendly (or unfriendly) its policies.

Once distributed to regions and communities on a *per capita* basis, investment funds are channeled to regional and community enterprises by public banks. Enterprises in need of investment (say, to expand production) apply to area banks for funds. Banks assess applications on the basis of a) profitability, b) job creation, and c) any other democratically chosen criteria, such as ecological impact. This mixed standard implies that while profitability matters, it is not *all* that matters. Projects that further socially chosen goals may be chosen over more profitable, but less socially desirable alternatives.

Summing up, Schweickart's model strategically transplants certain core elements of capitalism into a broadly socialist framework. We get markets and profit-seeking enterprises, but also workplace democracy and social control over investment. The result, Schweickart argues, is an economy that outperforms all rivals—whether socialist or capitalist—in terms of values dear to socialist hearts, such as equality, economic stability, human development, democracy, and environmentalism. ED thus promises to deliver "socialism that would really work," to quote the title of one of Schweickart's early articles on the topic.

Evaluating Economic Democracy

Perhaps it would really work, but would it be *socialism*? This, in essence, is the main criticism of Schweickart's model (and of market socialism more generally).

That his proposal would work—that it is feasible—seems relatively uncontroversial. Markets work. Self-managed enterprises work, as illustrated by decades of empirical evidence. Social control over investment is the only truly novel piece of Schweickart's model, but its basic mechanisms—the capital assets tax, the national investment fund, the system of public banks allocating funds on the basis of profitability as well as other socially chosen considerations—raise no obvious feasibility worries. Granted, neoclassical economists will complain that because ED regulates and interferes with markets in various ways, it sacrifices efficiency. But "less than perfectly efficient" does not mean "infeasible". And efficiency isn't the only thing we want from an economy anyway. Better to sacrifice some efficiency, Schweickart would argue, for gains in employment, more equitable development across regions, greater democratic empowerment at work, and so on. So all things considered, market socialism seems eminently feasible. This is perhaps its greatest selling point.

But is it desirable? Critics right and left will argue that it is not. Those on the right will complain that ED limits basic economic freedoms, such as the formal freedom to own the means of production, to hire wage labor, and to run a business in a un-democratic fashion. Market socialists will reply that not all formal freedoms are worth protecting. They will further suggest that ED will enhance *effective* economic freedom for the vast majority, even if this means diminishing economic freedom, both formal and effective, for those elites who would, absent ED, enjoy greater workplace control and authority. Under capitalism, most workers control no productive property and enjoy no real say over their work. Economic power is monopolized by a tiny class of owners. Under ED, by contrast, economic hierarchies are flattened. Economic power within the enterprise is distributed equally to all workers on a one worker, one vote basis. Consequently, everyone has the effective freedom to shape workplace decisions. Seen from this angle, ED enhances rather than reduces economic freedom.

Market socialism attracts critical fire from the left as well as the right. It is a strange form of socialism indeed, leftist critics will argue, that features anarchic market production for profit rather than planned production for use. With markets and profits come competition, greed, fear, and the diminution of community; with markets and profits come consumerism, ever-expanding hours of work, and the ecologically insane desire for never-ending economic growth.

Schweickart replies that these worries are overblown. Yes, ED features competition; yes, there will be advertising and some degree of consumerism; yes, enterprises may, under certain circumstances, seek to grow. But the details make a difference. Competition, consumerism, and economic growth are all held in check in ED by countervailing forces. Social control over investment means that we can democratically determine the overall rate and direction of economic growth. We can prioritize environmental aims, for instance, over the rapacious quest, so characteristic of capitalism, for additional output at whatever cost. Workplace democracy means that we can choose shorter working hours in exchange for reduced consumption opportunities. Moreover, because democratic firms seek to maximize profit *per-worker* (rather than *total* profit, as do capitalist firms), they will not expand as aggressively as their capitalist counterparts. But reduced expansion means less output that needs to be sold, which, in turn, reduces demand for advertising and marketing. In short, for all of these reasons ED is absolutely compatible with the socialist vision of a less-consumerist, more leisurely, ecologically sane world, or so defenders of market socialism would argue.

References

- Socialism: plato.stanford.edu, Retrieved 14 August, 2020
- Examples-of-socialism: examples.yourdictionary.com, Retrieved 19 April, 2020
- Difference-between-communism-and-socialism-195448: thoughtco.com, Retrieved 25 May, 2020
- 10-biggest-pros-and-cons-of-socialism: greengarageblog.org, Retrieved 26 July, 2020
- The-principles-of-socialism: counterpunch.org, Retrieved 06 June, 2020

Types of Socialism 2

- Religious Socialism
- Utopian Socialism
- Revolutionary Socialism
- State Socialism
- Market Socialism
- Ethical Socialism
- Socialist Mode of Production
- Neosocialism
- Democratic Socialism
- Yellow Socialism

Socialism is branched into various types such as religious socialism, revolutionary socialism, state socialism, eco-socialism, neosocialism, yellow socialism, etc. This chapter closely examines the different types of socialism to provide an extensive understanding of the subject.

Religious Socialism

One of the world's major economic-political ideologies is socialism, a system in which the production and distribution of goods is organized by a highly centralized government but controlled by the workers. The point of socialism is to ensure that the workers get a fair share of the value of their labor, and to put the benefits of industry back into society in a way that benefits everyone. There are countless variations and iterations of socialism, which is much more fluid and flexible than its cousins Marxism and Communism, and some people have even turned to their spiritual beliefs to advance socialist causes. A doctrine which blends socialist and religious ideologies is known as religious socialism. In general, religious socialism supports the idea that your economic decisions in this life can have important impacts on the afterlife.

Religious socialism is a broad theory, based loosely on the idea that some religious systems are compatible with socialism. As with the socialism itself, religious socialism largely rose out of the industrial revolutions of the 19th century. Socialists saw industrialization as stripping the workers of their agency and control over the value of their own labor. They believed that industrial capitalism, with no government regulation, was bad for society and oppressive of the poor.

Socialism shares a devotion to welfare with most major religions.

Socialism emerged with a focus on the welfare of the poor and the overall health of society. It was often moralistic, looking to create a stronger and better set of morals for society, and believed in the use of a centralized authority to distribute resources and welfare. Most of the world's religions embrace similar policies, from the focus on elevating the poor to welfare to the role of a central authority. Thus, religious socialism emerged from the pairing of these shared beliefs, as a way to promote and spread socialist ideologies within religious societies.

Socialism is a flexible doctrine, so there is no single theory of religious socialism. Instead, we see the concept of religious socialism applied to a variety of the world's major religions.

Utopian Socialism

Utopian socialism is the first current of modern socialism and socialist thought as exemplified by the work of Henri de Saint-Simon, Charles Fourier, Étienne Cabet,

Robert Owen and Henry George. Utopian socialism is often described as the presentation of visions and outlines for imaginary or futuristic ideal societies, with positive ideals being the main reason for moving society in such a direction. Later socialists and critics of utopian socialism viewed utopian socialism as not being grounded in actual material conditions of existing society and in some cases as reactionary. These visions of ideal societies competed with Marxist-inspired revolutionary social democratic movements.

As a term or label, it is most often applied to, or used to define, those socialists who lived in the first quarter of the 19th century who were ascribed the label utopian by later socialists as a pejorative in order to imply *naiveté* and to dismiss their ideas as fanciful and unrealistic. A similar school of thought that emerged in the early 20th century which makes the case for socialism on moral grounds is ethical socialism.

One key difference between utopian socialists and other socialists (including most anarchists) is that utopian socialists generally do not believe any form of class struggle or social revolution is necessary for socialism to emerge. Utopian socialists believe that people of all classes can voluntarily adopt their plan for society if it is presented convincingly. They feel their form of cooperative socialism can be established among like-minded people within the existing society and that their small communities can demonstrate the feasibility of their plan for society.

The thinkers identified as utopian socialist did not use the term utopian to refer to their ideas. Karl Marx and Friedrich Engels were the first thinkers to refer to them as utopian, referring to all socialist ideas that simply presented a vision and distant goal of an ethically just society as utopian. This utopian mindset which held an integrated conception of the goal, the means to produce said goal and an understanding of the way that those means would inevitably be produced through examining social and economic phenomena can be contrasted with scientific socialism which has been likened to Taylorism.

This distinction was made clear in Engels' work Socialism: Utopian and Scientific. Utopian socialists were seen as wanting to expand the principles of the French revolution in order to create a more rational society. Despite being labeled as utopian by later socialists, their aims were not always utopian and their values often included rigid support for the scientific method and the creation of a society based upon scientific understanding.

Development

The term utopian socialism was introduced by Karl Marx in "For a Ruthless Criticism of Everything" in 1843 and then developed in *The Communist Manifesto* in 1848, although shortly before its publication Marx had already attacked the ideas of Pierre-Joseph Proudhon in *Das Elend der Philosophie*. The term was used by later socialist thinkers to describe early socialist or quasi-socialist intellectuals who created hypothetical visions of egalitarian, communalist, meritocratic, or other notions of perfect societies without considering how these societies could be created or sustained.

In Das Elend der Philosophie, English title The Poverty of Philosophy, Marx criticized the economic and philosophical arguments of Proudhon set forth in The System of Economic Contradictions, or The Philosophy of Poverty. Marx accused Proudhon of wanting to rise above the bourgeoisie. In the history of Marx's thought and Marxism, this work is pivotal in the distinction between the concepts of utopian socialism and what Marx and the Marxists claimed as scientific socialism.

Although utopian socialists shared few political, social, or economic perspectives, Marx and Engels argued that they shared certain intellectual characteristics. In *The Communist Manifesto*, Marx and Engels wrote: "The undeveloped state of the class struggle, as well as their own surroundings, causes Socialists of this kind to consider themselves far superior to all class antagonisms. They want to improve the condition of every member of society, even that of the most favored. Hence, they habitually appeal to society at large, without distinction of class; nay, by preference, to the ruling class. For how can people, when once they understand their system, fail to see it in the best possible plan of the best possible state of society? Hence, they reject all political, and especially all revolutionary, action; they wish to attain their ends by peaceful means, and endeavor, by small experiments, necessarily doomed to failure, and by the force of example, to pave the way for the new social Gospel".

Marx and Engels used the term scientific socialism to describe the type of socialism they saw themselves developing. According to Engels, socialism was not "an accidental discovery of this or that ingenious brain, but the necessary outcome of the struggle between two historically developed classes – the proletariat and the bourgeoisie. Its task was no longer to manufacture a system of society as perfect as possible, but to examine the historical-economic succession of events from which these classes and their antagonism had of necessity sprung, and to discover in the economic conditions thus created the means of ending the conflict".

Critics have argued that utopian socialists who established experimental communities were in fact trying to apply the scientific method to human social organization and were therefore not utopian. For instance, Joshua Muravchik on the basis of Karl Popper's definition of science as "the practice of experimentation, of hypothesis and test" argued that "Owen and Fourier and their followers were the real 'scientific socialists.' They hit upon the idea of socialism, and they tested it by attempting to form socialist communities". Muravchik further argued that in contrast Marx made untestable predictions about the future and that Marx's view that socialism would be created by impersonal historical forces may lead one to conclude that it is unnecessary to strive for socialism because it will happen anyway.

Since the mid-19th century, Marxism and Marxism–Leninism overtook utopian socialism in terms of intellectual development and number of adherents. At one time almost half the population of the world lived under regimes that claimed to be Marxist. Currents like Saint-Simonianism and Fourierism attracted the interest of numerous later authors but failed to compete with the now dominant Marxist, Proudhonist, or Leninist schools on a political level. It has been noted that they exerted a significant influence on the emergence of new religious movements such as spiritualism and occultism.

Some communities of the modern intentional community movement such as kibbutzim could be categorized as utopian socialist.

Religious sects whose members live communally such as the Hutterites or Bruderhof Communities are not usually called utopian socialists, although their way of living is a prime example. Some have categorized them as religious socialists. The Hutterites, Bruderhof and Amish have appeared in several documentaries that question if communal living with a spiritual basis can ever be counted as utopia.

Classless modes of production in hunter-gatherer societies are referred to as primitive communism by Marxists to stress their classless nature.

A related concept is that of a socialist utopia, usually depicted in works of fiction as possible ways society can turn out to be in the future and often combined with notions of a technologically revolutionized economy.

Revolutionary Socialism

Revolutionary socialism is the socialist doctrine that social revolution is necessary in order to bring about structural changes to society. More specifically, it is the view that revolution is a necessary precondition for a transition from capitalism to socialism. Revolution is not necessarily defined as a violent insurrection; it is defined as seizure of political power by mass movements of the working class so that the state is directly controlled or abolished by the working class as opposed to the capitalist class and its interests. Revolutionary socialists believe such a state of affairs is a precondition for establishing socialism and orthodox Marxists believe that it is inevitable but not predetermined.

Revolutionary socialism encompasses multiple political and social movements that may define "revolution" differently from one another. These include movements based on orthodox Marxist theory, such as De Leonism, impossibilism, and Luxemburgism; as well as movements based on Leninism and the theory of vanguardist-led revolution, such as Maoism, Marxism–Leninism, and Trotskyism. Revolutionary socialism also includes non-Marxist movements, such as those found in anarchism, revolutionary syndicalism, and democratic socialism.

It is used in contrast to the reformism of social democracy and other evolutionary approaches to socialism. Revolutionary socialism is opposed to social movements that seek to gradually ameliorate the economic and social problems of capitalism through political reform.

Karl Marx and Friedrich Engels wrote:

> The proletariat, the lowest stratum of our present society, cannot stir, cannot raise itself up, without the whole superincumbent strata of official society being sprung into the air. Though not in substance, yet in form, the struggle of the proletariat with the bourgeoisie is at first a national struggle. The proletariat of each country must, of course, first of all settle matters with its own bourgeoisie. In depicting the most general phases of the development of the proletariat, we traced the more or less veiled civil war, raging within existing society, up to the point where that war breaks out into open revolution, and where the violent overthrow of the bourgeoisie lays the foundation for the sway of the proletariat. The Communists fight for the attainment of the immediate aims, for the enforcement of the momentary interests of the working class; The Communists disdain to conceal their views and aims. They openly declare that their ends can be attained only by the forcible overthrow of all existing social conditions. Let the ruling classes tremble at a Communistic revolution.

Twenty-four years after *The Communist Manifesto*, Marx and Engels admitted that in developed countries "labour may attain its goal by peaceful means". Marxist scholar Adam Schaff argued that Marx, Engels and Lenin have expressed such view "on many occasions". By contrast, the Blanquist view emphasised the overthrow by force of the ruling elite in government by an active minority of revolutionaries, who then proceed to implement socialist change, disregarding the state of readiness of society as a whole and the mass of the population in particular for revolutionary change.

In 1875, the Social Democratic Party of Germany (SPD) published a somewhat reformist Gotha Program, which was attacked by Marx in *Critique of the Gotha Program*, where he reiterated the need for dictatorship of the proletariat. The reformist viewpoint was introduced into Marxist thought by Eduard Bernstein, one of the leaders of the SPD. From 1896 to 1898, Bernstein published a series of articles entitled "Probleme des Sozialismus" ("Problems of Socialism"). These articles led to a debate on revisionism in the SPD and can be seen as the origins of a reformist trend within Marxism.

In 1900, Rosa Luxemburg wrote *Social Reform or Revolution*, a polemic against Bernstein's position. The work of reforms, Luxemburg argued, could only be carried on "in the framework of the social form created by the last revolution". In order to advance society to socialism from the capitalist 'social form', a social revolution will be necessary: Bernstein, thundering against the conquest of political power as a theory of Blanquist violence, has the misfortune of labeling as a Blanquist error that which has always been the pivot and the motive force of human history. From the first appearance of class societies, having class struggle as the essential content of their history, the conquest of political power has been the aim of all rising classes. Here is the starting point and end of every historic period In modern times, we see it in the struggle of the bourgeoisie against feudalism.

Vladimir Lenin attacked Bernstein's position in his *What Is To Be Done?* When Bernstein first put forward his ideas, the majority of the SPD rejected them. The 1899 Congress of the SPD reaffirmed the Erfurt programme as did the 1901 congress. The 1903 congress denounced "revisionist efforts".

On 4 August 1914, the SPD members of the Reichstag voted for the government's war budget while the French and Belgium socialists publicly supported and joined their governments. The Zimmerwald Conference in September 1915, attended by Lenin and Leon Trotsky, saw the beginning of the end of the uneasy coexistence of revolutionary socialists and reformist socialists in the parties of Second International. The conference adopted a proposal by Trotsky to avoid an immediate split with the Second International. At first opposed to it, in the end Lenin voted for Trotsky's resolution to avoid a split among anti-war socialists.

In December 1915 and March 1916, eighteen Social Democratic representatives, the Haase-Ledebour Group, voted against war credits and were expelled from the Social Democratic Party. Liebknecht wrote *Revolutionary Socialism in Germany* in 1916, arguing that this group was not a revolutionary socialist group despite their refusal to vote for war credits, further defining in his view what was meant by a revolutionary socialist.

Many revolutionary socialists argue that the Russian Revolution of October 1917 led by Vladimir Lenin follows the revolutionary socialist model of a revolutionary movement guided by a vangaurd party. By contrast, the October revolution is portrayed as a putsch or coup d'état along the lines of Blanquism.

Revolutionary socialists, particularly Trotskyists, argue that the Bolsheviks only seized power as the expression of the mass of workers and peasants, whose desires are brought into being by an organised force—the revolutionary party. Marxists such as Trotskyists argue that Lenin did not advocate seizing of power until he felt that the majority of the population, represented in the soviets, demanded revolutionary change and no longer supported the reformist government of Alexander Kerensky established in the earlier revolution of February 1917:

> " Lenin, after the experience of the reconnoiter, withdrew the slogan of the immediate overthrow of the Provisional Government. But he did not withdraw it for any set period of time, for so many weeks or months, but strictly in dependence upon how quickly the revolt of the masses against the conciliationists would grow ".

For these Marxists, the fact that the Bolsheviks won a majority (in alliance with the Left Socialist-Revolutionaries) in the second all-Russian congress of Soviets—democratically elected bodies—which convened at the time of the October revolution, shows that they had popular support of the masses of workers, peasants and soldiers, the vast majority of Russian society.

In his pamphlet *Lessons of October*, first published in 1924, Trotsky argued that military power lay in the hands of the Bolsheviks before the October Revolution was carried out, but this power was not used against the government until the Bolsheviks gained mass support.

The mass of the soldiers began to be led by the Bolshevik party after the July days of 1917 and followed only the orders of the Military Revolutionary Committee under the leadership of Trotsky in October (also termed the Revolutionary Military Committee in Lenin's collected works). Yet Trotsky only mobilised the Military Revolutionary Committee to seize power on the advent of the Second All-Russian Congress of Soviets of Workers' and Soldiers' Deputies, which began on 25 October 1917.

Following the October Revolution, the Communist International (also known as the Third International) was founded. This International became widely identified with communism, but also defined itself in terms of revolutionary socialism. However, in 1938 Trotskyists formed the Fourth International because they thought that the Third International turned to Marxism–Leninism—this latter International became identified with revolutionary socialism.

Emerging from the Communist International, but critical of the post-1924 Soviet Union, the Trotskyist tradition in Western Europe and elsewhere uses the term "revolutionary socialism". For instance, in 1932 the first issue of the first Canadian Trotskyist newspaper, *The Vanguard*, published an editorial entitled "Revolutionary Socialism vs Reformism". Today, many Trotskyist groups advocate "revolutionary socialism" as opposed to reformism and are considered—and consider themselves—"revolutionary socialists". Luxemburgism is another revolutionary socialist tradition.

State Socialism

State socialism is a classification for any socialist political and economic perspective advocating state ownership of the means of production either as a temporary measure in the transition from capitalism to socialism, or as characteristic of socialism itself.

State socialism is often used interchangeably with state capitalism in reference to the economic systems of Marxist–Leninist states such as the Soviet Union to highlight the role of state planning in these economies, with the critics of said system referring to it more commonly as state capitalism. Democratic and libertarian socialists claim that these states had only a limited number of socialist characteristics. However, Marxist–Leninists maintain that workers in the Soviet Union and other Marxist–Leninist states had genuine control over the means of production through institutions such as trade unions.

State socialism is held in contrast with libertarian socialism which rejects the view that socialism can be constructed by using existing state institutions or by governmental policies. By contrast, proponents of state socialism claim that the state—through practical considerations of governing—must play at least a temporary part in building socialism. It is possible to conceive of a democratic state that owns the means of production, but it is internally organized in a participatory, cooperative fashion, thereby achieving both social ownership of productive property and workplace democracy in day-to-day operations.

The philosophy of state socialism was first explicitly expounded by Ferdinand Lassalle. In contrast to Karl Marx's perspective, Lassalle rejected the concept of the state as a class-based power structure whose main function was to preserve existing class structures, therefore Lassalle also rejected the Marxist view that the state was destined to "wither away". Lassalle considered the state to be an entity independent of class allegiances and as an instrument of justice that would therefore be essential for the achievement of socialism.

Early concepts of state socialism were articulated by anarchist and libertarian philosophers who opposed the concept of the state. In *Statism and Anarchy*, Mikhail Bakunin identified a statist tendency within the Marxist movement which he contrasted to libertarian socialism and attributed to Marx's philosophy. Bakunin predicted that Marx's theory of transition from capitalism to socialism involving the working class seizing state power in a dictatorship of the proletariat would eventually lead to an usurpation of power by the state apparatus acting in its own self-interest, ushering in a new form of capitalism rather than establishing socialism.

As a political ideology, state socialism rose to prominence during the 20th century Bolshevik, Leninist and later Marxist–Leninist revolutions where single-party control over the state and by extension over the political and economic spheres of society was justified as a means to safeguard the revolution against counter-revolutionary insurrection and foreign invasion. The Stalinist theory of socialism in one country was an attempt to legitimize state-directed activity in an effort to accelerate the industrialization of the Soviet Union.

As a political ideology, state socialism is one of the major dividing lines in the broader socialist movement. It is often contrasted non-state or anti-state forms of socialism such as those that advocate direct self-management adhocracy and direct cooperative ownership and management of the means of production. Political philosophies contrasted to state socialism include libertarian socialist philosophies such as anarchism, De Leonism, economic democracy, free-market socialism, libertarian Marxism and syndicalism. These forms of socialism are opposed to hierarchical technocratic socialism, scientific management and state-directed economic planning.

The modern concept of state socialism, when used in reference to Soviet-style economic and political systems, emerged from a deviation in Marxist theory starting with Vladimir Lenin. In Marxist theory, socialism is projected to emerge in the most developed capitalist economies where capitalism suffers the greatest amount of internal contradictions and class conflict. On the other hand, state socialism became a revolutionary theory for the poorest, often quasi-feudal, countries of the world.

In such systems, the state apparatus is used as an instrument of capital accumulation, forcibly extracting surplus from the working class and peasantry for the purposes of modernizing and industrializing poor countries. Such systems are described as state capitalism because the state engages in capital accumulation. However, there is a clear difference between those two concepts. In state socialism, the state as a public entity engages in this activity in order to achieve socialism by re-investing the accumulated capital into the society whether be in more healthcare, education, employment or consumer goods whereas in capitalist societies the surplus extracted from the working class is spent in whatever needs the owners of the means of production wants.

Role of the State in Socialism

In the traditional view of socialism, thinkers like Friedrich Engels and Henri de Saint-Simon took the position that the state will change in nature in a socialist society, with the function of the state changing from one of political rule over people into a scientific administration of the processes of production. Specifically, the state would become a coordinating economic entity consisting of interdependent inclusive associations rather than a mechanism of class and political control, in the process ceasing to be a state in the traditional definition.

Preceding the Bolshevik-led revolution in Russia, many socialist groups such as anarchists, orthodox Marxist currents such as council communism and the Mensheviks, reformists and other democratic and libertarian socialists criticized the idea of using the state to conduct central planning and nationalization of the means of production as a way to establish socialism.

Political Perspectives

State socialism was traditionally advocated as a means for achieving public ownership of the means of production through nationalization of industry. This was intended to be a transitional phase in the process of building a socialist economy. The goals of nationalization were to dispossess large capitalists and consolidate industry so that profit would go toward public finance rather than private fortune. Nationalization would be the first step in a long-term process of socializing production, introducing employee management and reorganizing production to directly produce for use rather than profit.

Traditional social democrats and non-revolutionary democratic socialists argued for a gradual, peaceful transition from capitalism to socialism. They wish to neutralize or to abolish capitalism, respectively, but through political reform rather than revolution. This method of gradualism implies utilization of the existing state apparatus and machinery of government to gradually move society toward socialism and is sometimes derided by other socialists as a form of socialism from above or political elitism for relying on electoral means to achieve socialism.

In contrast, Marxist socialism and revolutionary socialism holds that a proletarian revolution is the only practical way to implement fundamental changes in the structure of society. Socialists who advocate representative democracy believe that after a certain period of time under socialism the state will "wither away" because class distinctions cease to exist and representative democracy would be replaced by direct democracy in the remaining public associations comprising the former state. Political power would be decentralized and distributed evenly among the population, producing a communist society.

The economic model adopted in the former Soviet Union, Eastern Bloc and other communist states is often described as a form of state socialism. The ideological basis for this system was the Marxist–Leninist theory of socialism in one country. The system that emerged in the 1930s in the Soviet Union was based on state ownership of the means of production and centralized planning, along with bureaucratic management of the workplace by state officials that were ultimately subordinate to the all-encompassing communist party. Rather than the producers controlling and managing production, the party controlled both the government machinery which directed the national economy on behalf of the communist party and planned the production and distribution of capital goods.

Because of this, classical and orthodox Marxists as well as Trotskyist groups denounced the communist states as being Stalinist and their economies as being state capitalist or representing deformed or degenerated workers' states, respectively. Within the socialist movement, there is criticism towards the use of the term socialist states in relation to countries such as China and previously of Soviet Union and Eastern and Central European states before what some term the "collapse of Stalinism" in 1989.

Trotskyism argues that the leadership of the communist states was corrupt and that it abandoned Marxism in all but name. In particular, some Trotskyist schools call those countries degenerated workers' states to contrast them with proper socialism (i.e. workers' states) while other Trotskyist schools call them state capitalist to emphasize the lack of true socialism and presence of defining capitalist characteristics (wage labor, commodity production and bureaucratic control over workers).

Otto von Bismarck implemented a set of social programs between 1883 and 1889 following his anti-socialist laws, partly as remedial measures to appease the working class and detract support for the Social Democratic Party of Germany (SPD). Bismarck's biographer A. J. P. Taylor said: "It would be unfair to say that Bismarck took up social welfare solely to weaken the Social Democrats; he had had it in mind for a long time, and believed in it deeply. But as usual he acted on his beliefs at the exact moment when they served a practical need". When a reference was made to his friendship with Ferdinand Lassalle (a nationalist and state-oriented socialist), Bismarck said that he was a more practical socialist than the Social Democrats. These policies were informally referred to as State Socialism by liberal and conservative opponents and the term was later adopted by supporters of the programs in a further attempt to detract the working class from the SPD, with the goal of making the working class content with a nationalist-oriented capitalist welfare state.

Bismarck made the following statement on his social welfare programs: "Whoever has pensions for his old age is far more easier to handle than one who has no such prospect. Look at the difference between a private servant in the chancellery or at court; the latter will put up with much more, because he has a pension to look forward to".

Criticism

Many democratic and libertarian socialists, including anarchists, mutualists and syndicalists, criticize state socialism for advocating a workers' state instead of abolishing the bourgeois state apparatus outright. They use the term state socialism in contrast with their own form of socialism which involves either collective ownership (in the form of worker cooperatives) or common ownership of the means of production without centralized state planning. Those libertarian socialists believe there is no need for a state in a socialist system because there would be no class to suppress and no need for an institution based on coercion and therefore regard the state being a remnant of capitalism. Most hold that statism is itself antithetical to true socialism, the goal of which is the eyes of socialists such as William Morris, who wrote as follows in a *Commonweal* article: "State Socialism? — I don't agree with it; in fact I think the two words contradict one another, and that it is the business of Socialism to destroy the State and put Free Society in its place".

Classical and orthodox Marxists also view state socialism as an oxymoron, arguing that while an association for managing production and economic affairs would exist in socialism, it would no longer be a state in the Marxist definition which is based on domination by one class. Preceding the Bolshevik-led revolution in Russia, many socialist groups—including reformists, orthodox Marxist currents such as council communism and the Mensheviks as well as anarchists and other libertarian socialists—criticized the idea of using the state to conduct planning and nationalization of the means of production as a way to establish socialism. Lenin himself acknowledged his policies as state capitalism.

Some Trotskyists following on from Tony Cliff deny that it even is socialism, calling it instead state capitalism. Other Trotskyists agree that these states could not be described as socialist, but deny that they were state capitalist. They support Leon Trotsky's analysis of pre-restoration Soviet Union as a workers' state that had degenerated into a bureaucratic dictatorship which rested on a largely nationalized industry run according to a plan of production and claimed that the former Stalinist states of Central and Eastern Europe were deformed workers' states based on the same relations of production as the Soviet Union.

Those socialists who oppose any system of state control whatsoever believe in a more decentralized approach which puts the means of production directly into the hands of the workers rather than indirectly through state bureaucracies—which they claim represent a new elite or class. This leads them to consider state socialism a form of state capitalism (an economy based on centralized management, capital accumulation and wage labor, but with the state owning the means of production) which Engels stated would be the final form of capitalism rather than socialism. Furthermore, state ownership or nationalization has nothing to do with socialism by itself, having been historically carried out for various different purposes under a wide variety of different political and economic systems.

State socialism is often referred to by detractors simply as socialism. For example, Austrian School economists such as Friedrich Hayek and Ludwig von Mises continually used the term socialism as a synonym for central planning and state socialism. This is notable in the United States, where socialism is a pejorative term to mean state socialism used by conservatives and libertarians to taint liberal and progressive policies, proposals and public figures.

Market Socialism

Market socialism is a type of economic system involving the public, cooperative or social ownership of the means of production in the framework of a market economy. Market socialism differs from non-market socialism in that the market mechanism is utilized for the allocation of capital goods and the means of production. Depending on the specific model of market socialism, profits generated by socially owned firms (i.e. net revenue not reinvested into expanding the firm) may variously be used to directly remunerate employees, accrue to society at large as the source of public finance or be distributed amongst the population in a social dividend.

Market socialism is distinguished from the concept of the mixed economy because models of market socialism are complete and self-regulating systems, unlike the mixed economy. Market socialism also contrasts with social democratic policies implemented within capitalist market economies. While social democracy aims to achieve greater economic stability and equality through policy measures such as taxes, subsidies and social welfare programs, market socialism aims to achieve similar goals through changing patterns of enterprise ownership and management.

Although economic proposals involving social ownership with factor markets have existed since the early 19th century, the term market socialism only emerged in the 1920s during the socialist calculation debate. Contemporary market socialism emerged from the debate on socialist calculation during the early-to-mid 20th century among socialist economists who believed that a socialist economy could neither function on the basis of calculation in natural units nor through solving a system of simultaneous equations for economic coordination, and that capital markets would be required in a socialist economy.

Early models of market socialism trace their roots to the work of Adam Smith and the theories of classical economics which consisted of proposals for cooperative enterprises operating in a free-market economy. The aim of such proposals was to eliminate exploitation by allowing individuals to receive the full product of their labor while removing the market-distorting effects of concentrating ownership and wealth in the hands of a small class of private owners. Among early advocates of market socialism were the Ricardian socialist economists and mutualist philosophers. In the early 20th century, Oskar Lange and Abba Lerner outlined a neoclassical model of socialism which included a role for a central planning board (CPB) in setting prices equal to marginal cost to achieve Pareto efficiency. Although these early models did not rely on conventional markets, they were labeled market socialist for their utilization of financial prices and calculation. In more recent models proposed by American neoclassical economists, public ownership of the means of production is achieved through public ownership of equity and social control of investment.

Classical Economics

The key theoretical basis for market socialism is the negation of the underlying expropriation of surplus value present in other, exploitative, modes of production. Socialist theories that favored the market date back to the Ricardian socialists and anarchist economists, who advocated a free market combined with public ownership or mutual ownership of the means of production.

Proponents of early market socialism include the Ricardian socialist economists, the classical liberal philosopher John Stuart Mill and the anarchist philosopher Pierre-Joseph Proudhon. These models of socialism entailed perfecting or improving the market mechanism and free price system by removing distortions caused by exploitation, private property and alienated labor.

This form of market socialism has been termed free-market socialism because it does not involve planners.

John Stuart Mill

Mill's early economic philosophy was one of free markets that he moved toward a more socialist bent, adding chapters to his *Principles of Political Economy* in defence of a socialist outlook, and defending some socialist causes. Within this revised work he also made the radical proposal that the whole wage system be abolished in favour of a co-operative wage system. Nonetheless, some of his views on the idea of flat taxation remained, albeit altered in the third edition of the Principles of Political Economy to reflect a concern for differentiating restrictions on unearned incomes which he favoured; and those on earned incomes, which he did not favour.

Mill's Principles, first published in 1848, was one of the most widely read of all books on economics in the period. As Adam Smith's Wealth of Nations had during an earlier period, Mill's Principles dominated economics teaching. In the case of Oxford University, it was the standard text until 1919, when it was replaced by Alfred Marshall's Principles of Economics.

In later editions of Principles of Political Economy, Mill would argue that "as far as economic theory was concerned, there is nothing in principle in economic theory that precludes an economic order based on socialist policies".

Mill also promoted substituting capitalist businesses with worker cooperatives, writing:

> " The form of association, however, which if mankind continue to improve, must be expected in the end to predominate, is not that which can exist between a capitalist as chief, and work-people without a voice in the management, but the association of the labourers themselves on terms of equality, collectively owning the capital with which they carry on their operations and working under managers elected and removable by themselves ".

Mutualism

Pierre-Joseph Proudhon developed a theoretical system called mutualism which attacks the legitimacy of existing property rights, subsidies, corporations, banking and rent. Proudhon envisioned a decentralized market where people would enter the market with equal power, negating wage slavery. Proponents believe that cooperatives, credit unions and other forms of worker ownership would become viable without being subject to the state. Market socialism has also been used to describe some individualist anarchist works which argue that free markets help workers and weaken capitalists.

Individualist Anarchism in the United States

For American anarchist historian Eunice Minette Schuster, "it is apparent that Proudhonian Anarchism was to be found in the United States at least as early as 1848 and that it was not conscious of its affinity to the Individualist Anarchism of Josiah Warren and Stephen Pearl Andrews. William B. Greene presented this Proudhonian Mutualism in its purest and most systematic form". Josiah Warren is widely regarded as the first American anarchist, and the four-page weekly paper he edited during 1833, *The Peaceful Revolutionist*, was the first anarchist periodical published, an enterprise for which he built his own printing press, cast his own type, and made his own printing plates.

Warren was a follower of Robert Owen and joined Owen's community at New Harmony, Indiana. Josiah Warren termed the phrase "cost the limit of price", with "cost" here referring not to monetary price paid but the labor one exerted to produce an item. Therefore, "he proposed a system to pay people with certificates indicating how many hours of work they did. They could exchange the notes at local time stores for goods that took the same amount of time to produce". He put his theories to the test by establishing an experimental "labor for labor store" called the Cincinnati Time Store where trade was facilitated by notes backed by a promise to perform labor. The store proved successful and operated for three years after which it was closed so that Warren could pursue establishing colonies based on mutualism. These included Utopia and Modern Times. Warren said that Stephen Pearl Andrews' *The Science of Society*, published in 1852, was the most lucid and complete exposition of Warren's own theories.

Later, Benjamin Tucker fused the economics of Warren and Proudhon and published these ideas in *Liberty* calling them "Anarchistic-Socialism". Tucker said: "The fact that one class of men are dependent for their living upon the sale of their labour, while another class of men are relieved of the necessity of labour by being legally privileged to sell something that is not labour. And to such a state of things I am as much opposed as any one. But the minute you remove privilege every man will be a labourer exchanging with fellow-labourers. What Anarchistic-Socialism aims to abolish is usury it wants to deprive capital of its reward". Left-wing market anarchism is a modern branch of free-market anarchism that is based on a revival of such market socialist theories.

Neoclassical Economics

Beginning in the early 20th century, neoclassical economic theory provided the theoretical basis for more comprehensive models of market socialism. Early neoclassical models of socialism included a role for a central planning board (CPB) in setting prices equal marginal cost to achieve Pareto efficiency. Alhough these early models did not rely on conventional markets, they were labeled market socialist for their utilization of financial prices and calculation. Alternative outlines for market socialism involve models where socially owned enterprises or producer co-operatives operate within free markets under the criterion of profitability. In recent models proposed by American neoclassical economists, public ownership of the means of production is achieved through public ownership of equity and social control of investment.

The earliest models of neoclassical socialism were developed by Leon Walras, Enrico Barone and Oskar R. Lange. Lange and Fred M. Taylor proposed that central planning boards set prices through "trial and error", making adjustments as shortages and surpluses occurred rather than relying on a free price mechanism. If there were shortages, prices would be raised; if there were surpluses, prices would be lowered. Raising the prices would encourage businesses to increase production, driven by their desire to increase their profits, and in doing so eliminate the shortage. Lowering the prices would encourage businesses to curtail production to prevent losses, which would eliminate the surplus. Therefore, it would be a simulation of the market mechanism, which Lange thought would be capable of effectively managing supply and demand.

Although the Lange–Lerner model was often labelled as market socialism, it is better described as market simulation because factor markets did not exist for the allocation of capital goods. The objective of the Lange–Lerner model was explicitly to replace markets with a non-market system of resource allocation.

H. D. Dickinson published two articles proposing a form of market socialism, namely "Price Formation in a Socialist Community" and "The Problems of a Socialist Economy". Dickinson proposed a mathematical solution whereby the problems of a socialist economy could be solved by a central planning agency. The central agency would have the necessary statistics on the economy, as well as the capability of using statistics to direct production. The economy could be represented as a system of equations. Solution values for these equations could be used to price all goods at marginal cost and direct production. Hayek argued against the proposal to simulate markets with equations. Dickinson adopted the Lange-Taylor proposal to simulate markets through trial and error.

The Lange–Dickinson version of market socialism kept capital investment out of the market. Lange insisted that a central planning board would have to set capital accumulation rates arbitrarily. Lange and Dickinson saw potential problems with bureaucratization in market socialism. According to Dickinson, "the attempt to check irresponsibility will tie up managers of socialist enterprises with so much red tape and bureaucratic regulation that they will lose all initiative and independence". In The Economics of Control: Principles of Welfare Economics, Abba Lerner admitted that capital investment would be politicized in market socialism.

Economists active in the former Yugoslavia, including Czech-born Jaroslav Vanek and Croat-born Branko Horvat, promoted a model of market socialism dubbed the Illyrian model, where firms were socially owned by their employees and structured on workers' self-management and competed with each other in open and free markets.

American economists in the latter half of the 20th century developed models based such as coupon socialism (by the economist John Roemer) and economic democracy (by the philosopher David Schweickart).

Pranab Bardhan and John Roemer proposed a form of narket socialism where there was a stock market that distributed shares of the capital stock equally among citizens. In this stock market, there is no buying or selling of stocks, which leads to negative externalities associated with a concentration of capital ownership. The Bardhan and Roemer model satisfied the main requirements of both socialism (workers own all the factors of production, not just labour) and market economies (prices determine efficient allocation of resources). New Zealand economist Steven O'Donnell expanded on the Bardhan and Roemer model and decomposed the capital function in a general equilibrium system to take account of entrepreneurial activity in market socialist economies. O'Donnell set up a model that could be used as a blueprint for transition economies and the results suggested that although market socialist models were inherently unstable in the long term, they would provide in the short term the economic infrastructure necessary for a successful transition from planned to market economies.

In the early 21st century, the Marxian economist Richard D. Wolff refocused Marxian economics giving it a microfoundational focus. The core idea was that transition from capitalism to socialism required the reorganization of the enterprise from a top-down hierarchical capitalist model to a model where all key enterprise decisions (what, how, and where to produce and what to do with outputs) were made on a one-worker, one vote basis. Wolff called them workers self-directed enterprises (WSDEs). How they would interact with one another and with consumers was left open to democratic social decisions and could entail markets or planning, or likely mixtures of both.

Anti-equilibrium Economics

Another form of market socialism has been promoted by critics of central planning and generally of neoclassical general equilibrium theory. The most notable of these economists were Alec Nove and Janos Kornai. In particular, Alec Nove proposed what he called feasible socialism, a mixed economy consisting of state-run enterprises, autonomous publicly owned firms, cooperatives and small-scale private enterprise operating in a market economy that included a role for macroeconomic planning.

In Practice

A number of market socialist elements have existed in various economies.

The economy of the former Socialist Federal Republic of Yugoslavia is widely considered to be a model of market-based socialism which was based on the predominance of socially-owned cooperatives, workers' self-management and market allocation of capital.

Some of the economic reforms introduced during the Prague Spring by Alexander Dubček, the leader of Czechoslovakia, included elements of market socialism.

The Mondragon Corporation in the Basque Country and Coop in Italy are widely cited as highly successful co-operative enterprises based on worker- or consumer-ownership and democratic management.

Peter Drucker described the United States system of regulated pension funds providing capital to financial markets as "pension fund socialism". William H. Simon characterized pension fund socialism as "a form of market socialism", concluding that it was promising but perhaps with prospects more limited than those envisioned by its enthusiasts.

The economy of Cuba under the rule of Raúl Castro has been described as attempting market socialist reforms.

Similar policies to the market socialist proposal of a social dividend and basic income scheme have been implemented on the basis of public ownership of natural resources in Alaska (Alaska Permanent Fund) and in Norway (The Government Pension Fund of Norway).

Belarus under Alexander Lukashenko is sometimes described as market-socialist.

Ethiopia under Abiy Ahmed has recently been described as market socialist.

Relation to Political Ideologies

Marxism–Leninism

The phrase market socialism has occasionally been used in reference to any attempt by a Soviet-type planned economy to introduce market elements into its economic system. In this sense, market socialism was first attempted during the 1920s in the Soviet Union as the New Economic Policy (NEP) before being abandoned. Later, elements of market socialism were introduced in Hungary (where it was nicknamed goulash communism), Czechoslovakia and Yugoslavia in the 1970s and 1980s. The contemporary Economy of Belarus has been described as a market socialist system. The Soviet Union attempted to introduce a market system with its perestroika reforms under Mikhail Gorbachev. During the later stages there was talk within top circles that the Soviet Union should move toward a market-based socialist system.

Historically, these kinds of market socialist systems attempt to retain state ownership of the commanding heights of the economy such as heavy industry, energy and infrastructure while introducing decentralised decision making and giving local managers more freedom to make decisions and respond to market demands. Market socialist systems also allow private ownership and entrepreneurship in the service and other secondary economic sectors. The market is allowed to determine prices for consumer goods and agricultural products, and farmers are allowed to sell all or some of their products on the open market and keep some or all of the profit as an incentive to increase and improve production.

Socialism with Chinese Characteristics

The term market socialism has been used to refer to reformed economic systems in Marxist–Leninist states, most notably in reference to the contemporary economy of the People's Republic of China, where a free price system is used for the allocation of capital goods in both the state and private sectors. However, Chinese political and economic proponents of the socialist market economy do not consider it to be a form of market socialism in the neoclassical sense and many Western economists and political scientists question the degree to which this model constitutes a form of market socialism, often preferring to describe it as state capitalism.

Although similar in name, market socialism differs markedly from the socialist market economy and socialist-oriented market economy models practiced in the contemporary People's Republic of China and Socialist Republic of Vietnam, respectively. Officially these economic systems represent market economies that are in the long-term process of transition toward socialism. Key differences between models of market socialism and the Chinese and Vietnamese models include the role of private investment in enterprises, the lack of a social dividend or basic income system to equitably distribute state profits among the population and the existence and role of financial markets in the Chinese model—markets which are absent in the market socialist literature.

The Chinese experience with socialism with Chinese characteristics is frequently referred to as a socialist market economy where the commanding heights are state-owned, but a substantial portion of both the state and private sectors of economy are governed by market practices, including a stock exchange for trading equity and the utilization of indirect macroeconomic market mechanisms (i.e. fiscal, monetary and industrial policies) to influence the economy in the same manner governments affect the economy in capitalist economies. The market is the arbitrator for most economic activity, with economic planning being relegated to macro-economic government indicative planning that does not encompass the microeconomic decision-making that is left to the individual organizations and state-owned enterprises. This model includes a significant amount of privately owned firms that operate as a business for profit, but only for consumer goods and services.

In the Chinese system, directive planning based on mandatory output requirements and quotas were displaced by market mechanisms for most of the economy, including both the state and private sectors, although the government engages in indicative planning for large state enterprises. In comparison with the Soviet-type planned economy, the Chinese socialist market model is based on the corporatization of state institutions, transforming them into joint-stock companies. As of 2008, there were 150 state-owned corporations directly under the central government. These state-owned corporations have been reformed and become increasingly dynamic and a major source of revenue for the state in 2008, leading the economic recovery in 2009 during the wake of the global financial crises.

This economic model is defended from a Marxist–Leninist perspective which states that a planned socialist economy can only emerge after first developing the basis for socialism through the establishment of a market economy and commodity-exchange economy; and that socialism would only emerge after this stage has exhausted its historical necessity and gradually transforms itself into socialism. Proponents of this model argue that the economic system of the former Soviet Union and its satellite states attempted to go from a natural economy to a planned economy by decree, without passing through the necessary market economy phase of development.

Democratic Socialism

Some democratic socialists advocate forms of market socialism, some of which are based on self-management. Others advocate for a non-market participatory economy based on decentralized economic planning.

Anarchism

The French philosopher Pierre Joseph Proudhon is the first person to call himself an anarchist and considered among its most influential theorists. He is considered by many to be the "father of anarchism". He became a member of the French Parliament after the revolution of 1848, whereon he referred to himself as a federalist. His best-known assertion is that "Property is theft!", contained in his first major work What Is Property?, published in 1840. The book's publication attracted the attention of the French authorities. It also attracted the scrutiny of Karl Marx, who started a correspondence with its author. The two influenced each other: they met in Paris while Marx was exiled there. Their friendship finally ended when Marx responded to Proudhon's The Philosophy of Poverty with the provocatively titled The Poverty of Philosophy. The dispute became one of the sources of the split between the anarchist and Marxian wings of the International Working Men's Association. Mutualism is an economic theory and anarchist school of thought that advocates a society where each person might possess a means of production, either individually or collectively, with trade representing equivalent amounts of labor in the free market. Integral to the scheme was the establishment of a mutual-credit bank that would lend to producers at a minimal interest rate, just high enough to cover administration. Mutualism is based on a labor theory of value that holds that when labor or its product is sold, in exchange, it ought to receive goods or services embodying "the amount of labor necessary to produce an article of exactly similar and equal utility".

Mutualism originated from the writings of philosopher Pierre-Joseph Proudhon. Mutualists oppose the idea of individuals receiving an income through loans, investments and rent as they believe these individuals are not laboring. Though Proudhon opposed this type of income, he expressed that he had never intended "to forbid or suppress, by sovereign decree, ground rent and interest on capital. I think that all these manifestations of human activity should remain free and voluntary for all: I ask for them no modifications, restrictions or suppressions, other than those which result naturally and of necessity from the universalization of the principle of reciprocity which I propose". Insofar as they ensure the worker's right to the full product of their labor, mutualists support markets (or artificial markets) and property in the product of labor. However, they argue for conditional titles to land, whose ownership is legitimate only so long as it remains in use or occupation (which Proudhon called "possession"), advocating personal property but not private property.

Josiah Warren is widely regarded as the first American anarchist and the four-page weekly paper he edited during 1833, *The Peaceful Revolutionist*, was the first anarchist periodical published. For American anarchist historian Eunice Minette Schuster, "it is apparent that Proudhonian Anarchism was to be found in the United States at least as early as 1848 and that it was not conscious of its affinity to the Individualist Anarchism of Josiah Warren and Stephen Pearl Andrews. William B. Greene presented this Proudhonian Mutualism in its purest and most systematic form". Later, the American individualist anarchist Benjamin Tucker "was against both the state and capitalism, against both oppression and exploitation. While not against the market and property he was firmly against capitalism as it was, in his eyes, a state-supported monopoly of social capital (tools, machinery, etc.) which allows owners to exploit their employees, i.e. to avoid paying workers the full value of their labour. He thought that the "labouring classes are deprived of their earnings by usury in its three forms, interest, rent and profit". Therefore, "*Liberty* will abolish interest; it will abolish profit; it will abolish monopolistic rent; it will abolish taxation; it will abolish the exploitation of labour; it will abolish all means whereby any labourer can be deprived of any of his product". This stance puts him squarely in the libertarian socialist tradition and, unsurprisingly, Tucker referred to himself many times as a socialist and considered his philosophy to be "anarchistic socialism".

French individualist anarchist Emile Armand shows clearly opposition to capitalism and centralized economies when he said that the individualist anarchist "inwardly he remains refractory – fatally refractory – morally, intellectually, economically (The capitalist economy and the directed economy, the speculators and the fabricators of single systems are equally repugnant to him.)". He argued for a pluralistic economic logic when he said that "Here and there everything happening – here everyone receiving what they need, there each one getting whatever is needed according to their own capacity. Here, gift and barter – one product for another; there, exchange – product for representative value. Here, the producer is the owner of the product, there, the product is put to the possession of the collectivity". The Spanish individualist anarchist Miguel Gimenez Igualada thought that "capitalism is an effect of government; the disappearance of government means capitalism falls from its pedestal vertiginously. That which we call capitalism is not something else but a product of the State, within which the only thing that is being pushed forward is profit, good or badly acquired. And so to fight against capitalism is a pointless task, since be it State capitalism or Enterprise capitalism, as long as Government exists, exploiting capital will exist. The fight, but of consciousness, is against the State". His view on class division and technocracy are as follows "Since when no one works for another, the profiteer from wealth disappears, just as government will disappear when no one pays attention to those who learned four things at universities and from that fact they pretend to govern men. Big industrial enterprises will be transformed by men in big associations in which everyone will work and enjoy the product of their work. And from those easy as well as beautiful problems anarchism deals with and he who puts them in practice and lives them are anarchists. The priority which without rest an anarchist must make is that in which no one has to exploit anyone, no man to no man, since that non-exploitation will lead to the limitation of property to individual needs".

Left-wing market anarchism is a form of left-libertarianism and individualist anarchism associated with scholars such as Kevin Carson, Roderick T. Long, Charles W. Johnson, Brad Spangler, Samuel Edward Konkin III, Sheldon Richman, Chris Matthew Sciabarra and Gary Chartier, who stress the value of radically free markets, termed freed markets to distinguish them from the common conception which these libertarians believe to be riddled with statist and capitalist privileges. Referred to as left-wing market anarchists or market-oriented left-libertarians, proponents of this approach strongly affirm the classical liberal ideas of free markets and self-ownership while maintaining that taken to their logical conclusions these ideas support anti-capitalist, anti-corporatist, anti-hierarchical, pro-labor positions in economics; anti-imperialism in foreign policy; and thoroughly liberal or radical views regarding cultural and social issues such as gender, sexuality and race.

The genealogy of contemporary market-oriented left-libertarianism, sometimes labeled left-wing market anarchism, overlaps to a significant degree with that of Steiner–Vallentyne left-libertarianism as the roots of that tradition are sketched in the book *The Origins of Left-Libertarianism*. Carson–Long-style left-libertarianism is rooted in 19th-century mutualism and in the work of figures such as Thomas Hodgskin and the American individualist anarchists Benjamin Tucker and Lysander Spooner. While with notable exceptions market-oriented libertarians after Tucker tended to ally with the political right, relationships between such libertarians and the New Left thrived in the 1960s, laying the groundwork for modern left-wing market anarchism. Left-wing market anarchism identifies with left-libertarianism which names several related but distinct approaches to politics, society, culture and political and social theory, which stress both individual freedom and social justice. Unlike right-libertarians, they believe that neither claiming nor mixing one's labor with natural resources is enough to generate full private property rights and maintain that natural resources (land, oil, gold and trees) ought to be held in some egalitarian manner, either unowned or owned collectively. Those left-libertarians who support private property do so under the condition that recompense is offered to the local or global community.

Criticism

Market abolitionists such as David McNally argue in the Marxist tradition that the logic of the market inherently produces inequitable outcomes and leads to unequal exchanges, arguing that Adam Smith's moral intent and moral philosophy espousing equal exchange was undermined by the practice of the free market he championed—the development of the market economy involved coercion, exploitation and violence that Smith's moral philosophy could not countenance. McNally criticizes market socialists for believing in the possibility of fair markets based on equal exchanges to be achieved by purging parasitical elements from the market economy such as private ownership of the means of production, arguing that market socialism is an oxymoron when socialism is defined as an end to wage labour.

Ethical Socialism

Ethical socialism is a political philosophy that appeals to socialism on ethical and moral grounds as opposed to economic, egoistic, and consumeristic grounds. It emphasizes the need for a morally conscious economy based upon the principles of altruism, cooperation, and social justice while opposing possessive individualism.

In contrast to socialism inspired by rationalism, historical materialism, neoclassical economics, and Marxist theory which base their appeals for socialism on grounds of economic efficiency, rationality, or historical inevitability, ethical socialism focuses on the moral and ethical reasons for advocating socialism.

Ethical socialism had a profound impact on the social democratic movement and reformism during the later half of the 20th century, particularly in Great Britain. Ethical socialism is distinct in its focus on criticism of the ethics of capitalism and not merely criticism of the economic, systemic, and material issues of capitalism. When the Social Democratic Party of Germany (SPD) renounced orthodox Marxism during the Godesberg Program in the 1950s, ethical socialism became the official philosophy within the SPD.

The term ethical socialism initially originated as a pejorative by the Marxian economist Rosa Luxemburg against reformist, Marxist revisionist Eduard Bernstein and his supporters, who evoked neo-Kantian liberal ideals and ethical arguments in favour of socialism. Self-recognized ethical socialists soon arose in Britain such as the Christian socialist R. H. Tawney and its ideals were connected to Christian socialist, Fabian, and guild socialist ideals. Ethical socialism was an important ideology within the British Labour Party. Ethical socialism has been publicly supported by British Prime Ministers Ramsay MacDonald, Clement Attlee, and Tony Blair.

The utopian socialists, one of the first currents of modern socialist thought, presented visions and outlines for imaginary or futuristic ideal societies, characterized by the establishment of a moral economy, with positive ideals based on moral and ethical grounds being the main reason for moving society in such a direction. Before Marxists established a hegemony over definitions of socialism, "the term socialism was a broad concept" which referred to one or more of various theories aimed at solving the labour problem through radical changes in the capitalist economy. Descriptions of the problem, explanations of its causes and proposed solutions (for example, abolition of private property, or supporting cooperatives and public ownership, among others) varied among socialist philosophies.

Themes

R. H. Tawney denounced self-seeking amoral and immoral behaviour that he claimed is supported by capitalism. Tawney opposed what he called the "acquisitive society" that causes private property to be used to transfer surplus profit to "functionless owners", i.e. capitalist rentiers. However, he did not denounce managers as a whole, believing that management and employees could join together in a political alliance for reform. Tawney supported the pooling of surplus profit through means of progressive taxation to redistribute these funds to provide social welfare (including public health care, public education, and public housing) and the nationalization of strategic industries and services. He supported worker participation in the business of management in the economy as well as consumer, employee, employer and state cooperation in regulating the economy.

Although Tawney supported a substantial role for public enterprise in the economy, he stated that where private enterprise provided a service that was commensurate with its rewards that was functioning private property, then a business could be usefully and legitimately be left in private hands. Thomas Hill Green supported the right of equal opportunity for all individuals to be able freely appropriate property, but claimed that acquisition of wealth did not imply that an individual could do whatever they wanted to once that wealth was in their possession. Green opposed "property rights of the few" that were preventing the ownership of property by the many.

Ethical socialism was advocated and promoted by former British Prime Minister Tony Blair, who has been influenced by John Macmurray who himself was influenced by Green. Blair has defined ethical socialism with similar notions promoted by earlier ethical socialists, such as emphasis on the common good, rights, and responsibilities, and support of an organic society in which individuals flourish through cooperation. Blair believes that the Labour Party ran into problems in the 1960s and 1970s when it "abandoned" ethical socialism and believes that the Labour Party's recovery required a return to the ethical socialist values last promoted by the Attlee Labour government.

Socialist Mode of Production

All historical social formations have been characterized by a combination of economic modes of production. We conventionally speak of these modes of production being structured into dominant and subordinate modes, so that we speak of whole periods in which a particular mode of production is dominant. Thus we talk of capitalist societies or slave societies, even though slavery and capitalism may co-exist within a given society.

How does one decide which mode of production dominates a society?

One answer would be to look at the state, which social class dominates. One might on these grounds say that for most of the ante-bellum period the USA was dominated by the slave mode of production, in the sense that the representatives of the slave owners dominated the political system. But behind such political dominance stands wealth. A class can control the state if the economic system they represent provides them with the resources to do so. The shift of political control over the US from slavers to industrialists echoed economic development.

To control the state, a class must control the greater part of a society's surplus product. Underlying political dominance is control over surplus labour.

What differentiate the contesting forms of economy are two things:

- The specific mode in which the social division of labour is organised.
- The particular way in which a surplus product is extracted.

For a mode of production to rise to dominance it must be able to reproduce its form of the division of labour and its form of surplus extraction on an expanded scale. This expansion can in the end only be protected by political power. Competing modes of production must, finally, resolve their rivalry by force or the threat of force. The argument over competing expansions by slavery and capitalism onto new lands to the west falls in the end by the *ultimo ratio Regis*, the voice of the cannon. The competing expansions of the communist and capitalist modes of production on a world scale are resolved in favour of the latter by Star Wars and the threat of nuclear annihilation.

But to win, the victor must have out mobilised and out-produced the vanquished. It must have commanded more labour and more productive labour; it must have had a greater freely disposable surplus to squander on the demands of total war.

We are to talk about possible futures, ones in which the communist system again comprises a part. We can not consider their social structure without talking about the struggle, economic, political and military between the capitalism and communism.

Following the fall of communism, there has been a temptation for western socialists to concentrate on coming up with schemes to address apparent failings of the communist system in the supply of consumer goods. Roemer and others have implied that the adoption of some form of market reforms would have improved consumer goods supply and averted the crisis. This is often associated with the advocacy of political reforms towards free elections. We believe that reforms of this sort could only have accelerated the triumph of capital.

It is a mistake, to which we ourselves have fallen prey, to concentrate too much attention on issues like shortages of consumer goods under socialism, or lower living standards relative to the US. These were not decisive issues. Were living standards the key, it would have been the USA and not the USSR that would have fallen. In 1989, real wages in the US were lower than they had been in 1973, whilst those in the USSR had risen even during what was called the 'period of stagnation' under Breshnev. It was stagnation only in comparison to the much more rapid growth of the Stalin and Kruschev years. If a failure to deliver rising living standards explained the fall of the Soviet system, the survival of the subsequent Yeltsin regime during which real wages have fallen by an extent unprecedented in peacetime history can only be miraculous.

We see other causes of crisis arising from:

- The form of appropriation of the surplus product.
- The scale and disposition of this product.
- The specific forms of class antagonism engendered by the communist mode of production.
- The constitutional forms of the socialist states.

Note that follow Marx in talking only of the capitalist and communist modes of production, eschewing the Soviet orthodoxy which, basing itself on the language of German social democracy, introduced a third mode of production: socialism. We follow Mao i We see the self-described socialist countries as having been social formations defined by an articulated combination of capitalist and communist modes of production. This articulation is both internal, in the relationship between economic forms by which reproduction occurred, externally defined by the politico-military struggle with the capitalist block.

Our purpose in this paper is:

- To characterise the fundamental features of the communist mode of production.
- Discuss how a future communism could structure its social institutions the better to emerge as victor in the next cold war.

We shall talk about both economic and political levels. In discussing the economic level we examine communism's characteristic form of the division of labour and surplus extraction and how these can be improved by information technology. In discussing the political level we look at the weaknesses of hitherto existing socialist state constitutions and propose forms, based on historical precedent, that we hope would be more robust.

Economic Level

Division of Labour

Social Labour and value: All societies must divide their labour between different concrete activities. Labour time is the fundamental productive resource that they have at their disposition. It is, in Smith's words, the original currency by which we purchase our wants from nature. Smith's analogy with money is apt, just as money is abstract purchasing power, able to buy any commodity; labour is abstract productive power. Labour turns its hand to any trade. By altering how it spends its labour, society alters what it consumes.

If we want to know what it cost a society to produce something, expressing this in terms of a long dead currency, be it thaler or solidus, tells us little. Translate cost into a percentage of social labour time and we get a handle on it.

In market economies, this social labour cost is represented, more or less precisely, in an object's price. By an inversion of signs engendered by the possibility of sale, the cost of producing something comes to be seen as something positive, its value.

Money and information: The adaptability of labour means that, considered in the abstract, it can be measured in hours: a scalar. We can then associate with each product a scalar quantity, its value, being the labour required making it. This list of pairs {($product_1$, $value_1$), ($product_2$ $value_2$),} is homeomorphic to a price list. Money prices or labour values can equally well serve as units of account. They both act as operators mapping elements of heterogeneous types onto a single measuring scale. They formally identical when it comes to comparing the costs of alternative economic options.

But the existence of money involves more than just a price list for all commodities. It also implies, and this is not adequately emphasized in the Marxian analysis of money, existence of a credit account list. This is of the form {($subject_1$ $credit_1$), ($subject_2$ $credit_2$)....} associating with each juridical subject a monetary credit or debit. The list may exist in the form of ledger entries in the banks, database entries in Visa's computers, or more primitively, coins in purposes. All of these are just different historically evolved technologies for recording the same sort of information.

Whilst price lists and value lists may at first sight seem equally useful in cost accounting, credit account lists imply something quite different. Here money appears not as a neutral metric, but as, what Smith called, the power to command the labour of others. Credit accounts encode social hierarchy. Throughout history the index of membership of the upper classes was the ability to command others to do things. Thus the persistence of such accounts in socialist societies is an index of the survival of capitalist forms of domination, of lordship.

Economic computation: Any economy must have some cybernetic mechanism by which the allocation of labour between different branches of production is regulated. Another mechanism must exist by which the proportionate division between surplus and necessary labour time is controlled.

This control process involves three movements:

- A movement of people.
- A movement of products.
- A movement of symbols.

A movement of symbols is what we associate with computation or calculation. Such symbolic calculation takes place in ledgers, but also through the movement of physical symbols – coin or notes, between agents. But considered as a whole, the economic algorithm can include steps that move people and products. It is characteristic of market economies that their economic algorithm relies on the movement of people where communism could move symbols.

Market computation: In a market economy the public symbolic moment of the economic algorithm is concerned solely with lordship, the abstract power of command: money. Public symbolic calculation is concerned with the manipulation of credit accounts. It ensures that for every routine movement of products from the ownership of subject X to that of Y there is a balancing adjustment of their powers of domination.

Hidden behind this there is a private symbolic manipulation carried out in the production planning divisions of corporations. Here the symbols, the numbers stand not for social power but for things, turbine blades, impeller blades, fan ducting. Here the characteristic operation is not the account transaction but the parts explosion. This form of symbolic computation is the germ of communist planning.

The other moment of the economic algorithm involves the movement of things and people. Products are assigned to uses, people to jobs. In a market economy these two movements, the symbolic and physical form an interlinked cycle. The rate at which ownership of products changes, their rate of sale, and thus the rate of credits to the accounts of the producing firms, influences the price of the product. This is a purely symbolic change. It also influences the production plans of the firms, another symbolic change but now a private one. Finally it influences their employment levels, actually altering the division of labour in society. We are all familiar with this feedback loop.

The computational capacity of a system is determined by its degree of parallelism and its cycle time. The advocates of market cybernetics eulogise its parallelism. They are silent about its cycles. The breathless euphoria of NASDAQ may cycle in seconds, but such symbolic markets are pure computations of domination and lordship. Markets for products are different. Their cycle times are of the order of 18 months for stock building cycles, of the order of 7 years for fixed investment. The goals of the agents are purely symbolic, profit, the growth of domination. The actual process of economic adjustment involves slower physical changes. From the dislocation of cycle times stem the instabilities, recessions and booms to which market economies are subject. Equilibration, to the extent that it is possible, occurs ex post, but given the long cycle time of the algorithm, it effectively never occurs. Chaos reigns, the infamous anarchy of capitalist production.

Market like allocation under communism: Marx famously envisaged communism as having two phases. The first of these retained the principle of bourgeois right: what people got back from society in the form of goods would be proportional to the labour that they performed. It would be modified form of bourgeois right in that there would be no property income. But the reciprocity that underlies commodity exchange would persist. Workers would be paid in labour tokens and would be allocated products containing an equivalent amount of labour. The number of labour tokens that they were paid would be somewhat less than the hours because of deductions for social security and the like.

Although this scheme does not involve a market proper, and he was at pains to point out that labour tokens were not money (they were to be cancelled on use like a theatre ticket), it is market like. Whilst a gross balance between issue of labour tokens and production of consumer goods can be achieved relatively simply, there remains the problem of adjusting the composition of the consumer goods bundle.

A communist economy can use market like mechanisms here.

We will put forward a lemma, which we can prove elsewhere, that there will always exist a composition of the consumer goods bundle such that the 'sale' of all products at their labour values will exactly balance supply and demand. Assume, unrealistically, that changes in consumer taste were the driving force for changes in demand. The planning authorities would have two types of indicator that they could use to steer the composition of the consumer goods bundle towards this mix.

- They could use the rate of change of buffer stocks as an indicator of demand and adjust output accordingly.
- They could, as specified in elementary economics textbooks, adjust the selling price in labour tokens so that goods in short supply rose above their values. They could then increase the production of all goods whose prices were above their values and reduce output for those below their values.

In the latter case the deviation of price from value acts in the way a higher rate of profit would in a capitalist economy. Which of these mechanisms was used is essentially a pragmatic question.

Plan computation and computerised planning: The key difference between communist economies and market economies is that the former adjust the division of labour by means of calculations in kind, the latter do it by means of calculations in money. Market calculation is the calculus of domination. Planning is the unmediated calculation of products and labour: the famous *system of material balances*.

The implementation of material balances has, in the past, been partial. The information processing techniques needed to fully implement material balances did not exist. They do now.

Where the market is an ex-post system, the plan is ex-ante. The plan is a symbolic representation of future production. In a planned economy, the moment of economic computation is purely symbolic, a manipulation of figures that precedes the issue of directives. Since at no moment in the computation do people and products have to move, the computation precedes the physical allocation of resources. This algorithmic structure frees communism from the cyclical crises of market economies.

However the general laws of computability and complexity theory can not be evaded. The preparation of a complete, balanced and disaggregated plan is Turing computable; algorithms exist for it. But not every thing that is computable in principle is computable in practice. A five year plan that takes 50 years to prepare is no good to anyone. Opponents of socialism have made much of the impossible complexity of the millions of equations that would have to be solved.

It sounded formidable but we now solve millions of equations on a routine basis. Weather forecasts involve evaluating the temperature pressure and wind velocities for millions of discrete space time positions. Weather forecasts share with plans the criterion of promptness. It is no good having an algorithm that will forecast tomorrow's weather if it takes two days to do the calculations. The key issues here are the complexity of the algorithms and the speed of the computers used. By complexity of an algorithm is meant the rate at which the running time grows with the size of the problem. For an algorithm to be tractable, the running time must grow relatively slowly with the problem size. The reason why the millions of equations needed for short range weather forecasts are tractable lies in the fact that they involve local interactions. Each cubic kilometer of air interacts only with its nearest neighbours. This bounds the complexity involved in solving the equations.

We have outlined elsewhere, plan balancing algorithms of low complexity. Plans, like weather simulations, are characterised by local interactions. Modern supercomputers could, were they suitably programmed, derive a balanced plan for a major industrial economy as expeditiously as they, today, predict tomorrows weather. This removes what has long been a major practical objection to planning.

With the ability to plan in detail, the problems that arose with aggregative planning, like perverse incentives to produce a few heavy items when directives were in terms of weight of product delivered, do not arise.

It is difficult to gauge the economic impact of a more efficient planning system. What would have been the percentage increase in output?

What would be the percentage increase in annual growth?

The most that you can say is that an increase in efficiency boosts the potential surplus product. If this were reinvested in new plant and equipment it could bring a long term increase in growth rates. But it is hard to judge just how decisive this might have been had it been available to the Soviets. It is not as if their system of central planning was actually unviable. It may have been bureaucratic and behind the times in terms of information technology, but it did work. It maintained and regulated a complex division of labour supporting a quarter of a billion people and provided them with forty years of continuous economic growth post 1945. Perhaps the decisive issue is not the efficiency or otherwise of the plan, but other factors; the existence of money, the production and allocation of the surplus, the class structure of socialism.

Surplus Product

We define as surplus any output over and above that necessary to reproduce the current productive apparattus and current productive population. Modes of production are distinguished by their specific form of surlus extraction.

Exploitative and Non-exploitative Surpluses

The production of a surplus product has typically been tied up with exploitation, whereby the surplus is appropriated by a class of non-producers and used for their benefit rather than that of the direct producers. But surplus production need not necessarily be exploitative. Where the class of non-producers are those past working age, their consumption of part of the surplus is hardly exploitative. More generally, if the direct producers or their children benefit from the use of the surplus product, its is not exploitation.

Unproductive uses of the surplus, like defence, are more problematic. The citizens of a socialist state may have little option but to devote time and children to their defence against external threat, but such expenditures cut into their living standards, and, in the event of conflict, bring loss and heartbreak. Such expenditure can approach the condition of exploitation.

Judgement has, in the end, to rest upon whether the use of the surplus is agreed by the producers to be in their benefit. This entails some form of collective voluntary decision about how much surplus to produce – for this impinges on working hours, and about how the surplus is to be used. The decision need only be voluntary at the collective level, it may appear coercive to the individual. I may have voted against an increase in pensions, but if the majority approve the impost I am forced to go along with it.

How then is a surplus to be produced and appropriated in a communist economy.

Mechanism of Surplus Production under Capitalism

In the capitalist case it is apparently clear, to socialists at least, how the surplus is produced and appropriated. Firms hire workers, employ them to produce goods and services, these sell for more than the wages paid, the surplus is profit. Out of the profits, the firms pay dividends to shareholders, who thereby receive an income without doing any work, and any profits left over are reinvested by the firms in equipment to make them even more profitable.

But all of this is symbolic, a movement of monetary signs. Behind it there is a real material process. The actual production of a surplus implies that employees have to work harder and longer than they would if the firm was just to break even. Since they gain nothing from the profits, there must be some form of coercive work discipline to make them work long and hard. There must be managers and overseers with the power to hire and fire. There must be monitoring of work.. There may be a mechanical discipline imposed by the production line. Such discipline avails little unless wages are held down. Typically this is effected by an over-supply of labour, competition from the unemployed keeping wages below the full value that workers produce.

Behind these proximate causes lie deeper ones. A surplus implies something about productivity. If workers can produce the value of their wages in 4 hours, leaving them 4 hours to work to produce profits, then if productivity doubled, they could produce their wage in 2 hours, leaving them 6 hours to produce profits. The combination of profit with long term rises in real wages is only possible through constant improvements in the productivity of labour. A capitalist economy builds in incentives to firms to employ labour saving machinery and thus improve both their individual profits, and indirectly, the scale of the social surplus.

Alongside the appropriation of the surplus as profit, there exists in every capitalist country another channel for the surplus, one both older and newer – the state and its taxes. Before capitalism and after it, the public power endures, with the primordial right to surplus labour. Originally this takes the form of a personal obligation to labour or serve as a soldier. The latter can persist to this day, but generally these duties were, by all states with an effective bureaucracy, commuted. Instead of performing the labour myself I can get somebody else to do it, provided that I can surrender to the state a certificate showing that they have performed it for me. These certificates can take various forms, tally sticks, paper vouchers or the metal disks stamped with royal insignia that we call coin. With the formation of a standing army, the personal military service is performed by a minority whose service is certified by the queen's shilling. The obligation, however, remains general and those who do not serve must render coin in lieu: tax. The coin then circulate, as the only way others can obtain coin is by selling goods and services. The coin are tokens of labour performed for the state, and the payment of tax a performance of these services by proxy. Money's lordship is the delegation of sovereign power.

Under the twin pressures of social democracy and inter-state competition the share of the social working day claimed by the state grows. It expands to cover not just part of the surplus, but part of the labour necessary for social reproduction – education, the provision of transport infrastructure etc.

The state has to maintain a balance between the rate at which it issues exemption certificates – it money purchases and disbursements of benefits, and the rate at which it collects the certificates back in the form of tax revenues. A shortfall in the rate of tax collection devalues the certificates leading to inflation, a shortfall in expenditure leads to recession.

Mechanism of Surplus Production under Communism

The specifically communist way of producing a surplus is to plan for it. The plan specifies the physical composition of the whole product. When it specifies that this will involve the production of a 10,000 tanks, 2000 warplanes, 15 new power stations etc, it is defining the surplus product. These products by their nature form no part of current consumption.

This mode of surplus production is quite distinct from what happens in capitalist countries: either the appropriation of profit by private firms or the collection of taxes by the state.

The decisive difference arises from the fact that the means of production are in unitary public ownership. The proprietors appropriate capitalist surplus, but they are many, and profit appears as the accidental outcome of market turbulence. The capitalist state is unitary but does not own the means of production so its appropriation of the surplus has to be indirect, by means of money taxes.

Turnover Taxes

The magnitude and composition of the social surplus under communism is determined, targets being met, by the structure of the plan. However some money-like form of allocation can persist for the distribution of part of the necessary product, workers are paid some form of tokens for their work. They individually 'buy' back from the state some of the goods that they consume. Marx pointed out in *The Critique of the Gotha Program,* that the production of a surplus precluded workers individually receiving the full productof their labour, instead there must be some sort of deduction to support those unable to work, net investment etc. Failing this more labour tokens will be handed out than are cancelled in exchange for consumer goods. In a capitalist economy this would result in inflation, or a devaluation of the labour token. Depending on pricing policy in a socialist economy, the result is either inflation or the development of chronic shortages, as worker's purchasing power exceeds the planned allocation of consumer goods.

In the USSR the deductions to cover the social surplus were hidden. Only a minor part of the state's revenue was met by income taxes. Instead the major source of state revenue was the profits of publicly owned enterprises.

It should be noted that although it appeared that the state financed its surplus production through turnover taxes, this is an arse foremost way of thinking about it. In reality, as the owner of the means of production the state had no need to finance its expenditure. The products that it used for investment or the armed forces belonged to it to start out with, and did not have to be purchased. The only reason that the turnover taxes were required was to ensure that the issue of roubles balances the issue of goods through state shops in return for these roubles. In practice, because of the inflexibility of prices upwards, and the tendancy to raise wages faster than the growth of the planned consumer goods bundle, there was a persistent buildup of rouble balances in workers accounts. The excess purchasing power in conjunction with fixed prices was the precondition for visible shortages.

The invisiblity of the state revenues, the fact that they did not appear as an explicit deduction from wages, or as an explicit markup in the fashion of western Value Added Taxes may, in the short run, have been politically advantageous. It meant that the government would not face unpopularity from explicit tax rises. On the other hand, this did not remove the temptation to court popularity by holding prices down. The fall of the Gierek and Gomulka governments in Poland followed attempts to raise food prices. The long term political consequences of this form of hidden taxation were generalised shortages and a distrust in the currency. These, in the Polish case certainly, contributed to the general crisis of socialism in the 1980s.

In the USSR a similar effect was produced in the Gorbachov period by the twin 'reforms' of banning alcohol thus forfeiting the Vodka tax, and, following the advice of market socialist reformers, allowing enterprises to retain the greater part of their profits. The deficit in state finances led to the drastic overvaluation of the rouble, shortages and suppressed inflation. These, both in the Polish and Russian cases strengthened the hands of those economists and politicians who advocated shock treatment- the general freeing of prices and abandonment of planning controls: effectively the full reintroduction of capitalism.

A complicating factor in this was the fact that a considerable portion of the necessary product in the socialist economies was distributed on the basis of need rather than being paid for. Education, housing and medical care were provided either free or well below value. This followed on from the conception in the *Critique of the Gotha Program*, that such distribution on the basis of need would be characteristic of the higher phase of communism. The result was that the wage paid to workers in state enterprises was below the value of labour power, the remaining costs of labour reproduction being met by the social wage. In conjunction with the form of taxation this had two invidious consequences:

- By raising the total share of the product that was not marketed, it made the system even more prone to suppressed inflation in the event of tax shortfalls.
- It led to the systematic undervaluation of labour inputs at the enterprise level. This encouraged deliberate overmanning and the use of labour intesive rather than machine intensive production techniques. This undermined what Marx called, in the context of capitalist economy, the production of relative surplus value; i.e., the reduction of the necessary labour time through productivity enhancements. We would hypothesise that over several plan periods this reduced the level of the potential surplus product.

The long term compression of the surplus product meant that the needs of defence and of investment came more and more into conflict – hence the falling share of net investment in the plans of the 70s and 80s. From being a deficiency in the financing of the surplus, the turnover tax system became a deficiency in the actual production of a surplus.

Income or Poll Taxes

The deficiencies of the soviet tax system could have been remedied by the introduction of a proportional income tax accompanied by a break even pricing policy. This would, given the political will to raise taxes, have had two effects:

- Suppressed demand for consumer goods could have been contained, eliminating generalised visible shortages.
- The cost of employing labour at the enterprise level would no longer have been systematically underestimated. This would have discouraged labour hoarding and encouraged the use of labour saving techniques.

For ideological reasons we have advocated fixed poll taxes rather than proportional income taxes. This advocacy is a relatively secondary issue but we see it as having 3 advantages:

- In the absence of significant income differentials, the redistributionist argument for income taxes in a capitalist economy is lacking.
- Poll taxes maintain an high incentive to work, by paying workers the full value of their product at the margin.
- Poll taxes emphasise the general duty to perform work for the community before work for oneself.

Uniform Poll Taxes

Whatever tax regime is used by a socialist economy, it is essential that persistent shortfalls in tax collection do not occur. This involves some political mechanism to bring tax collection and government expenditure into balance.

Neosocialism

Neosocialism was the name of a political faction that existed in France during the 1930s and in Belgium around the same time and which included several revisionist tendencies in the French Section of the Workers' International (SFIO). During the 1930s the faction gradually distanced itself from revolutionary Marxism and reformist socialism, while stopping short of merging into traditional class-collaborative socialism of radical-socialist progressivism; instead they advocated a revolution from above which they termed as a constructive revolution. In France this brought them into conflict with the Socialist Party's traditional policy of anti-governmentalism, and the neosocialists were expelled from SFIO.

From the start this linked them to fascist politics in France, and neosocialists expressed admiration for Italian Fascism. This tendency later emerged as an ideological orientation in its own right with the Neosocialist Party, which advocated authoritarianism and antisemitic policies as well as intimate cooperation with the Nazis.

In the wake of the Great Depression, a group of deputies led by Henri de Man in Belgium (the leader of the Belgian Labour Party's right-wing, and founder of the ideology of *planisme*, i.e. planism, meaning economic planning) and in France by Marcel Déat and Pierre Renaudel (leader of the SFIO's right wing), René Belin of the General Confederation of Labour, the Young Turk current of the Radical-Socialist Party (Pierre Mendès-France) argued that the unprecedented scale of the global economic crisis, and the sudden success of national-populist parties across Europe, meant that time had run out for socialists to slowly pursue either of the traditional stances of the parliamentary left: gradual, progressive reformism or Marxist-inspired popular revolution. Instead, influenced by Henri de Man's planism, they promoted a "constructive revolution" headed by the state, where a democratic mandate would be sought to develop technocracy and a planned economy.

This approach saw great success in the Belgian Labour Party in 1933-1934, where it was adopted as official policy with the support of the party's right (De Man) and left (Paul-Henri Spaak) wings, though by 1935 enthusiasm had waned. Such ideas also influenced the non-conformist movement on the French right.

Marcel Déat published in 1930 Perspectives socialistes (Socialist Perspectives), a revisionist work closely influenced by Henri de Man's planism. Along with over a hundred articles written in La vie socialiste (The Socialist Life), the review of the SFIO's right-wing, Perspective socialistes marked the shift of Déat from classical socialism to neosocialism. Déat replaced class struggle with class collaboration and national solidarity, advocated corporatism as a model of social organisation, replaced the notion of socialism with anti-capitalism and supported a technocratic state which would plan the economy and in which parliamentarism would be replaced by political technocracy.

The neosocialist faction inside of the SFIO which included the senior party figures Marcel Déat and Pierre Renaudel was expelled at the November 1933 party congress, partly for its admiration for Italian fascism, and largely for its revisionist stances: the neosocialists advocated alliances with the middle classes and favoured making compromises with the bourgeois Radical-Socialist Party to enact the SFIO's program one issue at a time. After having been expelled from the SFIO, Marcel Déat and his followers created the Socialist Party of France – Jean Jaurès Union; by the close of 1935 the emergence of the Popular Front had stolen the thunder for much of the neo-socialists' tactical and policy proposals, and the Jean Jaurès Union merged with the more traditional class-collaborative Independent Socialists and Socialist Republicans to form the small Socialist Republican Union. Within the General Confederation of Labour trade union, neosocialism was represented by René Belin's *Syndicats* (then *Redressements*)'s faction. On the other hand, Henri de Man's planism influenced the left-wing of the progressive-centrist Radical-Socialist Party, known as Young Turks (among them Pierre Mendès-France).

At first the neosocialists remained part of the broader left. Déat led his splinter party into the Socialist Republican Union, a merger of various revisionist socialist parties, and participated in the Popular Front coalition of 1936. But disillusionment in democracy eventually caused many neosocialists to distance themselves from the traditional left and call for more authoritarian government. After 1936 many evolved toward a form of participatory and national socialism which led them to join with the reactionary right and support the collaborationist Vichy regime during World War II. For instance, René Belin and Marcel Déat became members of the Vichy government. As a result, Déat's neosocialism was discredited in France after the war.

Democratic Socialism

Democratic socialists believe that both the economy and society should be run democratically—to meet public needs, not to make profits for a few. To achieve a more just society, many structures of our government and economy must be radically transformed through greater economic and social democracy so that ordinary Americans can participate in the many decisions that affect our lives.

Democracy and socialism go hand in hand. All over the world, wherever the idea of democracy has taken root, the vision of socialism has taken root as well—everywhere but in the United States. Because of this, many false ideas about socialism have developed in the US.

Democratic socialists do not want to create an all-powerful government bureaucracy. But we do not want big corporate bureaucracies to control our society either. Rather, we believe that social and economic decisions should be made by those whom they most affect.

Today, corporate executives who answer only to themselves and a few wealthy stockholders make basic economic decisions affecting millions of people. Resources are used to make money for capitalists rather than to meet human needs. We believe that the workers and consumers who are affected by economic institutions should own and control them.

Social ownership could take many forms, such as worker-owned cooperatives or publicly owned enterprises managed by workers and consumer representatives. Democratic socialists favor as much decentralization as possible. While the large concentrations of capital in industries such as energy and steel may necessitate some form of state ownership, many consumer-goods industries might be best run as cooperatives.

Democratic socialists have long rejected the belief that the whole economy should be centrally planned. While we believe that democratic planning can shape major social investments like mass transit, housing, and energy, market mechanisms are needed to determine the demand for many consumer goods.

Socialists have been among the harshest critics of authoritarian Communist states. Just because their bureaucratic elites called them "socialist" did not make it so; they also called their regimes "democratic." Democratic socialists always opposed the ruling party-states of those societies, just as we oppose the ruling classes of capitalist societies. We applaud the democratic revolutions that have transformed the former Communist bloc. However, the improvement of people's lives requires real democracy without ethnic rivalries and new forms of authoritarianism. Democratic socialists will continue to play a key role in that struggle throughout the world.

Moreover, the fall of Communism should not blind us to injustices at home. We cannot allow all radicalism to be dismissed as "Communist." That suppression of dissent and diversity undermines America's ability to live up to its promise of equality of opportunity, not to mention the freedoms of speech and assembly.

In the short term we can't eliminate private corporations, but we can bring them under greater democratic control. The government could use regulations and tax incentives to encourage companies to act in the public interest and outlaw destructive activities such as exporting jobs to low-wage countries and polluting our environment. Public pressure can also have a critical role to play in the struggle to hold corporations accountable. Most of all, socialists look to unions to make private business more accountable.

We don't agree with the capitalist assumption that starvation or greed are the only reasons people work. People enjoy their work if it is meaningful and enhances their lives. They work out of a sense of responsibility to their community and society. Although a long-term goal of socialism is to eliminate all but the most enjoyable kinds of labor, we recognize that unappealing jobs will long remain. These tasks would be spread among as many people as possible rather than distributed on the basis of class, race, ethnicity, or gender, as they are under capitalism. And this undesirable work should be among the best, not the least, rewarded work within the economy. For now, the burden should be placed on the employer to make work desirable by raising wages, offering benefits and improving the work environment. In short, we believe that a combination of social, economic, and moral incentives will motivate people to work.

Although no country has fully instituted democratic socialism, the socialist parties and labor movements of other countries have won many victories for their people. We can learn from the comprehensive welfare state maintained by the Swedes, from Canada's national health care system, France's nationwide childcare program, and Nicaragua's literacy programs. Lastly, we can learn from efforts initiated right here in the US, such as the community health centers created by the government in the 1960s. They provided high quality family care, with community involvement in decision-making. Many northern European countries enjoy tremendous prosperity and relative economic equality thanks to the policies pursued by social democratic parties. These nations used their relative wealth to insure a high standard of living for their citizens—high wages, health care and subsidized education. Most importantly, social democratic parties supported strong labor movements that became central players in economic decision-making. But with the globalization of capitalism, the old social democratic model becomes ever harder to maintain. Stiff competition from low-wage labor markets in developing countries and the constant fear that industry will move to avoid taxes and strong labor regulations has diminished (but not eliminated) the ability of nations to launch ambitious economic reform on their own. Social democratic reform must now happen at the international level. Multinational corporations must be brought under democratic controls, and workers' organizing efforts must reach across borders.

Now, more than ever, socialism is an international movement. As socialists have always known, the welfare of working people in Finland or California depends largely on standards in Italy or Indonesia. As a result, we must work towards reforms that can withstand the power of multinationals and global banks, and we must fight for a world order that is not controlled by bankers and bosses.

No, we are not a separate party. Like our friends and allies in the feminist, labor, civil rights, religious, and community organizing movements, many of us have been active in the Democratic Party. We work with those movements to strengthen the party's left wing, represented by the Congressional Progressive Caucus.

The process and structure of American elections seriously hurts third party efforts.

Winner-take-all elections instead of proportional representation, rigorous party qualification requirements that vary from state to state, a presidential instead of a parliamentary system, and the two-party monopoly on political power have doomed third party efforts. We hope that at some point in the future, in coalition with our allies, an alternative national party will be viable. For now, we will continue to support progressives who have a real chance at winning elections, which usually means left-wing Democrats.

Although capitalism will be with us for a long time, reforms we win now—raising the minimum wage, securing a national health plan, and demanding passage of right-to-strike legislation—can bring us closer to socialism. Many democratic socialists actively work in the single-issue organizations that advocate for those reforms. We are visible in the reproductive freedom movement, the fight for student aid, gay, lesbian, bisexual and transgender organizations, anti-racist groups, and the labor movement.

It is precisely our socialist vision that informs and inspires our day-to-day activism for social justice. As socialists we bring a sense of the interdependence of all struggles for justice. No single-issue organization can truly challenge the capitalist system or adequately secure its particular demands. In fact, unless we are all collectively working to win a world without oppression, each fight for reforms will be disconnected, maybe even self-defeating.

Yellow Socialism

Yellow socialism was the name applied to a form of revisionist socialism which became prominent in the early twentieth century prior to World War I, as an alternative to Marxism (sometimes called "red socialism"). Yellow socialists rejected class struggle, the general strike and revolutionary socialism in general.

The term "yellow socialism" was coined by a former member of the French Socialist Party, Pierre Biétry, in 1904 when he founded the "Fédération Nationale des Jaunes de France" (*National Federation of Yellows*), a right wing socialist group that rejected Marxism, class struggle and labour militancy. Over the next two decades revolutionary socialists would deride all revisionists as "yellow socialists" whether they accepted the label for themselves or not.

In the United States, yellow socialism was associated with the business unionism of Samuel Gompers (and thus described as "yellow unionism").

Yellow socialists and yellow unionists were criticised by more radical socialists for their concessions to nationalism and occasional engagement in chauvinism such as opposition to immigration (for supposedly flooding the labour market and reducing wages or denying jobs to native-born citizens), and sometimes even racism or anti-Semitism.

In Europe, during World War I, yellow socialism became associated with the social democratic parties who supported their own states in the war rather than taking an internationalist position against the conflict.

However, the "Berne International" (or "Two-and-a-half International") which met at Zimmerwald in 1915 was also described by Lenin as "yellow socialist", despite its opposition to the war, for its rejection of revolutionary socialism. After the war, the term "yellow socialism" fell into disuse, and the yellow socialists were absorbed into the larger post-war social democratic movement. Over time, the social democrats evolved towards their modern form, and many of the views held by the yellow socialists disappeared from the movement.

References

- Religious-socialism-definition-theory-criticism: study.com, Retrieved 24 July, 2020
- Ellman, Michael (2014). Socialist Planning, Third Edition. Cambridge University Press. p. 11. ISBN 1107427320
- What-is-democratic-socialism: dsausa.org, Retrieved 10 August, 2020
- Newman, Michael. (2005) Socialism: A Very Short Introduction, Oxford University Press, ISBN 0-19-280431-6
- Yellow-socialism, encyclopedia: academickids.com, Retrieved 14 April, 2020
- Bockman, Johanna (2011). Markets in the name of Socialism: The Left-Wing origins of Neoliberalism. Stanford University Press. ISBN 978-0-8047-7566-3

Theories of Socialism

3

- **Marx's Concept of Socialism**
- **Marxism–Leninism**
- **Mutualism**
- **Socialism in One Country**
- **Scientific Socialism**

There are many theories that are studied under the domain of socialism. Some of them are Marx's concept of socialism, Marxism-Leninism, mutualism, scientific socialism theory, etc. The topics elaborated in this chapter will help in gaining a better perspective of these theories studied under socialism.

Marx's Concept of Socialism

Marx's concept of socialism follows from his concept of man. It should be clear by now that according to this concept, socialism is not a society of regimented, automatized individuals, regardless of whether there is equality of income or not, and regardless of whether they are well fed and well clad. It is not a society in which the individual is subordinated to the state, to the machine, to the bureaucracy. Even if the state as an "abstract capitalist" were the employer, even if "the entire social capital were united in the hands either of a single capitalist or a single capitalist corporation," this would not be socialism. In fact, as Marx says quite clearly in the Economic and Philosophical Manuscripts, "communism as such is not the aim of human development." What, then, is the aim?

Quite clearly the aim of socialism is man. It is to create a form of production and an organization of society in which man can overcome alienation from his product, from his work, from his fellow man, from himself and from nature; in which he can return to himself and grasp the world with his own powers, thus becoming one with the world.

Socialism for Marx was, as Paul Tillich put it, "a resistance movement against the destruction of love in social reality."

Marx expressed the aim of socialism with great clarity at the end of the third volume of Capital: "In fact, the realm of freedom does not commence until the point is passed where labor under the compulsion of necessity and of external utility is required. In the very nature of things it lies beyond the sphere of material production in the strict meaning of the term. Just as the savage must wrestle with nature, in order to satisfy his wants, in order to maintain his life and reproduce it, so civilized man has to do it, and he must do it in all forms of society and under all possible modes of production. With his development the realm of natural necessity expands, because his wants increase; but at the same time the forces of production increase, by which these wants are satisfied. The freedom in this field cannot consist of anything else but of the fact that socialized man, the associated producers, regulate their interchange with nature rationally, bring it under their common control, instead of being ruled by it as by some blind power; they accomplish their task with the least expenditure of energy and under conditions most adequate to their human nature and most worthy of it. But it always remains a realm of necessity. Beyond it begins that development of human power, which is its own end, the true realm of freedom, which, however, can flourish only upon that realm of necessity as its basis."

Marx expresses here all essential elements of socialism. First, man produces in an associated, not competitive way; he produces rationally and in an unalienated way, which means that he brings production under his control, instead of being ruled by it as by some blind power. This clearly excludes a concept of socialism in which man is manipulated by a bureaucracy, even if this bureaucracy rules the whole state economy, rather than only a big corporation. It means that the individual participates actively in the planning and in the execution of the plans; it means, in short, the realization of political and industrial democracy. Marx expected that by this new form of an unalienated society man would become independent, stand on his own feet, and would no longer be crippled by the alienated mode of production and consumption; that he would truly be the master and the creator of his life, and hence that he could begin to make living his main business, rather than producing the means for living. Socialism, for Marx, was never as such the fulfillment of life, but the condition for such fulfillment. When man has built a rational, nonalienated form of society, he will have the chance to begin with what is the aim of life: the "development of human power, which is its own end, the true realm of freedom." Marx, the man who every year read all the works of Aeschylus and Shakespeare, who brought to life in himself the greatest works of human thought, would never have dreamt that his idea of socialism could be interpreted as having as its aim the well-fed and well-clad "welfare" or "workers' " state. Man, in Marx's view, has created in the course of history a culture which he will be free to make his own when he is freed from the chains, not only of economic poverty, but of the spiritual poverty created by alienation. Marx's vision is based on his faith in man, in the inherent and real potentialities of the essence of man which have developed in history. He looked at socialism as the condition of human freedom and creativity, not as in itself constituting the goal of man's life.

For Marx, socialism (or communism) is not flight or abstraction from, or loss of the objective world which men have created by the objectification of their faculties. It is not an impoverished return to unnatural, primitive simplicity. It is rather the first real emergence, the genuine actualization of man's nature as something real. Socialism, for Marx, is a society which permits the actualization of man's essence, by overcoming his alienation. It is nothing less than creating the conditions for the truly free, rational, active and independent man; it is the fulfillment of the prophetic aim: the destruction of the idols.

That Marx could be regarded as an enemy of freedom was made possible only by the fantastic fraud of Stalin in presuming to talk in the name of Marx, combined with the fantastic ignorance about Marx that exists in the Western world. For Marx, the aim of socialism was freedom, but freedom in a much more radical sense than the existing democracy conceives of it-freedom in the sense of independence, which is based on man's standing on his own feet, using his own powers and relating himself to the world productively. "Freedom," said Marx, "is so much the essence of man that even its opponents realize it No man fights freedom; he fights at most the freedom of others. Every kind of freedom has therefore always existed, only at one time as a special privilege, another time as a universal right."

Socialism, for Marx, is a society which serves the needs of man. But, many will ask, is not that exactly what modern capitalism does? Are not our big corporations most eager to serve the needs of man? And are the big advertising companies not reconnaissance parties which, by means of great efforts, from surveys to "motivation analysis," try to find out what the needs of man are? Indeed, one can understand the concept of socialism only if one understands Marx's distinction between the true needs of man, and the synthetic, artificially produced needs of man.

As follows from the whole concept of man, his real needs are rooted in his nature; this distinction between real and false needs is possible only on the basis of a picture of the nature of man and the true human needs rooted in his nature. Man's true needs are those whose fulfillment is necessary for the realization of his essence as a human being. As Marx put it: "The existence of what I truly love is felt by me as a necessity, as a need, without which my essence cannot be fulfilled, satisfied, complete." Only on the basis of a specific concept of man's nature can Marx make the difference between true and false needs of man. Purely subjectively, the false needs are experienced as being as urgent and real as the true needs, and from a purely subjective viewpoint, there could not be a criterion for the distinction. (In modern terminology one might differentiate between neurotic and rational healthy needs). Often man is conscious only of his false needs and unconscious of his real ones. The task of the analyst of society is precisely to awaken man so that he can become aware of the illusory false needs and of the reality of his true needs. The principal goal of socialism, for Marx, is the recognition and realization of man's true needs, which will be possible only when production serves man, and capital ceases to create and exploit the false needs of man.

Marx's concept of socialism is a protest, as is all existentialist philosophy, against the alienation of man; if, as Aldous Huxley put it, "our present economic, social and international arrangements are based, in large measure, upon organized lovelessness," then Marx's socialism is a protest against this very lovelessness, against man's exploitation of man, and against his exploitativeness towards nature, the wasting of our natural resources at the expense of the majority of men today, and more so of the generations to come. The unalienated man, who is the goal of socialism as we have shown before, is the man who does not "dominate" nature, but who becomes one with it, who is alive and responsive toward objects, so that objects come to life for him.

Does not all this mean that Marx's socialism is the realization of the deepest religious impulses common to the great humanistic religions of the past? Indeed it does, provided we understand that Marx, like Hegel and like many others, expresses his concern for man's soul, not in theistic, but in philosophical language.

Marx fought against religion exactly because it is alienated, and does not satisfy the true needs of man. Marx's fight against God is, in reality, a fight against the idol that is called God. Already as a young man he wrote as the motto for his dissertation "Not those are godless who have contempt for the gods of the masses but those who attribute the opinions of the masses to the gods." Marx's atheism is the most advanced form of rational mysticism, closer to Meister Eckhart or to Zen Buddhism than are most of those fighters for God and religion who accuse him of "godlessness."

It is hardly possible to talk about Marx's attitude toward religion without mentioning the connection between his philosophy of history, and of socialism, with the Messianic hope of the Old Testament prophets and the spiritual roots of humanism in Greek and Roman thinking. The Messianic hope is, indeed, a feature unique in Occidental thought. The prophets of the Old Testament are not only, like Lao Tzu or Buddha, spiritual leaders; they are also political leaders. They show man a vision of how he ought to be, and confront him with the alternatives between which he must choose. Most of the Old Testament prophets share the idea that history has a meaning, that man perfects himself in the process of history, and that he will eventually create a social order of peace and justice. But peace and justice for the prophets do not mean the absence of war and the absence of injustice. Peace and justice are concepts which are rooted in the whole of the Old Testament concept of man. Man, before he has consciousness of himself, that is, before he is human, lives in unity with nature (Adam and Eve in Paradise). The first act of Freedom, which is the capacity to say "no," opens his eyes, and he sees himself as a stranger in the world, beset by conflicts with nature, between man and man, between man and woman. The process of history is the process by which man develops his specifically human qualities, his powers of love and understanding; and once he has achieved full humanity he can return to the lost unity between himself and the world. This new unity, however, is different from the preconscious one which existed before history began. It is the at-onement of man with himself, with nature, and with his fellow man, based on the fact that man has given birth to himself in the historical process. In Old Testament thought, God is revealed in history ("the God of Abraham, the God of Isaac, the God of Jacob"), and in history, not in a state transcending history, lies the salvation of man. This means that man's spiritual aims are inseparably connected with the transformation of society; politics is basically not a realm that can be divorced from that of moral values and of man's self-realization.

Related thoughts arose in Greek (and Hellenistic) and Roman thinking. From Zeno, the founder of Stoic philosophy, to Seneca and Cicero, the concepts of natural law and of the equality of man exercised a powerful influence on the minds of men and, together with the prophetic tradition, are the foundations of Christian thinking.

While Christianity, especially since Paul, tended to transform the historical concept of salvation into an "other-worldly," purely spiritual one, and while the Church became the substitute for the "good society," this transformation was by no means a complete one. The early Church fathers express a radical criticism of the existing state; Christian thought of the late Middle Ages criticizes secular authority and the state from the standpoint of divine and natural law. This viewpoint stresses that society and the state must not be divorced from the spiritual values rooted in revelation and reason ("intellect" in the scholastic meaning of the word). Beyond this, the Messianic idea was expressed even in more radical forms in the Christian sects before the Reformation, and in the thinking of many Christian groups after the Reformation, down to the Society of Friends of the present time.

The mainstream of Messianic thinking after the Reformation, however, was expressed no longer in religious thought, but in philosophical, historical and social thought. It was expressed somewhat obliquely in the great utopias of the Renaissance, in which the new world is not in a distant future, but in a distant place. It was expressed in the thinking of the philosophers of the enlightenment and of the French and English Revolutions. It found its latest and most complete expression in Marx's concept of socialism. Whatever direct influence Old Testament thinking might have had on him through socialists like Moses Hess, no doubt the prophetic Messianic tradition influenced him indirectly through the thought of the enlightenment philosophers and especially through the thought stemming from Spinoza, Goethe, Hegel. What is common to prophetic, thirteenth-century Christian thought, eighteenth-century enlightenment, and nineteenth-century socialism, is the idea that State (society) and spiritual values cannot be divorced from each other; that politics and moral values are indivisible. This idea was attacked by the secular concepts of the Renaissance (Machiavelli) and again by the secularism of the modern state. It seems that Western man, whenever he was under the influence of gigantic material conquests, gave himself unrestrictedly to the new powers he had acquired and, drunk with these new powers, forgot himself. The elite of these societies became obsessed with the wish for power, luxury, and the manipulation of men, and the masses followed them. This happened in the Renaissance with its new science, the discovery of the globe, the prosperous City States of Northern Italy; it happened again in the explosive development of the first and the present second industrial revolutions.

But this development has been complicated by the presence of another factor. If the state or the society is meant to serve the realization of certain spiritual values, the danger exists that a supreme authority tells man -and forces him to think and behave in a certain way. The incorporation of certain objectively valid values into social life tends to produce authoritarianism. The spiritual authority of the Middle Ages was the Catholic Church. Protestantism fought this authority, at first promising greater independence for the individual, only to make the princely state the undisputed and arbitrary ruler of man's body and soul. The rebellion against princely authority occurred in the name of the nation, and for a while the national state promised to be the representative of freedom. But soon the national state devoted itself to the protection of the material interests of those who owned capital, and could thus exploit the labor of the majority of the population. Certain classes of society protested against this new authoritarianism and insisted on the freedom of the individual from the interference of secular authority. This postulate of liberalism, which tended to protect "freedom from," led, on the other hand, to the insistence that state and society must not attempt to realize "freedom to," that is to say, liberalism had to insist not only on separation from State and Church, but had also to deny that it was the function of the state to help realize certain spiritual and moral values; these values were supposed to be entirely a matter for the individual.

Socialism (in its Marxist and other forms) returned to the idea of the "good society" as the condition for the realization of man's spiritual needs. It was antiauthoritarian, both as far as the Church and the State are concerned, hence it aimed at the eventual disappearance of the state and at the establishment of a society composed of voluntarily co-operating individuals. Its aim was a reconstruction of society in such a way as to make it the basis for man's true return to himself, without the presence of those authoritarian forces which restricted and impoverished man's mind.

Thus, Marxist and other forms of socialism are the heirs of prophetic Messianism, Christian Chiliastic sectarianism, thirteenth-century Thomism, Renaissance Utopianism, and eighteenth-century enlightenment. It is the synthesis of the prophetic-Christian idea of society as the plane of spiritual realization, and of the idea of individual freedom. For this reason, it is opposed to the Church because of its restriction of the mind, and to liberalism because of its separation of society and moral values. It is opposed to Stalinism and Krushchevism, for their authoritarianism as much as their neglect of humanist values.

Socialism is the abolition of human self-alienation, the return of man as a real human being. "It is the definitive resolution of the antagonism between man and nature, and between man and man. It is the true solution of the conflict between existence and essence, be tween objectification and self-affirmation, between freedom and necessity, between individual and species. It is a solution of the riddle of history and knows itself to be this solution". For Marx, socialism meant the social order which permits the return of man to himself, the identity between existence and essence, the overcoming of the separateness and antagonism between subject and object, the humanization of nature; it meant a world in which man is no longer a stranger among strangers, but is in his world, where he is at home.

Marxism–Leninism

Marxism–Leninism is a political philosophy and self-proclaimed science that seeks to establish a socialist state and then develop it further into socialism and eventually communism, a classless social system with common ownership of the means of production and with full social and economic equality of all members of society. Marxist–Leninists espouse a wide array of views depending on their understanding of orthodox Marxism and Leninism, but they generally support the idea of a vanguard party, a communist party-led state, state-dominance over the economy, internationalism and opposition to bourgeois democracy, capitalism, imperialism and racism. As an ideology, it was developed by Joseph Stalin in the late 1920s based on his understanding and synthesis of both orthodox Marxism and Leninism. It was the official state ideology of the Soviet Union and the other ruling parties making up the Eastern Bloc as well as the political parties of the Communist International after Bolshevisation. Today, Marxism–Leninism is the ideology of Stalinist and Maoist political parties around the world and remains the official ideology of the ruling parties of China, Cuba, Laos and Vietnam.

After the death of Vladimir Lenin in 1924, Marxism–Leninism became a distinct philosophical movement in the Soviet Union when Stalin and his supporters gained control of the party. It rejected the common notions among Marxists at the time of world revolution as a prerequisite for building socialism in Russia in favour of the concept of socialism in one country. According to its supporters, the gradual transition from capitalism to socialism was signified with the introduction of the first five-year plan and the 1936 Soviet Constitution. The internationalism of Marxism–Leninism was expressed in supporting revolutions in foreign countries (e.g. initially through the Communist International or through the concept of socialist-leaning countries after de-Stalinisation). By the late 1920s, Stalin established ideological orthodoxy among the Russian Communist Party (Bolsheviks), the Soviet Union and the Communist International to establish universal Marxist–Leninist praxis. In the late 1930s, Stalin's official textbook History of the Communist Party of the Soviet Union (Bolsheviks) made the term Marxism–Leninism common political-science usage among communists and non-communists.

The goal of Marxism–Leninism is the revolutionary transformation of a capitalist state into a socialist state by way of two-stage revolution led by a vanguard party of professional revolutionaries drawn from the proletariat. To realise the two-stage transformation of the state, the vanguard party establishes the dictatorship of the proletariat (as opposed to that of the bourgeoisie) and determines policy through democratic centralism. The Marxist–Leninist communist party is the vanguard for the political, economic and social transformation of a capitalist society into a socialist society which is the lower stage of socio-economic development and progress towards the upper-stage communist society which is stateless and classless. It features public ownership of the means of production, accelerated industrialisation, pro-active development of society's productive forces (research and development) and nationalised natural resources.

Joseph Stalin, Vladimir Lenin and Mikhail Kalinin in 1919.

In the establishment of socialism in the former Russian Empire, Bolshevism was the ideological basis for the Soviet Union. As the vanguard party who guide the establishment and development of socialism, the communist party represented their policies as correct. Because Leninism was the revolutionary means to achieving socialism in the praxis of government, the relationship between ideology and decision-making inclined to pragmatism and most policy decisions were taken in light of the continual and permanent development of Marxist–Leninist ideology, i.e. ideological adaptation to actual conditions.

Within five years of the death of Vladimir Lenin, Joseph Stalin completed his rise to power and was the leader of the Soviet Union who theorised and applied the socialist theories of Lenin and Karl Marx as political expediencies used to realise his plans for the Soviet Union and for world socialism. The book *Concerning Questions of Leninism* represented Marxism–Leninism as a separate communist ideology and featured a global hierarchy of communist parties and revolutionary vanguard parties in each country of the world. With that, Stalin's application of Marxism–Leninism to the situation of the Soviet Union became Stalinism, the official state ideology until his death in 1953. In Marxist political discourse, the term Stalinism, denoting and connoting the theory and praxis of Stalin, has two usages, namely praise of Stalin by Marxist–Leninists who believe Stalin successfully developed Lenin's legacy and criticism of Stalin by Marxist–Leninists and other Marxists who repudiate Stalin's political purges, social-class repressions and bureaucratic terrorism.

Mao Zedong with Anna Louise Strong, the American journalist who reported and explained the Chinese Communist Revolution to the West.

As the Left Opposition to Stalin within the Soviet party and government, Leon Trotsky and Trotskyists argued that Marxist–Leninist ideology contradicted Marxism and Leninism in theory, therefore Stalin's ideology was not socialist philosophy useful for the implementation of socialism in Russia. Moreover, Trotskyists within the party identified their anti-Stalinist communist ideology as Bolshevik–Leninism and supported the permanent revolution to differentiate themselves from Stalin's justification and implementation of socialism in one country.

After the Sino-Soviet split of the 1960s, the Communist Party of China and the Communist Party of the Soviet Union claimed to be the sole heir and successor to Stalin concerning the correct interpretation of Marxism–Leninism and ideological leader of world communism. In that vein, Mao Zedong Thought, Mao Zedong's updating and adaptation of Marxism–Leninism to Chinese conditions in which revolutionary praxis is primary and ideological orthodoxy is secondary, represents urban Marxism–Leninism adapted to pre-industrial China. The claim that Mao Zedong had adapted Marxism–Leninism to Chinese conditions evolved into the idea that he had updated it in a fundamental way applying to the world as a whole. Consequently, Mao Zedong Thought became the official state ideology of the People's Republic of China as well as the ideological basis of communist parties around the world which sympathised with China. In the late 1970s, the Peruvian communist party Shining Path developed and synthesized Maoism into Marxism–Leninism–Maoism, a contemporary variety of Marxism–Leninism that is a supposed higher level of Marxism–Leninism that can be applied universally.

Following the Sino-Albanian split of the 1970s, a small portion of Marxist–Leninists began to downplay or repudiate the role of Mao Zedong in the Marxist–Leninist international movement in favour of the Albanian Labor Party and a stricter adherence to Stalin. The Sino-Albanian split was caused by Albania's rejection of China's *Realpolitik* of Sino–American rapprochement, specifically the 1972 Mao–Nixon meeting which the anti-revisionist Albanian Labor Party perceived as an ideological betrayal of Mao Zedong's own Three Worlds Theory that excluded such political rapprochement with the West. To the Albanian Marxist–Leninists, the Chinese dealings with the United States indicated Mao Zedong's lessened, practical commitments to ideological orthodoxy and proletarian internationalism. In response to Mao Zedong's apparently unorthodox deviations, Enver Hoxha, head of the Albanian Labor Party, theorised an anti-revisionist Marxism–Leninism, referred to as Hoxhaism, that retained orthodox Marxism–Leninism when compared to the ideology of the post-Stalin Soviet Union.

In North Korea, Marxism–Leninism was officially superseded in 1977 by Juche. However, the government is still sometimes referred to as Marxist–Leninist, or more commonly as Stalinist, due to its political and economic structure. In the other four existing Marxist–Leninist socialist states, namely China, Cuba, Laos and Vietnam, the ruling parties hold Marxism–Leninism as their official ideology, although they give it different interpretations in terms of practical policy.

Although Marxism–Leninism was created after Vladimir Lenin's death during the regime of Josef Stalin in the Soviet Union, continuing to be the official state ideology after de-Stalinisation and of other Marxist–Leninist states, the basis for elements of Marxism–Leninism predate this. The philosophy of Marxism–Leninism originated as the pro-active, political praxis of the Bolshevik faction of the Russian Social Democratic Labour Party in realising political change in Tsarist Russia. Lenin's leadership transformed the Bolsheviks into the party's political vanguard which was composed of professional revolutionaries who practised democratic centralism to elect leaders and officers as well as to determine policy through free discussion, then decisively realised through united action. The vanguardism of proactive, pragmatic commitment to achieving revolution was the Bolsheviks' advantage in out-manoeuvring the liberal and conservative political parties who advocated social democracy without a practical plan of action for the Russian society they wished to govern. Leninism allowed the Bolshevik party to assume command of the October Revolution in 1917.

Twelve years before the October Revolution in 1917, the Bolsheviks had failed to assume control of the February Revolution of 1905 because the centres of revolutionary action were too far apart for proper political coordination. To generate revolutionary momentum from the Tsarist army killings on Bloody Sunday, the Bolsheviks encouraged workers to use political violence in order to compel the bourgeois social classes (the nobility, the gentry and the bourgeoisie) to join the proletarian revolution to overthrow the absolute monarchy of the Tsar of Russia. Most importantly, the experience of this revolution caused Lenin to conceive of the means of sponsoring socialist revolution through agitation, propaganda and a well-organised, disciplined and small political party.

Despite secret-police persecution by the Okhrana (Department for Protecting the Public Security and Order), émigré Bolsheviks returned to Russia to agitate, organise and lead, but then they returned to exile when peoples' revolutionary fervour failed in 1907. The failure of the February Revolution exiled Bolsheviks, Mensheviks, Socialist Revolutionaries and anarchists such as the Black Guards from Russia. Membership in both the Bolshevik and Menshevik ranks diminished from 1907 to 1908 while the number of people taking part in strikes in 1907 was 26% of the figure during the year of the Revolution of 1905, dropping to 6% in 1908 and 2% in 1910. The 1908–1917 period was one of disillusionment in the Bolshevik party over Lenin's leadership, with members opposing him for scandals involving his expropriations and methods of raising money for the party. This political defeat was aggravated by Tsar Nicholas II's political reformations of Imperial Russian government. In practise, the formalities of political participation (the electoral plurality of a multi-party system with the State Duma and the Russian Constitution of 1906) were the Tsar's piecemeal and cosmetic concessions to social progress because public office remained available only to the aristocracy, the gentry and the bourgeoisie. These reforms resolved neither the illiteracy, the poverty, nor malnutrition of the proletarian majority of Imperial Russia.

In Swiss exile, Lenin developed Marx's philosophy and extrapolated decolonisation by colonial revolt as a reinforcement of proletarian revolution in Europe. In 1912, Lenin resolved a factional challenge to his ideological leadership of the RSDLP by the Forward Group in the party, usurping the all-party congress to transform the RSDLP into the Bolshevik party. In the early 1910s, Lenin remained highly unpopular and was so unpopular amongst international socialist movement that by 1914 it considered censoring him. Unlike the European socialists who chose bellicose nationalism to anti-war internationalism, whose philosophical and political break was consequence of the internationalist–defencist schism among socialists, the Bolsheviks opposed the Great War. That nationalist betrayal of socialism was denounced by a small group of socialist leaders who opposed the Great War, including Rosa Luxemburg, Karl Liebknecht and Lenin, who said that the European socialists had failed the working classes for preferring patriotic war to proletarian internationalism. To debunk patriotism and national chauvinism, Lenin explained in the essay *Imperialism, the Highest Stage of Capitalism* that capitalist economic expansion leads to colonial imperialism which is then regulated with nationalist wars such as the Great War among the empires of Europe. To relieve strategic pressures from the Western Front, Imperial Germany impelled the withdrawal of Imperial Russia from the war's Eastern Front by sending Lenin and his Bolshevik cohort in a diplomatically-sealed train, anticipating them partaking in revolutionary activity.

In March 1917, the abdication of Tsar Nicholas II led to the Russian Provisional Government, who then proclaimed the Russian Republic. Later in the October Revolution, the Bolshevik's seizure of power against the Provisional Government resulted in their establishment of the Russian Soviet Federative Socialist Republic, yet parts of Russia remained occupied by the counter-revolutionary White Movement of anti-communists who had united to form the White Army to fight the Russian Civil War against the

Bolshevik government. Moreover, despite the White–Red civil war, Russia remained a combatant in the Great War that the Bolshevik's had quit with the Treaty of Brest-Litovsk which then provoked the Allied Intervention to the Russian Civil War by the armies of seventeen countries, featuring Great Britain, France, Italy, the United States and Imperial Japan.

Elsewhere, the successful October Revolution in Russia had facilitated the German Revolution of 1918–1919 and revolutions and interventions in Hungary which produced the First Hungarian Republic and the Hungarian Soviet Republic. In Berlin, the German government and their Freikorps mercenaries fought and defeated the Spartacist uprising which began as a general strike. In Munich, the local Freikorps fought and defeated the Bavarian Soviet Republic. In Hungary, the disorganised workers who had proclaimed the Hungarian Soviet Republic were fought and defeated by the royal armies of the Kingdom of Romania and the Kingdom of Yugoslavia as well as the army of the First Republic of Czechoslovakia. These communist forces were soon crushed by anti-communist forces and attempts to create an international communist revolution failed. However, a successful revolution occurred in Asia, when the Mongolian Revolution of 1921 established the Mongolian People's Republic.

As promised to the Russian peoples in October 1917, the Bolsheviks quit Russia's participation in the Great War on 3 March 1918. That same year, the Bolsheviks consolidated government power by expelling the Mensheviks, the Socialist Revolutionaries and the Left Socialist-Revolutionaries from the soviets. The Bolshevik government then established the Cheka (All-Russian Extraordinary Commission) secret police to eliminate anti–Bolshevik opposition in the country. Initially, there was strong opposition to the Bolshevik régime because they had not resolved the food shortages and material poverty of the Russian peoples as promised in October 1917. From that social discontent, the Cheka reported 118 uprisings, including the Kronstadt rebellion against the economic austerity of the War Communism imposed by the Bolsheviks. The principal obstacles to Russian economic development and modernisation were great material poverty and the lack of modern technology which were conditions that orthodox Marxism considered unfavourable to communist revolution. Agricultural Russia was sufficiently developed for establishing capitalism, but it was insufficiently developed for establishing socialism. For Bolshevik Russia, the 1921–1924 period featured the simultaneous occurrence of economic recovery, famine and a financial crisis. By 1924, considerable economic progress had been achieved and by 1926 the Bolshevik government had achieved economic production levels equal to Russia's production levels in 1913.

Initial Bolshevik economic policies from 1917 to 1918 were cautious, with limited nationalisations of the means of production which had been private property of the Russian aristocracy during the Tsarist monarchy. Lenin was immediately committed to avoid antagonising the peasantry by making efforts to coax them away from the Socialist Revolutionaries, allowing a peasant takeover of nobles' estates while no immediate nationalisations were enacted on peasants' property. The Decree on Land fulfilled Lenin's promised redistribution of Russia's arable land to the peasants, who reclaimed their farmlands from the aristocrats, ensuring the peasants' loyalty to the Bolshevik party. To overcome the civil war's economic interruptions, the policy of War Communism, a regulated market, state-controlled means of distribution and nationalisation of large-scale farms, was adopted to requisite and distribute grain in order to feed industrial workers in the cities whilst the Red Army was fighting the White Army's attempted restoration of the Romanov dynasty as absolute monarchs of Russia. Moreover, the politically unpopular forced grain-requisitions discouraged peasants from farming resulted in reduced harvests and food shortages that provoked labour strikes and food riots. In the event, the Russian peoples created an economy of barter and black market to counter the Bolshevik government's voiding of the monetary economy.

In 1921, the New Economic Policy restored some private enterprise to animate the Russian economy. As part of Lenin's pragmatic compromise with external financial interests in 1918, Bolshevik state capitalism temporarily returned 91% of industry to private ownership or trusts until the Soviet Russians learned the technology and the techniques required to operate and administrate industries. Importantly, Lenin declared that the development of socialism would not be able to be pursued in the manner originally thought by Marxists. A key aspect that affected the Bolshevik regime was the backward economic conditions in Russia that were considered unfavourable to orthodox Marxist theory of communist revolution. At the time, orthodox Marxists claimed that Russia was ripe for the development of capitalism, not yet for socialism. Lenin advocated the need of the development of a large corps of technical intelligentsia to assist the industrial development of Russia and advance the Marxist economic stages of development as it had too few technical experts at the time. In that vein, Lenin explained it as follows: "Our poverty is so great that we cannot, at one stroke, restore full-scale factory, state, socialist production". He added that the development of socialism would proceed according to the actual material and socio-economic conditions in Russia and not as abstractly described by Marx for industrialised Europe in the 19th century. To overcome the lack of educated Russians who could operate and administrate industry, Lenin advocated the development of a technical intelligentsia who would propel the industrial development of Russia to self-sufficiency.

As he neared death after suffering strokes, Lenin's Testament named Trotsky and Stalin as the most able men in the Central Committee, but he harshly criticised them. Lenin said that Stalin should be removed from being the General Secretary of the party and that he be replaced with "some other person who is superior to Stalin only in one respect, namely, in being more tolerant, more loyal, more polite, and more attentive to comrades". Upon his death, Lenin's political testament was read aloud to the Central Committee, who choose to ignore Lenin's ordered removal of Stalin as General Secretary because enough members believed Stalin had been politically rehabilitated in 1923.

Stalin and Nikolai Bukharin expediently joined forces to achieve Stalin's control of the All-Union Communist Party (Bolsheviks) and expel Trotsky from the party.

Consequent to personally spiteful disputes about the praxis of Leninism, the October Revolution veterans Lev Kamenev and Grigory Zinoviev said that the true threat to the ideological integrity of the party was Trotsky, who was a personally charismatic political leader as well as the commanding officer of the Red Army in the Russian Civil War and revolutionary partner of the dead Lenin. To thwart Trotsky's likely election to head the party, Stalin, Kamenev and Zinoviev formed a troika that featured Stalin as General Secretary, the *de facto* centre of power in the party and the country. The direction of the party was decided in confrontations of politics and personality between Stalin's troika and Trotsky over which Marxist policy to pursue, either Trotsky's policy of permanent revolution or Stalin's policy of socialism in one country. Trotsky's permanent revolution advocated rapid industrialisation, elimination of private farming and having the Soviet Union promote the spread of communist revolution abroad. Stalin's socialism in one country stressed moderation and development of positive relations between the Soviet Union and other countries to increase trade and foreign investment. To politically isolate and oust Trotsky from the party, Stalin expediently advocated socialism in one country, a policy to which he was indifferent. In 1925, the 14th Congress of the All-Union Communist Party (Bolsheviks) chose Stalin's policy, defeating Trotsky as a possible leader of the party and of the Soviet Union.

In the 1925–1927 period, Stalin dissolved the troika and disowned the centrist Kamenev and Zinoviev for an expedient alliance with the three most right-wing from the Bolshevik period, namely Alexei Rykov, Nikolai Bukharin and Mikhail Tomsky (leader of the All-Russian Central Council of Trade Unions). In 1927, the party endorsed Stalin's policy of socialism in one country as the Soviet Union's national policy and expelled the leftist Trotsky and the centrists Kamenev and Zinoviev from the Politburo. In 1929, Stalin politically controlled the party and the Soviet Union by way of deception and administrative acumen. In that time, Stalin's centralised, socialism in one country régime had negatively associated Lenin's revolutionary Bolshevism with Stalinism, i.e. government by command-policy to realise projects such as the rapid industrialisation of cities and the collectivisation of agriculture. Such Stalinism also subordinated the interests (political, national and ideological) of Asian and European communist parties to the geopolitical interests of the Soviet Union.

In the 1928–1932 period of the first five-year plan, Stalin affected the dekulakization of the farmlands of the Soviet Union, a politically radical dispossession of the kulak class of peasant-landlords from the Tsarist social order of monarchy. As Old Bolshevik revolutionaries, Bukharin, Rykov and Tomsky recommended amelioration of the dekulakization to lessen the negative social impact in the relations between the Soviet peoples and the party, but Stalin took umbrage and then accused them of uncommunist philosophical deviations from Lenin and Marx. That implicit accusation of ideological deviationism licensed Stalin to accuse Bukharin, Rykov and Tomsky of plotting against the party and the appearance of impropriety then compelled the resignations of the Old Bolsheviks from government and from the Politburo. Stalin then completed his political purging of the party by exiling Trotsky from the Soviet Union in 1929. Afterwards, the political opposition to the practical régime of Stalinism was denounced as Trotskyism (Bolshevik–Leninism), described as a deviation from Marxism–Leninism, the state ideology of the Soviet Union.

Political developments in the Soviet Union included Stalin dismantling the remaining elements of democracy from the party by extending his control over its institutions and eliminating any possible rivals. The party's ranks grew in numbers, with the party modifying its organisation to include more trade unions and factories. The ranks and files of the party were populated with members from the trade unions and the factories, whom Stalin controlled because there were no other Old Bolsheviks to contradict Marxism–Leninism. In the late 1930s, the Soviet Union adopted the 1936 Soviet Constitution which ended weighted-voting preferences for workers, promulgated universal suffrage for every man and woman older than 18 years of age and organised the soviets (councils of workers) into two legislatures, namely the Soviet of the Union (representing electoral districts) and the Soviet of Nationalities (representing the ethnic groups of the country). By 1939, with the exception of Stalin himself, none of the original Bolsheviks of the October Revolution of 1917 remained in the party. Unquestioning loyalty to Stalin was expected by the regime of all citizens.

Stalin exercised extensive personal control over the party and unleashed an unprecedented level of violence to eliminate any potential threat to his regime. While Stalin exercised major control over political initiatives, their implementation was in the control of localities, often with local leaders interpreting the policies in a way that served themselves best. This abuse of power by local leaders exacerbated the violent purges and terror campaigns carried out by Stalin against members of the party deemed to be traitors. With the Great Purge, Stalin rid himself of internal enemies in the party and rid the Soviet Union of any alleged socially dangerous and counterrevolutionary person who might have offered legitimate political opposition to Marxism–Leninism.

Stalin allowed the secret police NKVD (People's Commissariat for Internal Affairs) to rise above the law and the GPU (State Political Directorate) to use political violence to eliminate any person who might be a threat, whether real, potential, or imagined. As an administrator, Stalin governed the Soviet Union by controlling the formulation of national policy, but he delegated implementation to subordinate functionaries. Such freedom of action allowed local communist functionaries much discretion to interpret the intent of orders from Moscow, but this allowed their corruption. To Stalin, the correction of such abuses of authority and economic corruption were responsibility of the NKVD. In the 1937–1938 period, the NKVD arrested 1.5 million people, purged from every stratum of Soviet society and every rank and file of the party, of which 681,692 people were killed as enemies of the state. To provide manpower (manual, intellectual and technical) to realise the construction of socialism in one country, the NKVD established the Gulag system of forced-labour camps for regular criminals and political dissidents, for culturally insubordinate artists and politically incorrect intellectuals and for homosexual people and religious anti-communists.

Beginning in 1928, Stalin's five-year plans for the national economy of the Soviet Union achieved the rapid industrialisation (coal, iron and steel, electricity and petroleum, among others) and the collectivisation of agriculture. It achieved 23.6% of collectivisation within two years and 98.0% of collectivisation within thirteen years. As the revolutionary vanguard, the communist party organised Russian society to realise rapid industrialisation programs as defence against Western interference with socialism in Bolshevik Russia. The five-year plans were prepared in the 1920s whilst the Bolshevik government fought the internal Russian Civil War and repelled the external Allied intervention to the Russian Civil War. Vast industrialisation was initiated mostly based with a focus on heavy industry.

A 1929 metallurgical combine in Magnitogorsk demonstrates the Soviet Union's rapid industrialisation in the 1920s and 1930s.

During the 1930s, the rapid industrialisation of the country accelerated the Soviet people's sociological transition from poverty to relative plenty when politically illiterate peasants passed from Tsarist serfdom to self-determination and became politically aware urban citizens. The Marxist–Leninist economic régime modernised Russia from the illiterate, peasant society characteristic of monarchy to the literate, socialist society of educated farmers and industrial workers. Industrialisation led to a massive urbanisation in the country. Unemployment was virtually eliminated in the country during the 1930s.

Social developments in the Soviet Union included the relinquishment of the relaxed social control and allowance of experimentation under Lenin to Stalin's promotion of a rigid and authoritarian society based upon discipline, mixing traditional Russian values with Stalin's interpretation of Marxism. Organised religion was repressed, especially minority religious groups. Education was transformed. Under Lenin, the education system allowed relaxed discipline in schools that became based upon Marxist theory, but Stalin reversed this in 1934 with a conservative approach taken with the reintroduction of formal learning, the use of examinations and grades, the assertion of full authority of the teacher and the introduction of school uniforms. Art and culture became strictly regulated under the principles of socialist realism and Russian traditions that Stalin admired were allowed to continue.

Foreign policy in the Soviet Union from 1929 to 1941 resulted in substantial changes in the Soviet Union's approach to its foreign policy. In 1933, the Marxist–Leninist geopolitical perspective was that the Soviet Union was surrounded by capitalist and anti-communist enemies. As a result, the election of Adolf Hitler and his Nazi Party government in Germany initially caused the Soviet Union to sever diplomatic relations that had been established in the 1920s. In 1938, Stalin accommodated the Nazis and the anti-communist West by not defending Czechoslovakia, allowing Hitler's threat of pre-emptive war for the Sudetenland to annex the land and "rescue the oppressed German peoples" living in Czecho.

To challenge Nazi Germany's bid for European empire and hegemony, Stalin promoted anti-fascist front organisations to encourage European socialists and democrats to join the Soviet communists to fight throughout Nazi-occupied Europe, creating agreements with France to challenge Germany. After Germany and Britain signed the Munich Agreement which allowed the German occupation of Czechoslovakia, Stalin adopted pro-German policies for the Soviet Union's dealings with Nazi Germany. In 1939, the Soviet Union and Nazi Germany agreed to the Treaty of Non-aggression between Germany and the Union of Soviet Socialist Republics and to jointly invade and partition Poland, by way of which Nazi Germany started the Second World War.

In the 1941–1942 period of the Great Patriotic War, the German invasion of the Soviet Union was ineffectively opposed by the Red Army, who were poorly led, ill-trained and under-equipped. As a result, they fought poorly and suffered great losses of soldiers (killed, wounded and captured). The weakness of the Red Army was partly consequence of the Great Purge of senior officers and career soldiers whom Stalin considered politically unreliable. Strategically, the Wehrmacht's extensive and effective attack threatened the territorial integrity of the Soviet Union, and the political integrity of Stalin's model of a Marxist–Leninist state, when the Nazis were initially welcomed as liberators by the anti-communist and nationalist populations in the Byelorussian Soviet Socialist Republic, the Georgian Soviet Socialist Republic and the Ukrainian Soviet Socialist Republic.

The anti-Soviet nationalists' collaboration with the Nazi's lasted until the *Schutzstaffel* and the *Einsatzgruppen* began their *Lebensraum* killings of the Jewish populations, the local communists, the civil and community leaders—the Holocaust meant to realise the Nazi German colonisation of Bolshevik Russia. In response, Stalin ordered the Red Army to fight a total war against the Germanic invaders who would exterminate Slavic Russia. Hitler's attack against the Soviet Union (Nazi Germany's erstwhile ally) realigned Stalin's political priorities, from the repression of internal enemies to the existential defence against external attack. The pragmatic Stalin then entered the Soviet Union to the Grand Alliance, a common front against the Axis Powers (Nazi Germany, Fascist Italy and Imperial Japan).

In the continental European countries occupied by the Axis powers, the native communist party usually led the armed resistance (guerrilla warfare and urban guerrilla warfare) against fascist military occupation. In Mediterranean Europe, the communist Yugoslav Partisans led by Josip Broz Tito effectively resisted the German Nazi and Italian Fascist occupation. In the 1943–1944 period, the Yugoslav Partisans liberated territories with Red Army assistance and established the communist political authority that became the Socialist Federal Republic of Yugoslavia. To end the Imperial Japanese occupation of China in continental Asia, Stalin ordered Mao Zedong and the Communist Party of China to temporarily cease the Chinese Civil War against Chiang Kai-shek and the anti-communist Kuomintang as the Second United Front in the Second Sino-Japanese War.

Winston Churchill, Franklin D. Roosevelt and Stalin established the post-war order of the world with geopolitical spheres of influence under their hegemony at the Yalta Conference.

In 1943, the Red Army began to repel the Nazi invasion of the Soviet Union, especially at the Battle of Stalingrad and at the Battle of Kursk. The Red Army then repelled the Nazi and Fascist occupation armies from Eastern Europe until the Red Army decisively defeated Nazi Germany in the Berlin Strategic Offensive Operation. On concluding the Great Patriotic War, the Soviet Union was a military superpower with a say in determining the geopolitical order of the world. In accordance with the three-power Yalta Agreement, the Soviet Union purged native fascist collaborators from the Eastern European countries occupied by the Axis Powers and installed native Communist governments.

Upon Allied victory concluding the Second World War, the members of the Grand Alliance resumed their expediently suppressed, pre-war geopolitical rivalries and ideological tensions which disunity broke their anti-fascist wartime alliance into the anti-communist Western Bloc and the communist Eastern Bloc. The renewed competition for geopolitical hegemony resulted in the bi-polar Cold War, a protracted state of tension (military and diplomatic) between the Unted States and the Sovet Union which often threatened a Soviet–American nuclear war, but it usually featured proxy wars in the Third World.

The events that precipitated the Cold War in Europe were the Soviet and Yugoslav, Bulgarian and Albanian military interventions to the Greek Civil War on behalf of the Communist Party of Greece; and the Berlin Blockade by the Soviet Union. The event that precipitated the Cold War in continental Asia was the resumption of the Chinese Civil War fought between the anti-communist Kuomintang and the Communist Party of China. After military defeat exiled Generalissimo Chiang Kai-shek and his Kuomintang nationalist government to Formosa island (Taiwan), Mao Zedong established the People's Republic of China on 1 October 1949.

In the late 1940s, the geopolitics of the Eastern Bloc countries under the hegemony of Stalinist Russia featured an official-and-personal style of socialist diplomacy that failed Stalin and Tito when Tito refused to subordinating Yugoslavia to the Soviet Union. In 1948, circumstance and cultural personality aggravated the matter into the Yugoslav–Soviet split that resulted from Tito's rejection of Stalin's demand to subordinate the Socialist Federal Republic of Yugoslavia to the geopolitical agenda (economic and military) of the Soviet Union, i.e. Tito at Stalin's disposal. Stalin punished Tito's refusal by denouncing him as an ideological revisionist of Marxism–Leninism; by denouncing Yugoslavia's practice of Titoism as socialism deviated from the cause of world communism; and by expelling the Communist Party of Yugoslavia from the Communist Information Bureau (Cominform). The break from the Eastern Bloc allowed the development of a socialism with Yugoslav characteristics which allowed doing business with the capitalist West to develop the socialist economy and the establishment of Yugoslavia's diplomatic and commercial relations with countries of the Eastern Bloc and the Western Bloc. Yugoslavia's international relations matured into the Non-Aligned Movement of countries without political allegiance to any power bloc.

At the death of Stalin in 1953, Nikita Khrushchev became leader of the Soviet Union and of the Communist Party of the Soviet Union and then consolidated an anti-Stalinist government. In a secret meeting at the 20th Congress of the Communist Party of the Soviet Union, Khrushchev denounced Stalin and Stalinism in the speech *On the Cult of Personality and Its Consequences* in which he specified and condemned Stalin's dictatorial excesses and abuses of power such as the Great purge and the cult of personality. Khrushchev introduced the de-Stalinisation of the party and of the Soviet Union. He realised this with the dismantling of the Gulag archipelago of forced-labour camps and freeing the prisoners as well as allowing Soviet civil society greater political freedom of expression, especially for public intellectuals of the intelligentsia such as the novelist Aleksandr Solzhenitsyn, whose literature obliquely criticised Stalin and the Stalinist police state. De-Stalinization also ended Stalin's national-purpose policy of socialism in one country and was replaced with proletarian internationalism, by way of which Khrushchev re-committed the Soviet Union to permanent revolution to realise world communism. In that geopolitical vein, Khrushchev presented de-Stalinization as the restoration of Leninism as the state ideology of the Soviet Union.

The Chinese Communist Revolution concluded when Mao Zedong declared the establishment of the People's Republic of China on 1 October 1949.

In the 1950s, the de-Stalinisation of the Soviet Union was ideological bad news for the People's Republic of China because Soviet and Russian interpretations and applications of Leninism and orthodox Marxism contradicted the Sinified Marxism–Leninism of Mao Zedong—his Chinese adaptations of Stalinist interpretation and praxis for establishing socialism in China. To realise that leap of Marxist faith in the development of Chinese socialism, the Communist Party of China developed Maoism as the official state ideology. As the specifically Chinese development of Marxism–Leninism, Maoism illuminated the cultural differences between the European-Russian and the Asian-Chinese interpretations and practical applications of Marxism–Leninism in each country. The political differences then provoked geopolitical, ideological and nationalist tensions, which derived from the different stages of development, between the urban society of the industrialised Soviet Union and the agricultural society of the pre-industrial China.

The theory versus praxis arguments escalated to theoretic disputes about Marxist–Leninist revisionism and provoked the Sino-Soviet split and the two countries broke their international relations (diplomatic, political, cultural and economic).

In Eastern Asia, the Cold War produced the Korean War, the first proxy war between the Eastern Bloc and the Western Bloc, resulted from dual origins, namely the nationalist Koreans' post-war resumption of their Korean Civil War and the imperial war for regional hegemony sponsored by the United States and the Soviet Union. The international response to the North Korean invasion of South Korea was realised by the United Nations Security Council, who voted for war despite the absent Soviet Union and authorised an international military expedition to intervene, expel the northern invaders from the south of Korea and restore the geopolitical *status quo ante* of the Soviet and American division of Korea at the 38th Parallel of global latitude. Consequent to Chinese military intervention in behalf of North Korea, the magnitude of the infantry warfare reached operational and geographic stalemate. Afterwards, the shooting war was ended with the Korean Armistice Agreement and the superpower Cold War in Asia then resumed as the Korean Demilitarized Zone.

The Sino–Soviet split facilitated Russian and Chinese rapprochement with the United States and expanded East–West geopolitics into a tri-polar Cold War that allowed Premier Nikita Khrushchev to meet with President John F. Kennedy in June 1961.

Consequent to the Sino-Soviet split, the pragmatic China established politics of détente with the United States in a effort to publicly challenge the Soviet Union for leadership of the international Marxist–Leninist movement. Mao Zedong's pragmatism permitted geopolitical rapprochement and facilitated President Richard Nixon's 1972 visit to China which subsequently ended the policy of the existence to Two Chinas when the United States sponsored the People's Republic of China to replace the Republic of China (Taiwan) as the representative of the Chinese people at the United Nations. In the due course of Sino-American rapprochement, China also assumed membership in the Security Council of the United Nations. In the post-Mao period of Sino-American détente, the Deng Xiaoping government affected policies of economic liberalisation that allowed continual growth for the Chinese economy. The ideological justification is socialism with Chinese characteristics, the Chinese adaptation of Marxism–Leninism.

Che Guevara and Fidel Castro (leader of the Republic of Cuba from 1959 until 2008) led the Cuban Revolution to victory in 1959.

Communist revolution erupted in the Americas in this period, including revolutions in Bolivia, Cuba, El Salvador, Grenada, Nicaragua, Peru and Uruguay. The Cuban Revolution led by Fidel Castro and Che Guevara deposed the military dictatorship of Fulgencio Batista and established the Republic of Cuba, a state formally recognised by the Soviet Union. In response, the United States launched a coup against the Castro government in 1961. However, the CIA's unsuccessful Bay of Pigs invasion by anti-communist Cuban exiles impelled the Republic of Cuba to side with the Soviet Union in the geopolitics of the bipolar Cold War. The Cuban missile crisis occurred when the United States opposed Cuba being armed with nuclear missiles by the Soviet Union. After a stalemate confrontation, the United States and the Soviet Union jointly resolved the nuclear-missile crisis by respectively removing United States missiles from Turkey and Italy and Soviet missiles from Cuba.

Both Bolivia, Canada and Uruguay faced Marxist–Leninist revolution in the 1960s and 1970s. In Bolivia, this included Che Guevara as a leader until being killed there by government forces. In 1970, the October Crisis occurred in Canada, a brief revolution in the province of Quebec, where the actions of the Marxist–Leninist and separatist Quebec Liberation Front (FLQ) featured the kidnap of James Cross, the British Trade Commissioner in Canada; and the killing of Pierre Laporte, the Quebec government minister. The political manifesto of the FLQ condemned English-Canadian imperialism in French Quebec and called for a independent, socialist Quebec. The Canadian government's harsh response included the suspension of civil liberties in Quebec and compelled the FLQ leaders' flight to Cuba. Uruguay faced Marxist–Leninist revolution from the Tupamaros movement from the 1960s to the 1970s.

In 1979, the Sandinista National Liberation Front (FSLN) led by Daniel Ortega won the Nicaraguan Revolution against the government of Anastasio Somoza Debayle to establish a socialist Nicaragua. Within months, the government of Ronald Reagan sponsored the counter-revolutionary Contras in the secret Contra War against the

Sandinista government. In 1989, the Contra War concluded with the signing of the Tela Accord at the port of Tela, Honduras. The Tela Accord required the subsequent, voluntary demobilization of the Contra guerrilla armies and the FSLN army. In 1990, a second national election installed to government a majority of non-Sandinista political parties, to whom the FSLN handed political power. Since 2006, the FSLN has returned to government, winning every legislative and presidential election in the process.

Daniel Ortega led the Sandinista National Liberation Front to victory in the Nicaraguan Revolution in 1990.

The Salvadoran Civil War featured the popularly supported Farabundo Martí National Liberation Front, an organisation of left-wing parties fighting against the right-wing military government of El Salvador. In 1983, the United States invasion of Grenada thwarted the assumption of power by the elected government of the New Jewel Movement, a Marxist–Leninist vanguard party led by Maurice Bishop.

In Asia, the Vietnam War was the second East–West war fought during the Cold War. In the First Indochina War, the Việt Minh led by Ho Chi Minh defeated the French re-establishment of European colonialism in Vietnam. To fill the geopolitical power vacuum caused by French defeat in southeast Asia, the United States then became the Western power supporting the client-state Republic of Vietnam headed by Ngo Dinh Diem. Despite possessing military superiority, the United States failed to safeguard South Vietnam from the guerrilla warfare of the Viet Cong sponsored by North Vietnam. On 30 January 1968, North Vietnam launched the Tet Offensive. Although a military failure for the guerrillas and the army, it was a successful psychological warfare operation that decisively turned international public opinion against the United States intervention to the Vietnamese civil war, with the military withdrawal of the United States from Vietnam in 1973 and the subsequent and consequent Fall of Saigon to the North Vietnamese army on 30 April 1975.

With the end of the Vietnam War, Marxist–Leninist regimes were established in Vietnam's neighbour states. This included Kampuchea and Laos. Consequent to the Cambodian Civil War, a coalition composed of Prince Norodom Sihanouk, the native Cambodian Marxist–Leninists and the Maoist Khmer Rouge led by Pol Pot established

Democratic Kampuchea, a Marxist–Leninist state that featured class warfare to restructure the society of old Cambodia and to be effected and realised with the abolishment of money and private property, the outlawing of religion, the killing of the intelligentsia and compulsory manual labour for the middle classes by way of death-squad state terrorism. To eliminate Western cultural influence, Kampuchea expelled all foreigners and effected the destruction of the urban bourgeoisie of old Cambodia, first by displacing the population of the capital city, Phnom Penh; and then by displacing the national populace to work farmlands to increase food supplies. Meanwhile, the Khmer Rouge purged Kampuchea of internal enemies (social class and political, cultural and ethnic) at the Killing Fields, the scope of which became crimes against humanity for the deaths of 2,700,000 people by mass murder and genocide. That social restructuring of Cambodia into Kampuchea included attacks against the Vietnamese ethnic minority of the country which aggravated the historical, ethnic rivalries between the Viet and the Khmer peoples. Beginning in September 1977, Kampuchea and the Socialist Republic of Vietnam continually engaged in border clashes. In 1978, Vietnam invaded Kampuchea and captured Phnom Penh in January 1979, deposed the Maoist Khmer Rouge from government and established the Cambodian Liberation Front for National Renewal as the government of Cambodia.

In Apartheid South Africa, a trilingual sign in English, Afrikaans and Zulu enforces the racist segregation of a Natal beach as exclusively "for the sole use of members of the white race group".

A new front of Marxist–Leninist revolution erupted in Africa between 1961 and 1979. Angola, Benin, Congo, Ethiopia, Guinea-Bissau Mozambique, Somalia and Zimbabwe became Marxist–Leninist states governed by their respective native peoples during the 1968–1980 period. Marxist–Leninist guerrillas fought the Portuguese Colonial War in three countries, namely Angola, Guinea-Bissau and Mozambique. In Ethiopia, a Marxist–Leninist revolution deposed the monarchy of Emperor Haile Selassie and established the Derg government of the Provisional Military Government of Socialist

Ethiopia. In Rhodesia, Robert Mugabe led the Zimbabwe War of Liberation that deposed white-minority rule and then established the Republic of Zimbabwe.

In Apartheid South Africa, the Afrikaner government of the Nationalist Party caused much geopolitical tension between the United States and the Soviet Union because of the Afrikaners' violent social control and political repression of the black and coloured populations of South Africa exercised under the guise of anti-communism and national security. The Soviet Union officially supported the overthrow of apartheid while the West and the United States in particular maintained official neutrality on the matter. In the 1976–1977 period of the Cold War, the United States and other Western countries found it morally untenable to politically support Apartheid South Africa, especially when the Afrikaner government killed 176 people (students and adults) in the police suppression of the Soweto uprising, a political protest against Afrikaner cultural imperialism upon the non-white peoples of South Africa, specifically the imposition of the Germanic language of Afrikaans as the standard language for education which black South Africans were required to speak when addressing white people and Afrikaners; and the police assassination of Steven Biko, a politically moderate leader of the internal resistance to apartheid in South Africa.

Under President Jimmy Carter, the West joined the Soviet Union and others in enacting sanctions against weapons trade and weapons-grade material to South Africa. However, forceful actions by the United States against Apartheid South Africa were diminished under President Reagan as the Reagan administration feared the rise of revolution in South Africa as had happened in Zimbabwe against white minority rule. In 1979, the Soviet Union intervened in Afghanistan to establish a Marxist–Leninist state, although the act was seen as an invasion by the West which responded to the Soviet military actions by boycotting the Moscow Olympics of 1980 and providing clandestine support to the Mujahideen, including Osama bin Laden, as a means to challenge the Soviet Union. The war became a Soviet equivalent of the Vietnam War to the United States and it remained a stalemate throughout the 1980s.

Soviet General Secretary Mikhail Gorbachev, who sought to end the Cold War between the Soviet-led Warsaw Pact and the United States-led NATO and other its other Western allies, in a meeting with President Ronald Reagan.

Social resistance to the policies of Marxist–Leninist regimes in Eastern Europe accelerated in strength with the rise of the Solidarity, the first non-Marxist–Leninist controlled trade union in the Warsaw Pact that was formed in the People's Republic of Poland in 1980.

In 1985, Mikhail Gorbachev rose to power in the Soviet Union and began policies of radical political reform involving political liberalisation, called perestroika and glasnost. Gorbachev's policies were designed at dismantling authoritarian elements of the state that were developed by Stalin, aiming for a return to a supposed ideal Leninist state that retained one-party structure while allowing the democratic election of competing candidates within the party for political office. Gorbachev also aimed to seek détente with the West and end the Cold War that was no longer economically sustainable to be pursued by the Soviet Union. The Soviet Union and the United States under President George H. W. Bush joined in pushing for the dismantlement of apartheid and oversaw the dismantlement of South African colonial rule over Namibia.

The fall of the Berlin Wall in 1989.

Meanwhile, the eastern European Marxist–Leninist states politically deteriorated in response to the success of the Polish Solidarity movement and the possibility of Gorbachev-style political liberalisation. In 1989, revolts began across Eastern Europe and China against Marxist–Leninist regimes. In China, the government refused to negotiate with student protestors, resulting in the Tiananmen Square attacks that stopped the revolts by force. The revolts culminated with the revolt in East Germany against the Marxist–Leninist regime of Erich Honecker and demands for the Berlin Wall to be torn down. The event in East Germany developed into a popular mass revolt with sections of the Berlin Wall being torn down and East and West Berliners uniting. Gorbachev's refusal to use Soviet forces based in East Germany to suppress the revolt was seen as a sign that the Cold War had ended. Honecker was pressured to resign from office and the new government committed itself to reunification with West Germany. The Marxist–Leninist regime of Nicolae Ceaușescu in Romania was forcefully overthrown in 1989 and Ceaușescu was executed. The other Warsaw Pact regimes also fell during the Revolutions of 1989, with the exception of the Socialist People's Republic of Albania that continued until 1992.

Unrest and eventual collapse of Marxism–Leninism also occurred in Yugoslavia, although for different reasons than those of the Warsaw Pact. The death of Josip Broz Tito in 1980 and the subsequent vacuum of strong leadership allowed the rise of rival ethnic nationalism in the multinational country. The first leader to exploit such nationalism for political purposes was Slobodan Milošević, who used it to seize power as president of Serbia and demanded concessions to Serbia and Serbs by the other republics in the Yugoslav federation. This resulted in a surge of Slovene and Croat nationalism in response and the collapse of the League of Communists of Yugoslavia in 1990, the victory of nationalists in multi-party elections in most of Yugoslavia's constituent republics and eventually civil war between the various nationalities beginning in 1991. Yugoslavia was dissolved in 1992.

The Soviet Union itself collapsed between 1990 and 1991, with a rise of secessionist nationalism and a political power dispute between Gorbachev and Boris Yeltsin, the new leader of the Russian Federation. With the Soviet Union collapsing, Gorbachev prepared the country to become a loose federation of independent states called the Commonwealth of Independent States. Hardline Marxist–Leninist leaders in the military reacted to Gorbachev's policies with the August Coup of 1991 in which hardline Marxist–Leninist military leaders overthrew Gorbachev and seized control of the government. This regime only lasted briefly as widespread popular opposition erupted in street protests and refused to submit. Gorbachev was restored to power, but the various Soviet republics were now set for independence. On 25 December 1991, Gorbachev officially announced the dissolution of the Soviet Union, ending the existence of the world's first Marxist–Leninist-led state.

Since the fall of the Eastern European Marxist–Leninist regimes, the Soviet Union and a variety of African Marxist–Leninist regimes, only a few Marxist–Leninist parties remained in power. This include China, Cuba, Laos and Vietnam. Most Marxist–Leninist communist parties outside of these nations have fared relatively poorly in elections. However, other parties have remained or became a relative strong force. This include Russia, where the Communist Party of the Russian Federation has remained a significant political force, winning the 1995 legislative election, almost winning the 1996 presidential election and generally remaining the second most popular party. In Ukraine, the Communist Party of Ukraine has also exerted influence and governed the country after the 1994 parliamentary election and again after the 2006 parliamentary election. However, the 2014 parliamentary election following the Russian invasion of Ukraine and the annexation of Crimea resulted in the loss of its 32 members and no parliamentary representation.

In Europe, several Marxist–Leninist parties remain strong. In Cyprus, Dimitris Christofias of AKEL won the 2008 presidential election. AKEL has consistently been the first and third most popular party, winning the 1970, 1981, 2001 and 2006 legislative elections. In the Czech Republic and Portugal, the Communist Party of Bohemia and Moravia and the Portuguese Communist Party have been the second and fourth most popular parties until the 2017 and 2009 legislative elections, respectively. Since 2017, the Communist Party of Bohemia and Moravia supports the ANO 2011–ČSSD minority government while the Portuguese Communist Party has provided confidence and supply along with the Ecologist Party "The Greens" and Left Bloc to the Socialist minority government from 2015 to 2019. In Greece, the Communist Party of Greece has led an interim and later national unity government between 1989 and 1990, constantly remaining the third or fourth most popular party. In Moldova, the Party of Communists of the Republic of Moldova won the 2001, 2005 and April 2009 parliamentary elections. However, the April 2009 Moldovan elections results were protested and another round was held in July, resulting in the formation of the Alliance for European Integration. Failing to elect the president, new parliamentary elections were held in November 2010 which resulted in roughly the same representation in the parliament. According to Ion Marandici, a Moldovan political scientist, the Party of Communists differs from those in other countries because it managed to appeal to the ethnic minorities and the anti-Romanian Moldovans. After tracing the adaptation strategy of the party, he found confirming evidence for five of the factors contributing to its electoral success, already mentioned in the theoretical literature on former Marxist–Leninist parties, namely the economic situation, the weakness of the opponents, the electoral laws, the fragmentation of the political spectrum and the legacy of the old regime. However, Marandici identified seven additional explanatory factors at work in the Moldovan case, namely the foreign support for certain political parties, separatism, the appeal to the ethnic minorities, the alliance-building capacity, the reliance on the Soviet notion of the Moldovan identity, the state-building process and the control over a significant portion of the media. It is due to these seven additional factors that the party managed to consolidate and expand its constituency. In the post-Soviet states, the Party of Communists are the only ones who have been in power for so long and did not change the name of the party.

In Asia, a number of Marxist–Leninist regimes and movements continue to exist. The People's Republic of China has continued the agenda of Deng Xiaoping's 1980s reforms by initiating significant privatisation of the national economy. At the same time, no corresponding political liberalisation has occurred as happened in previous years to Eastern European countries. The Naxalite–Maoist insurgency has continued between the governments of Bangladesh and India against various Marxist–Leninist movements, having been unabated since the 1960s. In India, the Manmohan Singh government depended on the parliamentary support of the Communist Party of India (Marxist) which has led state governments in Kerala, Tripura and West Bengal. The armed wing of the Communist Party of India (Maoist) has been fighting a war against the government of India since 1967 and is still active in half the country. Maoist rebels in Nepal engaged in a civil war from 1996 to 2006 that managed to topple the monarchy there and create a republic. Communist Party of Nepal (Unified Marxist–Leninist) leader Man Mohan Adhikari briefly became prime minister and national leader from 1994 to 1995 and the Maoist guerrilla leader Prachanda was elected prime minister by the Constituent Assembly of Nepal in 2008. Prachanda has since been deposed as prime minister, leading the Maoists, who consider Prachanda's removal to be unjust, to abandon their legalistic approach and return to their street actions and militancy and to lead sporadic general strikes using their substantial influence on the Nepalese labour movement. These actions have oscillated between mild and intense. In the Philippines, the Maoist-oriented Communist Party of the Philippines and its armed wing, the New People's Army, have been waging armed revolution against the existing Philippine government since 1968 and is still experiencing a low-scale guerrilla insurgency.

In Africa, several Marxist–Leninist states reformed themselves and maintained power. In South Africa, the South African Communist Party is a member of the Tripartite alliance alongside the African National Congress and the Congress of South African Trade Unions. The Economic Freedom Fighters is a pan-African, Marxist–Leninist party founded in 2013 by expelled former president of the African National Congress Youth League Julius Malema and his allies. Sri Lanka has had Marxist–Leninist ministers in their national governments. In Zimbabwe, former President Robert Mugabe of the Zimbabwe African National Union – Patriotic Front, the country's long standing leader, was a professed Marxist–Leninist.

In the Americas, there have been several insurgencies. In North America, the Revolutionary Communist Party, USA led by its chairman Bob Avakian organises for a revolution to overthrow the capitalist system and replace it with a socialist state. In South America, Colombia has been in the midst of a civil war which has been waged since 1964 between the Colombian government and aligned right-wing paramilitaries against two Marxist–Leninist guerrilla groups, namely the National Liberation Army and Revolutionary Armed Forces of Colombia. In Peru, there has been an internal conflict between the Peruvian government and Marxist–Leninist–Maoist militants such as the Shining Path.

Ideology

Economy

The goal of Marxist–Leninist political economy is the emancipation of men and women from the dehumanisation caused by mechanistic work that is psychologically alienating (without work–life balance) which is performed in exchange for wages that give limited financial-access to the material necessities of life (i.e. food and shelter). That personal and societal emancipation from poverty (material necessity) would maximise individual liberty by enabling men and women to pursue their interests and innate talents (artistic, industrial and intellectual) whilst working by choice, without the economic coercion of poverty. In the communist society of upper-stage economic development, the elimination of alienating labour (mechanistic work) depends upon the developments of high technology that improve the means of production and the means of distribution. To meet the material needs of a socialist society, the state uses a planned economy to co-ordinate the means of production and of distribution to supply and deliver the goods and services required throughout society and the national economy. The state serves as a safeguard for the ownership and as the coordinator of production through a universal economic plan.

For the purpose of reducing waste and increasing efficiency, scientific planning replaces market mechanisms and price mechanisms as the guiding principle of the economy. The state's huge purchasing power replaces the role of market forces, with macroeconomic equilibrium not being achieved through market forces but by economic planning based on scientific assessment. The wages of the worker are determined according to the type of skills and the type of work he or she can perform within the national economy. Moreover, the economic value of the goods and services produced is based upon their use value (as material objects) and not upon the cost of production (value) or the exchange value (marginal utility). The profit motive as a driving force for production is replaced by social obligation to fulfil the economic plan. Wages are set and differentiated according to skill and intensity of work. While socially utilised means of production are under public control, personal belongings or property of a personal nature that does not involve mass production of goods remains unaffected by the state.

Because Marxism–Leninism has historically been the state ideology of countries who were economically undeveloped prior to socialist revolution, or whose economies were nearly obliterated by war such as the German Democratic Republic, the primary goal before achieving communism was the development of socialism in itself. Such was the case in the Soviet Union, where the economy was largely agrarian and urban industry was in a primitive stage. To develop socialism, the Soviet Union underwent rapid industrialisation with pragmatic programs of social engineering that transplanted peasant populations to the cities, where they were educated and trained as industrial workers and then became the workforce of the new factories and industries. Likewise, the farmer populations worked the system of collective farms to grow food to feed the industrial workers in the industrialised cities. Since the mid-1930s, Marxism–Leninism has advocated an austere social-equality based upon asceticism, egalitarianism and self-sacrifice. In the 1920s, the Bolshevik party semi-officially allowed some limited, small-scale wage inequality to boost labour productivity in the economy of the Soviet Union. These reforms were promoted to encourage materialism and acquisitiveness in order to stimulate economic growth. This pro-consumerist policy has been advanced on the lines of industrial pragmatism as it advances economic progress through bolstering industrialisation.

In the economic praxis of Bolshevik Russia, there was a defining difference of political economy between socialism and communism. Lenin explained their conceptual similarity to Marx's descriptions of the lower-stage and the upper-stage of economic development, namely that immediately after a proletarian revolution in the socialist lower-stage society the practical economy must be based upon the individual labour contributed by men and women and that paid labour would be the basis of the communist upper-stage society that has realised the social precept of the slogan: "From each according to his ability, to each according to his needs".

International Relations

Marxism–Leninism aims to create an international communist society. It opposes colonialism and imperialism and advocates decolonisation and anti-colonial forces. It supports anti-fascist international alliances and has advocated the creation of popular fronts between communist and non-communist anti-fascists against strong fascist movements. This Marxist–Leninist approach to international relations derives from the analyses (political, economic, sociological and geopolitical) that Lenin presented in the essay Imperialism, the Highest Stage of Capitalism. Extrapolating from five philosophical bases of Marxism, namely that human history is the history of class struggle between a ruling class and an exploited class; that capitalism creates antagonistic social classes, i.e. the bourgeois exploiters and the exploited proletariat; that capitalism employs nationalist war to further private economic expansion; that socialism is an economic system that voids social classes through public ownership of the means of production and so will eliminate the economic causes of war; and that once the state (socialist or communist) withers away, so shall international relations wither away because they are projections of national economic forces, Lenin said that the capitalists' exhaustion of domestic sources of investment profit by way of price-fixing trusts and cartels, then prompts the same capitalists to export investment capital to undeveloped countries to finance the exploitation of natural resources and the native populations and to create new markets. That the capitalists' control of national politics ensures the government's military safeguarding of colonial investments and the consequent imperial competition for economic supremacy provokes international wars to protect their national interests.

In the vertical perspective (social-class relations) of Marxism–Leninism, the internal and international affairs of a country are a political continuum, not separate realms of human activity. This is the philosophic opposite of the horizontal perspectives (country-to-country) of the liberal and the realist approaches to international relations. Colonial imperialism is the inevitable consequence in the course of economic relations among countries when the domestic price-fixing of monopoly capitalism has voided profitable competition in the capitalist homeland. The ideology of New Imperialism, rationalised as a civilising mission, allowed the exportation of high-profit investment capital to undeveloped countries with uneducated, native populations (sources of cheap labour), plentiful raw materials for exploitation (factors for manufacture) and a colonial market to consume the surplus production, which the capitalist homeland cannot consume. The example is the European Scramble for Africa in which imperialism was safeguarded by the national military.

To secure the economic and settler colonies, foreign sources of new capital-investment-profit, the imperialist state seeks either political or military control of the limited resources (natural and human). The First World War resulted from such geopolitical conflicts among the empires of Europe over colonial spheres of influence. For the colonised working classes who create the wealth (goods and services), the elimination of war for natural resources (access, control and exploitation) is resolved by overthrowing the militaristic capitalist state and establishing a socialist state because a peaceful world economy is feasible only by proletarian revolutions that overthrow systems of political economy based upon the exploitation of labour.

Political System

Marxism–Leninism supports the creation of a one-party state led by a communist party as a means to develop socialism and then communism. The political structure of the Marxist–Leninist state involves the rule of a communist vanguard party over a revolutionary socialist state that represents the will and rule of the proletariat. Through the policy of democratic centralism, the communist party is the supreme political institution of the Marxist–Leninist state.

In Marxism–Leninism, elections are held for all positions within the legislative structure, municipal councils, national legislatures and presidencies. In most Marxist–Leninist states, this has taken the form of directly electing representatives to fill positions, although in some states such as People's Republic of China, the Republic of Cuba and the Socialist Federal Republic of Yugoslavia this system also included indirect elections such as deputies being elected by deputies as the next lower level of government. Marxism–Leninism asserts that society is united upon common interests represented through the communist party and other institutions of the Marxist–Leninist state.

Society

A 1920 Bolshevik pro-education propaganda which reads the following: "In order to have more, it is necessary to produce more. In order to produce more, it is necessary to know more."

Marxism–Leninism supports universal social welfare. The Marxist–Leninist state provides for the national welfare with universal healthcare, free public education (academic, technical and professional) and the social benefits (childcare and continuing education) necessary to increase the productivity of the workers and the socialist economy to develop a communist society. As part of the planned economy, the Marxist–Leninist state is meant to develop the proletariat's universal education (academic and technical) and their class consciousness (political education) to facilitate their contextual understanding of the historical development of communism as presented in Marx's theory of history.

Marxism–Leninism supports the emancipation of women and ending the exploitation of women. Marxist–Leninist policy on family law has typically involved the elimination of the political power of the bourgeoisie, the abolition of private property and an education that teaches citizens to abide by a disciplined and self-fulfilling lifestyle dictated by the social norms of communism as a means to establish a new social order. The judicial reformation of family law eliminates patriarchy from the legal system. This facilitates the political emancipation of women from traditional social inferiority and economic exploitation. The reformation of civil law made marriage secular into a "free and voluntary union" between persons who are social-and-legal equals; facilitated divorce; legalised abortion, eliminated bastardy ("illegitimate children"); and voided the political power of the bourgeoisie and the private property-status of the means of production. The educational system imparts the social norms for a self-disciplined and self-fulfilling way of life, by which the socialist citizens establish the social order necessary for realising a communist society. With the advent of a classless society and the abolition of private property, society collectively assume many of the roles traditionally assigned to mothers and wives, with women becoming integrated into industrial work. This has been promoted by Marxism–Leninism as the means to achieve women's emancipation.

Marxist–Leninist cultural policy modernises social relations among citizens by eliminating the capitalist value system of traditionalist conservatism, by which Tsarism classified, divided and controlled people with stratified social classes without any socio-economic mobility. It focuses upon modernisation and distancing society from the past, the bourgeoisie and the old intelligentsia. The socio-cultural changes required for establishing a communist society are realised with education and agitprop (agitation and propaganda) which reinforce communal and communist values. The modernisation of educational and cultural policies eliminates the societal atomisation, including anomie and social alienation, caused by cultural backwardness. Marxism–Leninism develops the New Soviet man, an educated and cultured citizen possessed of a proletarian class consciousness who is oriented towards the social cohesion necessary for developing a communist society as opposed to the antithetic bourgeois individualist associated with social atomisation.

Teleology

The Marxist–Leninist worldview is atheist, wherein all human activity results from human volition and not the will of supernatural beings (gods, goddesses and demons) who have direct agency in the public and private affairs of human society. The tenets of the Soviet Union's national policy of Marxist–Leninist atheism originated from the philosophies of Georg Wilhelm Friedrich Hegel and Ludwig Feuerbach as well as that of Karl Marx and Vladimir Lenin.

As a basis of Marxism–Leninism, the philosophy of materialism (the physical universe exists independently of human consciousness) is applied as dialectical materialism (a philosophy of science and nature) to examine the socio-economic relations among people and things as parts of a dynamic, material world that is unlike the immaterial world of metaphysics. Soviet astrophysicist Vitaly Ginzburg said that ideologically the

"Bolshevik communists were not merely atheists, but, according to Lenin's terminology, militant atheists" in excluding religion from the social mainstream, from education and from government.

Criticism

Marxism–Leninism has been widely criticised due to its relations with Stalinism, the Soviet Union and state repression in Marxist–Leninist states. Classical and orthodox Marxists were critical of Stalin's political economy and single-party government in the Soviet Union.

Italian left communist Amadeo Bordiga dismissed Marxism–Leninism as political opportunism that preserved capitalism because of the claim that the exchange of commodities would occur under socialism and that the use of popular front organisations by the Communist International and a political vanguard organised by organic centralism were politically more effective than a vanguard organised by democratic centralism. American Marxist Raya Dunayevskaya dismissed Marxism–Leninism as a type of state capitalism because state ownership of the means of production is a form of state capitalism and single-party rule is undemocratic whereas the dictatorship of the proletariat is democratic, further arguing that the doctrine is neither Marxism nor Leninism, but rather a composite ideology that Stalin used to expediently determine what is communism and what is not communism for the countries of the Eastern Bloc.

Trotskyists claim that Marxism–Leninism led to the establishment of a degenerated workers' state. Others such as philosopher Eric Voegelin claim that Marxism–Leninism is in its core inherently oppressive, arguing that the "Marxian vision dictated the Stalinist outcome not because the communist utopia was inevitable but because it was impossible". Criticism like this has itself been criticised for philosophical determinism, i.e. that the negative events in the movement's history were predetermined by their convictions. Historian Robert Vincent Daniels argues that Marxism was used to "justify Stalinism, but it was no longer allowed to serve either as a policy directive or an explanation of reality" during Stalin's rule. In complete contrast, E. Van Ree argues that Stalin continued to be in "general agreement" with the classical works of Marxism until his death.

Mutualism

Mutualism is an anarchist school of thought and economic theory that advocates a socialist society based on free markets and usufructs, i.e. occupation and use property norms. One implementation of this system involves the establishment of a mutual-credit bank that would lend to producers at a minimal interest rate, just high enough to cover administration. Mutualism is based on a version of the labor theory of value holding that when labor or its product is sold, it ought to receive in exchange goods or services embodying "the amount of labor necessary to produce an article of exactly similar and equal utility".

Mutualism originated from the writings of philosopher Pierre-Joseph Proudhon. Mutualists disagree with the idea of individuals receiving an income through loans, investments and rent as they believe these individuals are not laboring. Although opposed to this type of income, Proudhon expressed that he had never intended "to forbid or suppress, by sovereign decree, ground rent and interest on capital. I think that all these manifestations of human activity should remain free and voluntary for all: I ask for them no modifications, restrictions or suppressions, other than those which result naturally and of necessity from the universalization of the principle of reciprocity which I propose". Insofar as they ensure the worker's right to the full product of their labor, mutualists support markets and property in the product of labor, differentiating between capitalist private property (productive property) and personal property (private property). As a result, they argue for conditional titles to land, whose ownership is legitimate only so long as it remains in use or occupation (which Proudhon called possession), a type of private property with strong abandonment criteria. This contrasts with capitalist non-proviso Lockean sticky property, where owners maintain title more or less until they consent to gift or sell it.

As libertarian socialists, mutualists distinguish their market socialism from state socialism and do not advocate state control over the means of production. Instead, each person possesses a means of production, either individually or collectively, with trade representing equivalent amounts of labor in the free market. Benjamin Tucker said of Proudhon that "though opposed to socializing the ownership of capital, he aimed nevertheless to socialize its effects by making its use beneficial to all instead of a means of impoverishing the many to enrich the few by subjecting capital to the natural law of competition, thus bringing the price of its own use down to cost".

Although similar to the economic doctrines of the 19th-century American individualist anarchists, mutualism is in favor of large industries. Mutualism has been retrospectively characterized sometimes as being a form of individualist anarchism and as ideologically situated between individualist and collectivist forms of anarchism as well. Proudhon himself described the liberty he pursued as "the synthesis of communism and property". As a result, some consider mutualism to be part of free-market anarchism, individualist anarchism and market-oriented left-libertarianism while others regard it to be part of social anarchism.

As a term, mutualism has seen a variety of related uses. Charles Fourier first used the French term mutualisme in 1822, although the reference was not to an economic system. The first use of the noun mutualist was in the New-Harmony Gazette by an American Owenite in 1826. In the early 1830s, a French labor organization in Lyons called themselves the Mutuellists.

Pierre-Joseph Proudhon was involved with the Lyons mutualists and later adopted the name to describe his own teachings. In What Is Mutualism?, Clarence Lee Swartz gives his own account of the origin of the term, claiming that "the word "mutualism" seems to have been first used by John Gray, an English writer, in 1832". When Gray's 1825 Lecture on Human Happiness was first published in the United States in 1826, the publishers appended the Preamble and Constitution of the Friendly Association for Mutual Interests, Located at Valley Forge. 1826 also saw the publication of the Constitution of the Friendly Association for Mutual Interests at Kendal, Ohio.

By 1846, Proudhon was speaking of *mutualité* in his writings and he used the term *mutuellisme* at least as early as 1848 in his "Programme Révolutionnaire". In 1850, William Batchelder Greene used the term mutualism to describe a mutual credit system similar to that of Proudhon. In 1850, the American newspaper *The Spirit of the Age*, edited by William Henry Channing, published proposals for a mutualist township by Joshua King Ingalls and Albert Brisbane, together with works by Proudhon, Greene, Pierre Leroux and others.

Proudhon ran for the French Constituent Assembly in April 1848, but was not elected, although his name appeared on the ballots in Paris, Lyon, Besançon and Lille. He was successful in the complementary elections of June 4 and served as a deputy during the debates over the National Workshops, created by the 25 February 1848 decree passed by Republican Louis Blanc. The workshops were to give work to the unemployed. Proudhon was never enthusiastic about such workshops, perceiving them to be essentially charitable institutions that did not resolve the problems of the economic system. He was against their elimination unless an alternative could be found for the workers who relied on the workshops for subsistence.

Proudhon was surprised by the French Revolution of 1848. He participated in the February uprising and the composition of what he termed "the first republican proclamation" of the new republic. However, he had misgivings about the new provisional government headed by Jacques-Charles Dupont de l'Eure, who since the French Revolution in 1789 had been a longstanding politician, although often in the opposition. Proudhon published his own perspective for reform which was completed in 1849, *Solution du problème social* (*Solution of the Social Problem*), in which he laid out a program of mutual financial cooperation among workers. He believed this would transfer control of economic relations from capitalists and financiers to workers. The central part of his plan was the establishment of a bank to provide credit at a very low rate of interest and the issuing of exchange notes that would circulate instead of money based on gold.

Mutualism has been associated with two types of currency reform. Labor notes were first discussed in Owenite circles and received their first practical test in 1827 in the Time Store of former New Harmony member and individualist anarchist Josiah Warren. Mutual banking aimed at the monetization of all forms of wealth and the extension of free credit. It is most closely associated with William Batchelder Greene, but Greene drew from the work of Proudhon, Edward Kellogg and William Beck as well as from the land bank tradition.

Mutualism can in many ways be considered the original anarchy since Pierre-Joseph Proudhon was the first to identify himself as an anarchist. Although mutualism is generally associated with anarchism, it is not necessarily anarchist. Historian Wendy McElroy reports that American individualist anarchism received an important influence of three European thinkers. One of the most important of these influences was the French political philosopher Pierre-Joseph Proudhon, whose words "Liberty is not the Daughter But the Mother of Order" appeared as a motto on *Liberty*'s masthead. *Liberty* was an influential American individualist anarchist publication of Benjamin Tucker. For American anarchist historian Eunice Minette Schuster, "it is apparent that Proudhonian Anarchism was to be found in the United States at least as early as 1848 and that it was not conscious of its affinity to the Individualist Anarchism of Josiah Warren and Stephen Pearl Andrews. William B. Greene presented this Proudhonian Mutualism in its purest and most systematic form".

After 1850, Greene became active in labor reform. He was elected vice-president of the New England Labor Reform League, the majority of the members holding to Proudhon's scheme of mutual banking; and in 1869 president of the Massachusetts Labor Union. He then publishes *Socialistic, Mutualistic, and Financial Fragments*. He saw mutualism as the synthesis of "liberty and order". His "associationism is checked by individualism. "Mind your own business", "Judge not that ye be not judged". Over matters which are purely personal, as for example, moral conduct, the individual is sovereign as well as over that which he himself produces. For this reason, he demands "mutuality" in marriage—the equal right of a woman to her own personal freedom and property".

Tucker later connected his economic views with those of Proudhon, Warren and Karl Marx, taking sides with the first two while also arguing against American anti-socialists who declared socialism as imported, stating:

The economic principles of Modern Socialism are a logical deduction from the principle laid down by Adam Smith in the early chapters of his "Wealth of Nations," – namely, that labor is the true measure of price. Half a century or more after Smith enunciated the principle above stated, Socialism picked it up where he had dropped it, and in following it to its logical conclusions, made it the basis of a new economic philosophy. This seems to have been done independently by three different men, of three different nationalities, in three different languages: Josiah Warren, an American; Pierre J. Proudhon, a Frenchman; Karl Marx, a German Jew. That the work of this interesting trio should have been done so nearly simultaneously would seem to indicate that Socialism was in the air, and that the time was ripe and the conditions favorable for the appearance of this new school of thought. So far as priority of time is concerned, the credit seems to belong to Warren, the American, – a fact which should be noted by the stump orators who are so fond of declaiming against Socialism as an imported article.

Mutualist ideas found fertile ground in the 19th century in Spain. In Spain, Ramón de la Sagra established the anarchist journal *El Porvenir* in A Coruña in 1845 which was inspired by Proudhon's ideas. The Catalan politician Francesc Pi i Margall became the principal translator of Proudhon's works into Spanish and later briefly became president of Spain in 1873 while being the leader of the Democratic Republican Federal Party. According to George Woodcock, "these translations were to have a profound and lasting effect on the development of Spanish anarchism after 1870, but before that time Proudhonian ideas, as interpreted by Pi, already provided much of the inspiration for the federalist movement which sprang up in the early 1860's".

"During the Spanish revolution of 1873, Pi y Margall attempted to establish a decentralized, or cantonalist, political system on Proudhonian lines". Pi i Margall was a dedicated theorist in his own right, especially through book-length works such as La reacción y la revolución (Reaction and Revolution), Las nacionalidades (Nationalities) and La Federación (The Federation). For prominent anarcho-syndicalist Rudolf Rocker, "the first movement of the Spanish workers was strongly influenced by the ideas of Pi y Margall, leader of the Spanish Federalists and disciple of Proudhon. Pi y Margall was one of the outstanding theorists of his time and had a powerful influence on the development of libertarian ideas in Spain. His political ideas had much in common with those of Richard Price, Joseph Priestly, Thomas Paine, Jefferson, and other representatives of the Anglo-American liberalism of the first period. He wanted to limit the power of the state to a minimum and gradually replace it by a Socialist economic order".

According to historian of the First International G. M. Stekloff, in April 1856 "arrived from Paris a deputation of Proudhonist workers whose aim it was to bring about the foundation of a Universal League of Workers. The object of the League was the social emancipation of the working class, which, it was held, could only be achieved by a union of the workers of all lands against international capital. Since the deputation was one of Proudhonists, of course this emancipation was to be secured, not by political methods, but purely by economic means, through the foundation of productive and distributive co-operatives". Stekloff contines by saying that "it was in the 1863 elections that for the first time workers' candidates were run in opposition to bourgeois republicans, but they secured very few votes. A group of working-class Proudhonists (among whom were Murat and Tolain, who were subsequently to participate in the founding of the (First) International issued the famous Manifesto of the Sixty, which, though extremely moderate in tone, marked a turning point in the history of the French movement. For years and years the bourgeois liberals had been insisting that the revolution of 1789 had abolished class distinctions. The Manifesto of the Sixty loudly proclaimed that classes still existed. These classes were the bourgeoisie and the proletariat. The latter had its specific class interests, which none but workers could be trusted to defend. The inference drawn by the Manifesto was that there must be independent working-class candidates".

For Stekloff, "the Proudhonists, who were at that date the leaders of the French section of the International. They looked upon the International Workingmen's Association as a sort of academy or synagogue, where Talmudists or similar experts could "investigate" the workers' problem; wherein the spirit of Proudhon they could excogitate means for an accurate solution of the problem, without being disturbed by the stresses of a political campaign. Thus Fribourg, voicing the opinions of the Parisian group of the Proudhonists assured his readers that "the International was the greatest attempt ever made in modern times to aid the proletariat towards the conquest, by peaceful, constitutional, and moral methods, of the place which rightly belongs to the workers in the sunshine of civilisation". According to Stekoff, the Belgian Federation "threw in its lot with the anarchist International at its Brussels Congress, held in December, 1872. Those taking part in the socialist movement of the Belgian intelligentsia were inspired by Proudhonist ideas which naturally led them to oppose the Marxist outlook".

Mutualism also had a considerable influence in the Paris Commune. George Woodcock manifests that "a notable contribution to the activities of the Commune and particularly to the organization of public services was made by members of various anarchist factions, including the mutualists Courbet, Longuet, and Vermorel, the libertarian collectivists Varlin, Malon, and Lefrangais, and the bakuninists Elie and Elisée Reclus and Louise Michel".

19th-century mutualists considered themselves libertarian socialists and are still considered libertarian socialists to this day. While oriented towards cooperation, mutualists favor free market solutions, believing that most inequalities are the result of preferential conditions created by government intervention. Mutualism is something of a middle way between classical economics and socialism of the collectivist variety, with some characteristics of both. As for capital goods (man-made, non-land means of production), mutualist opinions differs on whether these should be commonly managed public assets or private property. Modern-day mutualist Kevin Carson considers mutualism to be free-market socialism. Proudhon supported labor-owned cooperative firms and associations, for "we need not hesitate, for we have no choice. It is necessary to form an association among workers because without that, they would remain related as subordinates and superiors, and there would ensue two castes of masters and wage-workers, which is repugnant to a free and democratic society" and so "it becomes necessary for the workers to form themselves into democratic societies, with equal conditions for all members, on pain of a relapse into feudalism". In the preface to his *Studies in Mutualist Political Economy*, Carson describes this work as "an attempt to revive individualist anarchist political economy, to incorporate the useful developments of the last hundred years, and to make it relevant to the problems of the twenty-first century".

Contemporary mutualists are among those involved in the Alliance of the Libertarian Left and in the Voluntary Cooperation Movement. Contemporary mutualist Kevin Carson holds that capitalism has been founded on "an act of robbery as massive as feudalism" and argues that capitalism could not exist in the absence of a state. He says that "it is state intervention that distinguishes capitalism from the free market". Carson does not define capitalism in the idealized sense, but he says that when he talks about capitalism he is referring to what he calls actually existing capitalism. He believes the term *laissez-faire* capitalism is an oxymoron because capitalism, he argues, is "organization of society, incorporating elements of tax, usury, landlordism, and tariff, which thus denies the Free Market while pretending to exemplify it". However, he says he has no quarrel with anarcho-capitalists who use the term *laissez-faire* capitalism and distinguish it from actually existing capitalism. Carson says he has deliberately chosen to resurrect an old definition of the term. However, many anarchists, including mutualists, continue to use the term and do not consider it an old definition of the term.

Carson argues that the centralization of wealth into a class hierarchy is due to state intervention to protect the ruling class by using a money monopoly, granting patents and subsidies to corporations, imposing discriminatory taxation and intervening militarily to gain access to international markets. Carson's thesis is that an authentic free-market economy would not be capitalism as the separation of labor from ownership and the subordination of labor to capital would be impossible, bringing a classless society where people could easily choose between working as a freelancer, working for a fair wage, taking part of a cooperative, or being an entrepreneur. As did Benjamin Tucker before him, he notes that a mutualist free-market system would involve significantly different property rights than capitalism is based on, particularly in terms of land and intellectual property.

Theory

The primary aspects of mutualism are free association, reciprocity and gradualism, or dual power. Mutualism is often described by its proponents as advocating an anti-capitalist free market. Mutualists argue that most of the economic problems associated with capitalism each amount to a violation of the cost principle, or as Josiah Warren interchangeably said, the cost the limit of price. It was inspired by the labor theory of value which was popularized—although not invented—by Adam Smith in 1776 (Proudhon mentioned Smith as an inspiration). The labor theory of value holds that the actual price of a thing (or the true cost) is the amount of labor that was undertaken to produce it. In Warren's terms, cost should be the limit of price, with cost referring to the amount of labor required to produce a good or service. Anyone who sells goods should charge no more than the cost to himself of acquiring these goods.

Contract and Federation

Mutualism holds that producers should exchange their goods at cost-value using systems of contract. While Proudhon's early definitions of cost-value were based on fixed assumptions about the value of labor-hours, he later redefined cost-value to include other factors such as the intensity of labor, the nature of the work involved and so on. He also expanded his notions of contract into expanded notions of federation. As Proudhon argued:

> "I have shown the contractor, at the birth of industry, negotiating on equal terms with his comrades, who have since become his workmen. It is plain, in

> fact, that this original equality was bound to disappear through the advantageous position of the master and the dependent position of the wage-workers. In vain does the law assure the right of each to enterprise. When an establishment has had leisure to develop itself, enlarge its foundations, ballast itself with capital, and assure itself a body of patrons, what can a workman do against a power so superior? "

Gradualism and Dual Power

Dual power is the process of building alternative institutions to the ones that already exist in modern society. Originally theorized by Proudhon, it has become adopted by many anti-state movements like autonomism and agorism. Proudhon described it as such:

> "Beneath the governmental machinery, in the shadow of political institutions, out of the sight of statemen and priests, society is producing its own organism, slowly and silently; and constructing a new order, the expression of its vitality and autonomy".

Dual power should not be confused with the dual power popularized by Vladimir Lenin as it was also theorized by Proudhon and it refers to a more specific scenario where a revolutionary entity intentionally maintains the structure of the previous political institutions until the power of the previous institution is weakened enough such that the revolutionary entity can overtake it entirely. Dual power as implemented by mutualists and agorists is the development of the alternative institution itself.

Free Association

Mutualists argue that association is only necessary where there is an organic combination of forces. For instance, an operation that requires specialization and many different workers performing their individual tasks to complete a unified product, i.e. a factory. In this situation, workers are inherently dependent on each other—and without association they are related as subordinate and superior, master and wage-slave.

An operation that can be performed by an individual without the help of specialized workers does not require association. Proudhon argued that peasants do not require societal form and only feigned association for the purposes of solidarity in abolishing rents, buying clubs and so on. He recognized that their work is inherently sovereign and free. In commenting on the degree of association that is preferable, Proudhon said:

> "In cases in which production requires great division of labour, it is necessary to form an association among the workersbecause without that they would remain isolated as subordinates and superiors, and there would ensue two industrial

> castes of masters and wage workers, which is repugnant in a free and democratic society. But where the product can be obtained by the action of an individual or a family, there is no opportunity for association".

For Proudhon, mutualism involved creating industrial democracy, a system where workplaces would be "handed over to democratically organised workers' associations. We want these associations to be models for agriculture, industry and trade, the pioneering core of that vast federation of companies and societies woven into the common cloth of the democratic social Republic". He urged "workers to form themselves into democratic societies, with equal conditions for all members, on pain of a relapse into feudalism". This would result in "capitalistic and proprietary exploitation, stopped everywhere, the wage system abolished, equal and just exchange guaranteed". Workers would no longer sell their labour to a capitalist but rather work for themselves in co-operatives.

As Robert Graham notes: "Proudhon's market socialism is indissolubly linked to his notions of industrial democracy and workers' self-management". K. Steven Vincent notes in his in-depth analysis of this aspect of Proudhon's ideas that "Proudhon consistently advanced a program of industrial democracy which would return control and direction of the economy to the workers". For Proudhon, "strong workers' associations would enable the workers to determine jointly by election how the enterprise was to be directed and operated on a day-to-day basis".

Mutual Credit

Mutualists argue that free banking should be taken back by the people to establish systems of free credit. They contend that banks have a monopoly on credit, just as capitalists have a monopoly on the means of production and landlords have a monopoly on land. Banks are essentially creating money by lending out deposits that do not actually belong to them, then charging interest on the difference. Mutualists argue that by establishing a democratically run mutual bank or credit union, it would be possible to issue free credit so that money could be created for the benefit of the participants rather than for the benefit of the bankers. Individualist anarchists noted for their detailed views on mutualist banking include Pierre-Joseph Proudhon, William Batchelder Greene and Lysander Spooner. Some modern forms of mutual credit are LETS and the Ripple monetary system project.

In a session of the French legislature, Proudhon proposed a government-imposed income tax to fund his mutual banking scheme, with some tax brackets reaching as high as 33 $\frac{1}{3}$ percent and 50 percent, but it was turned down by the legislature. This income tax Proudhon proposed to fund his bank was to be levied on rents, interest, debts and salaries. Specifically, Proudhon's proposed law would have required all capitalists and stockholders to disburse one-sixth of their income to their tenants and debtors and another sixth to the national treasury to fund the bank.

This scheme was vehemently objected to by others in the legislature, including Frédéric Bastiat. The reason given for the income tax's rejection was that it would result in economic ruin and that it violated "the right of property". In his debates with Bastiat, Proudhon did once propose funding a national bank with a voluntary tax of 1%. Proudhon also argued for the abolition of all taxes.

Property

Pierre-Joseph Proudhon was one of the most famous philosophers who articulated thoughts on the nature of property. He is known for claiming that "property is theft", but is less known for the claims that "property is liberty" and "property is impossible". According to Colin Ward, Proudhon did not see a contradiction between these slogans. This was because Proudhon distinguished between what he considered to be two distinct forms of property often bound up in the single label. To the mutualist, this is the distinction between property created by coercion and property created by labor. Property is theft "when it is related to a landowner or capitalist whose ownership is derived from conquest or exploitation and is only maintained through the state, property laws, police, and an army". Property is freedom for "the peasant or artisan family who have a natural right to a home, land they may cultivate, to tools of a trade" and the fruits of that cultivation—but not to ownership or control of the lands and lives of others. The former is considered illegitimate property, the latter legitimate property. Proudhon argued that property in the product of labor is essential to liberty while property that strayed from possession ("occupancy and use") was the basis for tyranny and would lead a society to destroy itself. The conception of entitlement property as a destructive force and illegitimate institution can be seen in this quote by Proudhon:

> "Then if we are associated for the sake of liberty, equality, and security, we are not associated for the sake of property; then if property is a natural right, this natural right is not social, but anti-social. Property and society are utterly irreconcilable institutions. It is as impossible to associate two proprietors as to join two magnets by their opposite poles. Either society must perish, or it must destroy property. If property is a natural, absolute, imprescriptible, and inalienable right, why, in all ages, has there been so much speculation as to its origin? – for this is one of its distinguishing characteristics. The origin of a natural right! Good God! who ever inquired into the origin of the rights of liberty, security, or equality? "

Clarence Lee Swartz says:

> "It is, therefore, one of the purposes of Mutualists, not only to awaken in the people the appreciation of and desire for freedom, but also to arouse in them a determination to abolish the legal restrictions now placed upon non-invasive human activities and to institute, through purely voluntary associations, such

> measures as will liberate all of us from the exactions of privilege and the power of concentrated capital".

Swartz also states that mutualism differs from anarcho-communism and other collectivist philosophies by its support of private property, arguing: "One of the tests of any reform movement with regard to personal liberty is this: Will the movement prohibit or abolish private property? If it does, it is an enemy of liberty. For one of the most important criteria of freedom is the right to private property in the products of ones labor. State Socialists, Communists, Syndicalists and Communist-Anarchists deny private property". However, Proudhon warned that a society with private property would lead to statist relations between people, arguing:

> "The purchaser draws boundaries, fences himself in, and says, 'This is mine; each one by himself, each one for himself.' Here, then, is a piece of land upon which, henceforth, no one has right to step, save the proprietor and his friends; which can benefit nobody, save the proprietor and his servants. Let these multiply, and soon the people will have nowhere to rest, no place of shelter, no ground to till. They will die of hunger at the proprietor's door, on the edge of that property which was their birth-right; and the proprietor, watching them die, will exclaim, 'So perish idlers and vagrants".

Unlike capitalist private-property supporters, Proudhon stressed equality. He thought that all workers should own property and have access to capital, stressing that in every cooperative "every worker employed in the association must have an undivided share in the property of the company". This distinction Proudhon made between different kinds of property has been articulated by some later anarchist and socialist theorists as one of the first distinctions between private property and personal property, with the latter having direct use-value to the individual possessing it.

Criticism

Anarchism

In Europe, a contemporary critic of Proudhon was the early libertarian communist Joseph Déjacque, who was able to serialise his book L'Humanisphère, Utopie anarchique (The Humanisphere: Anarchic Utopia) in his periodical Le Libertaire, Journal du Mouvement Social (Libertarian: Journal of Social Movement), published in 27 issues from 9 June 1858 to 4 February 1861 while living in New York. Unlike and against Proudhon, he argued that "it is not the product of his or her labor that the worker has a right to, but to the satisfaction of his or her needs, whatever may be their nature". In his critique of Proudhon, Déjacque also coined the word libertarian and argued that Proudhon was merely a liberal, a moderate, suggesting him to become "frankly and completely an anarchist" instead by giving up all forms of authority and property. Since then, the word libertarian has been used to describe this consistent anarchism which rejected private and public hierarchies along with property in the products of labour as well as the means of production. Libertarianism is frequently used as a synonym for anarchism and libertarian socialism.

One area of disagreement between anarcho-communists and mutualists stems from Proudhon's alleged advocacy of labour vouchers to compensate individuals for their labor as well as markets or artificial markets for goods and services. Peter Kropotkin, like other anarcho-communists, advocated the abolition of labor remuneration and questioned "how can this new form of wages, the labor note, be sanctioned by those who admit that houses, fields, mills are no longer private property, that they belong to the commune or the nation?". According to George Woodcock, Kropotkin believed that a wage system in any form, whether "administered by Banks of the People or by workers' associations through labor cheques", is a form of compulsion.

Collectivist anarchist Mikhail Bakunin was an adamant critic of Proudhonian mutualism as well, stating: "How ridiculous are the ideas of the individualists of the Jean Jacques Rousseau school and of the Proudhonian mutualists who conceive society as the result of the free contract of individuals absolutely independent of one another and entering into mutual relations only because of the convention drawn up among men. As if these men had dropped from the skies, bringing with them speech, will, original thought, and as if they were alien to anything of the earth, that is, anything having social origin".

Capitalism

Criticism from pro-capitalist market sectors has been common as well. Some critics object to the use of the term capitalism in reference to historical or actually existing economic arrangements which they term mixed economies. They reserve the term for the abstract ideal or future possibility of a genuinely free market. This sort of free-market capitalism may closely follow contemporary mutualist Kevin Carson's free-market anti-capitalism in its practical details, except for the fact that Carson does not recognize a right of an individual to protect land that he has transformed through labor or purchased to be protected when he is not using it. Like other mutualists, Carson only recognize occupancy and use as the standard for retaining legitimate control over something. As a result, Austrian School economist and Objectivist George Reisman charges that mutualism supports exploitation when it does not recognize a right of an individual to protect land that he has mixed his labor with if he happens to not be using it. Reisman sees the seizure of such land as the theft of the product of labor and has said: "Mutualism claims to oppose the exploitation of labor, i.e. the theft of any part of its product. But when it comes to labor that has been mixed with land, it turns a blind eye out foursquare on the side of the exploiter".

This is due to the different conception of property rights between capitalism and mutualism, with the latter supporting free access to capital, the means of production and natural resources, arguing that permanent private ownership of land and capital entails to monopolization, if there is not the equal liberty of access; and that a society with capitalist private property inevitably lead to statist relations between people. For mutualists, occupancy and use is "the only legitimate standard for establishing ownership of land, regardless of how many times it has changed hands". According to Carson, "an existing owner may transfer ownership by sale or gift; but the new owner may establish legitimate title to the land only by his own occupancy and use. A change in occupancy will amount to a change in ownership. Absentee landlord rent, and exclusion of homesteaders from vacant land by an absentee landlord, are both considered illegitimate by mutualists. The actual occupant is considered the owner of a tract of land, and any attempt to collect rent by a self-styled landlord is regarded as a violent invasion of the possessor's absolute right of property".

Socialism in One Country

Socialism in one country was a theory put forth by Joseph Stalin and Nikolai Bukharin in 1924 which was eventually adopted by the Soviet Union as state policy. The theory held that given the defeat of all the communist revolutions in Europe in 1917–1923 except Russia, the Soviet Union should begin to strengthen itself internally. This turn toward national communism was a shift from the previously held position by classical Marxism that socialism must be established globally. However, proponents of the theory argue that it contradicts neither world revolution nor world communism. The theory was in opposition to Leon Trotsky's theory of permanent revolution and the earlier communist left theory of world revolution.

The defeat of several proletarian revolutions in countries like Germany and Hungary ended Bolsheviks' hopes for an imminent world revolution and began promotion of socialism in one country by Joseph Stalin. In the first edition of The Foundations of Leninism, Stalin was still a follower of the orthodox Marxist idea that revolution in one country is insufficient. Vladimir Lenin died in January 1924 and by the end of that year in the second edition of the book Stalin's position started to turn around as he claimed that "the proletariat can and must build the socialist society in one country". In April 1925, Nikolai Bukharin elaborated the issue in his brochure Can We Build Socialism in One Country in the Absence of the Victory of the West-European Proletariat? and the Soviet Union adopted socialism in one country as state policy after Stalin's January 1926 article On the Issues of Leninism. 1925–1926 signaled a shift in the immediate activity of the Communist International from world revolution towards a defense of the Soviet state. This period was known up to 1928 as the Second Period, mirroring the shift in the Soviet Union from war communism to the New Economic Policy.

"In his 1915 article On the Slogan for a United States of Europe", Lenin had written:

> "Uneven economic and political development is an absolute law of capitalism. Hence, the victory of socialism is possible first in several or even in one capitalist

> country alone. After expropriating the capitalists and organising their own socialist production, the victorious proletariat of that country will arise against the rest of the world".

In January 1918, Lenin wrote:

> "I know that there are, of course, sages who think they are very clever and even call themselves Socialists, who assert that power should not have been seized until the revolution had broken out in all countries. They do not suspect that by speaking in this way they are deserting the revolution and going over to the side of the bourgeoisie. To wait until the toiling classes bring about a revolution on an international scale means that everybody should stand stock-still in expectation. That is nonsense".

After Lenin's death, Stalin used these quotes and others to argue that Lenin shared his view of socialism in one country. Grigory Zinoviev and Leon Trotsky vigorously criticized the theory of socialism in one country. In particular, Trotskyists often claimed and still claim that socialism in one country opposes both the basic tenets of Marxism and Lenin's particular beliefs that the final success of socialism in one country depends upon the revolution's degree of success in proletarian revolutions in the more advanced countries of Western Europe. At the Seventh Congress in March 1918, Lenin explained:

> "Regarded from the world-historical point of view, there would doubtlessly be no hope of the ultimate victory of our revolution if it were to remain alone, if there were no revolutionary movements in other countries. I repeat, our salvation from all these difficulties is an all Europe revolution. At all events, under all conceivable circumstances, if the German revolution does not come, we are doomed".

The exponents of socialism in one country contend that Stalin's theory was firmly in line with the basic tenets of Leninism in that the victory of socialism is possible in one or separate countries while other countries may continue to remain bourgeois for some time. To support this assertion, they quote Lenin, who said:

> "Socialism cannot achieve victory simultaneously *in all* countries. It will achieve victory first in one or several countries, while the others will for some time remain bourgeois or pre-bourgeois".

The defeat of all the 1917–1923 revolutions in Europe, except Russia, ended the Bolsheviks and especially Lenin's hopes for an imminent world revolution. In his 1918 *Letter to American Workers*, Lenin wrote:

> "We are banking on the inevitability of the world revolution, but this does not mean that we are such fools as to bank on the revolution inevitably coming on a definite and early date".

In his report to the Extraordinary Seventh Congress of the R.C.P.(B.) which met on 6 March 1918, Lenin said:

> "Yes, we shall see the world revolution, but for the time being it is a very good fairy-tale, a very beautiful fairy-tale—I quite understand children liking beautiful fairy-tales. But I ask, is it proper for a serious revolutionary to believe in fairy-tales? There is an element of reality in every fairy-tale. If you told children fairy-tales in which the cock and the cat did not converse in human language they would not be interested. In the same way, if you tell the people that civil war will break out in Germany and also guarantee that instead of a clash with imperialism we shall have a field revolution on a world-wide scale, the people will say you are deceiving them. In doing this you will be overcoming the difficulties with which history has confronted us only in your own minds, by your own wishes. It will be a good thing if the German proletariat is able to take action. But have you measured it, have you discovered an instrument that will show that the German revolution will break out on such-and-such a day? If the revolution breaks out, everything is saved. Of course! But if it does not turn out as we desire, if it does not achieve victory tomorrow—what then? Then the masses will say to you, you acted like gamblers—you staked everything on a fortunate turn of events that did not take place, you proved to be unequal to the situation that actually arose instead of the world revolution, which will inevitably come, but which has not yet reached maturity".

With the world revolution having altogether failed to materialize, the nascent Soviet Union found itself in a state of capitalist encirclement. According to the interpretation of Lenin's writings by the proponents of socialism in one country, Lenin laid down a long-term future course of action for the nascent Soviet state and its vanguard the R.C.P.(B.), enabling the young Soviet state needs to first start strengthening itself internally to survive. The plan was firstly based on building a close class alliance between the proletariat and the vast masses of the small peasantry (with assured proletarian leadership of the peasantry) and secondly constructing a complete socialist society in Russia whilst patiently awaiting and aiding the worldwide class struggle to first mature around the world before a mass based proletarian revolution on a worldwide scale is made possible. In his 1923 article titled *Our Revolution*, Lenin wrote:

> "You say that civilization is necessary for the building of socialism. Very good. But why could we not first create such prerequisites of civilization in our country by the expulsion of the landowners and the Russian capitalists, and then start moving toward socialism? Where, in what books, have you read that such sequence of events are impermissible or impossible? "

Another quote by Lenin further expounded on his ideas in his article titled *On Cooperation*, where he wrote:

> "Indeed, the power of the state over all large-scale means of production, political power in the hands of the proletariat, the alliance of this proletariat with

> the many millions of small and very small peasants, the assured proletarian leadership of the peasantry, etc. — is this not all that is necessary to build a complete socialist society out of cooperatives, out of cooperatives alone, which we formerly ridiculed as huckstering and which from a certain aspect we have the right to treat as such now, under NEP? Is this not all that is necessary to build a complete socialist society? It is still not the building of socialist society, but it is all that is necessary and sufficient for it".

Opponents of this interpretation, notably Leon Trotsky, have contended that the Lenin quotes adduced in support of socialism on one country are taken out of context. They argue that in the 1915 article *On the Slogan for a United States of Europe* the expression "triumph of socialism possible in a single capitalist country" in context refers only to the initial establishment of a proletarian political and economic regime and not to the eventual construction of a complete socialist society which would take generations. As for the quote from the 1923 article *On Cooperation*, Trotsky maintains that the passage speaking of "necessary and sufficient" prerequisites for the transition to socialism is concerned only with the "socio-organisational" and political prerequisites, but not with the "material-productive" and cultural ones which Russia still lacked.

Joseph Stalin

Stalin presented the theory of socialism in one country as a further development of Leninism based on Lenin's aforementioned quotations. In his 14 February 1938 article titled *Response to Comrade Ivanov*, formulated as an answer to a question of a "comrade Ivanov" mailed to *Pravda* newspaper, Stalin splits the question in two parts. The first side of the question is in terms of the internal relations within the Soviet Union, whether it is possible to construct the socialist society by defeating the local bourgeoisie and fostering the union of workers and peasants. Stalin quotes Lenin that "we have all that is necessary for the building of a complete socialist society" and claims that the socialist society has for the most part been indeed constructed. The second side of the question is in terms of external relations and whether the victory of the socialism is "final", i.e. whether capitalism cannot possibly be restored. Here, Stalin cites Lenin that the final victory is possible only on the international scale and only with the help of the workers of other countries.

Marxist writer Isaac Deutscher traces Stalin's socialism in one country policy to the publication of *The Foundations of Leninism* which emphasized the policy of isolationism and economic development in opposition to Trotsky's policy of permanent revolution.

Karl Marx and Friedrich Engels

On the question of socialist construction in a single country, Friedrich Engels wrote:

> "Will it be possible for this revolution to take place in one country alone?
>
> No. By creating the world market, big industry has already brought all the

> peoples of the Earth, and especially the civilized peoples, into such close relation with one another that none is independent of what happens to the others. Further, it has co-ordinated the social development of the civilized countries to such an extent that, in all of them, bourgeoisie and proletariat have become the decisive classes, and the struggle between them the great struggle of the day. It follows that the communist revolution will not merely be a national phenomenon but must take place simultaneously in all civilized countries—that is to say, at least in England, America, France, and Germany. It will develop in each of these countries more or less rapidly, according as one country or the other has a more developed industry, greater wealth, a more significant mass of productive forces. Hence, it will go slowest and will meet most obstacles in Germany, most rapidly and with the fewest difficulties in England. It will have a powerful impact on the other countries of the world, and will radically alter the course of development which they have followed up to now, while greatly stepping up its pace. It is a universal revolution and will, accordingly, have a universal range".

In 1848, Karl Marx and Engels claimed:

> "The Communists are further reproached with desiring to abolish countries and nationalities. The working men have no country. We cannot take from them what they have not got. Since the proletariat must first of all acquire political supremacy, must rise to be the leading class of the nation, must constitute itself the nation, it is, so far, itself national, though not in the bourgeois sense of the word".

In 1882, Marx and Engels wrote:

> "If the Russian Revolution becomes the signal for a proletarian revolution in the West, so that both complement each other, the present Russian common ownership of land may serve as the starting point for a communist development".

Scientific Socialism

The term *scientific socialism* was used by Friedrich Engels to characterize the doctrines that he and Karl Marx developed and distinguish them from other socialist doctrines, which he dismissed as utopian socialism. Engels regarded the Marx-Engels doctrines as scientific in that they laid bare the secret of capitalism through the discovery of surplus value, and explained (with a theory known in the USSR as historical materialism) how capitalism would inevitably be overthrown and replaced by socialism. The concept "scientific socialism" made Marxist doctrines more attractive to many than rival socialist doctrines by suggesting that equality and the end of exploitation were not only desirable but also inevitable.

Scientific socialism was introduced to Russia in the late ninenteenth century. After the Bolshevik victory in the civil war, scientific socialism became part of the official ideology of the USSR. The term itself was frequently used loosely to designate a doctrine concerning the development of a Soviet type of society. Much of the actual content of the doctrine varied over time in accordance with the concrete policies of the Soviet state.

Socialism as a comprehensive social system failed to spread to the advanced capitalist countries (although "pension fund socialism," the growth of government welfare and regulatory programs, the expansion of employee rights, state-owned industries, public education, and universal suffrage, were widespread and important). This failure, along with other developments such as the collapse of the USSR, indicated that scientific socialism was an imperfect guide to the future. By the end of the twentieth century, the term was mainly of historical interest.

Diverse Aspects of Socialism

4

- Anarchism
- Reformism
- Common Ownership
- Socialist State
- Socialist Market Economy
- Production for Use
- Social Ownership
- Lange Model
- Socialist Economics

Anarchism, reformism, blanquism, socialist state, social dividend, social ownership, socialist economics, Lange model, socialist law and realism, etc. are a few of the aspects within socialism. This chapter sheds light on these diverse aspects of socialism for a thorough understanding of the subject.

Anarchism

Anarchism is a political theory, which is skeptical of the justification of authority and power, especially political power. Anarchism is usually grounded in moral claims about the importance of individual liberty. Anarchists also offer a positive theory of human flourishing, based upon an ideal of non-coercive consensus building. Anarchism has inspired practical efforts at establishing utopian communities, radical and revolutionary political agendas, and various forms of direct action. This entry primarily describes "philosophical anarchism": it focuses on anarchism as a theoretical idea and not as a form of political activism. While philosophical anarchism describes a skeptical theory of political legitimation, anarchism is also a concept that has been employed in philosophical and literary theory to describe a sort of anti-foundationalism. Philosophical anarchism can mean either a theory of political life that is skeptical of attempts to justify state authority or a philosophical theory that is skeptical of the attempt to assert firm foundations for knowledge.

Varieties of Anarchism

There are various forms of anarchism. Uniting this variety is the general critique of centralized, hierarchical power and authority. Given that authority, centralization, and hierarchy show up in various ways and in different discourses, institutions, and practices, it is not surprising that the anarchist critique has been applied in diverse ways.

Political Anarchism

Anarchism is primarily understood as a skeptical theory of political legitimation. Anarchy is thus rule by no one or non-rule. Some argue that non-ruling occurs when there is rule by all—with consensus or unanimity providing an optimistic goal.

Political anarchists focus their critique on state power, viewing centralized, monopolistic coercive power as illegitimate. Anarchists thus criticize "the state". Bakunin provides a paradigm historical example, saying:

> "If there is a State, there must be domination of one class by another and, as a result, slavery; the State without slavery is unthinkable—and this is why we are the enemies of the State".

A more recent example comes from Gerard Casey who writes, "states are criminal organizations. All states, not just the obviously totalitarian or repressive ones" .

Such sweeping generalizations are difficult to support. Thus anarchism as political philosophy faces the challenge of specificity. States have been organized in various ways. Political power is not monolithic. Sovereignty is a complicated matter that includes divisions and distributions of power. Moreover, the historical and ideological context of a given anarchist's critique makes a difference in the content of the political anarchist's critique. Bakunin was responding primarily to a Marxist and Hegelian view of the state, offering his critique from within the global socialist movement; Casey is writing in the Twenty-First Century in the era of liberalism and globalization, offering his critique from within the movement of contemporary libertarianism. Some anarchists engage in broad generalizations, aiming for a total critique of political power. Others will present a localized critique of a given political entity. An ongoing challenge for those who would seek to understand anarchism is to realize how historically and ideologically diverse approaches fit under the general anarchist umbrella.

Religious Anarchism

The anarchist critique has been extended toward the rejection of non-political centralization and authority. Bakunin extended his critique to include religion, arguing against both God and the State. Bakunin rejected God as the absolute master, saying famously, "if God really existed, it would be necessary to abolish him".

There are, however, religious versions of anarchism, which critique political authority from a standpoint that takes religion seriously. Rapp has shown how anarchism can be found in Taoism. And Ramnath has identified anarchist threads in Islamic Sufism, in Hindu *bhakti* movements, in Sikhism's anti-caste efforts, and in Buddhism.

Christian anarchist theology views the kingdom of God as lying beyond any human principle of structure or order. Christian anarchists offer an anti-clerical critique of ecclesiastical and political power. Tolstoy provides an influential example. Tolstoy claims that Christians have a duty not to obey political power and to refuse to swear allegiance to political authority. Tolstoy was also a pacifist. Christian anarcho-pacifism views the state as immoral and unsupportable because of its connection with military power. But there are also non-pacifist Christian anarchists. Berdyaev, for example, builds upon Tolstoy and in his own interpretation of Christian theology. Berdyaev concludes: "The Kingdom of God is anarchy".

Christian anarchists have gone so far as to found separatist communities where they live apart from the structures of the state. Notable examples include New England transcendentalists such as William Garrison and Adin Ballou. These transcendentalists had an influence on Tolstoy.

Other notable Christians with anarchist sympathies include Peter Maurin and Dorothy Day of the Catholic Worker movement. In more recent years, Christian anarchism has been defended by Jacques Ellul who links Christian anarchism to a broad social critique. In addition to being pacifistic, Ellul says, Christian anarchism should also be "antinationalist, anticapitalist, moral, and antidemocratic". The Christian anarchist ought to be committed to "a true overturning of authorities of all kinds". When asked whether a Christian anarchist should vote, Ellul says no. He states, "anarchy first implies conscientious objection".

Theoretical Anarchism

Anarchist rejection of authority has application in epistemology and in philosophical and literary theory. One significant usage of the term shows up in American pragmatism. William James described his pragmatist philosophical theory as a kind of anarchism: "A radical pragmatist is a happy-go-lucky anarchistic sort of creature". James had anarchist sympathies, connected to a general critique of systematic philosophy. Pragmatism, like other anti-systematic and post-Hegelian philosophies, gives up on the search for an *arché* or foundation.

Anarchism thus shows up as a general critique of prevailing methods. An influential example is found in the work of Paul Feyerabend, whose *Against Method* provides an example of "theoretical anarchism" in epistemology and philosophy of science. Feyerabend explains:

> "Science is an essentially anarchic enterprise: theoretical anarchism is more humanitarian and more likely to encourage progress than its law-and-order alternatives".

His point is that science ought not be constrained by hierarchically imposed principles and strict rule following.

Post-structuralism and trends in post-modernism and Continental philosophy can also be anarchistic. So-called "post-anarchism" is a decentered and free-flowing discourse that deconstructs power, questions essentialism, and undermines systems of authority. Following upon the deconstructive and critical work of authors such as Derrida, Deleuze, Foucault, and others, this critique of the *arché* goes all the way down. If there is no *arché* or foundation, then we are left with a proliferation of possibilities. Emerging trends in globalization, cyber-space, and post-humanism make the anarchist critique of "the state" more complicated, since anarchism's traditional celebration of liberty and autonomy can be critically scrutinized and deconstructed.

Traditional anarchists were primarily interested in sustained and focused political activism that led toward the abolition of the state. The difference between free-flowing post-anarchism and traditional anarchism can be seen in the realm of morality. Anarchism has traditionally been critical of centralized moral authority—but this critique was often based upon fundamental principles and traditional values, such as autonomy or liberty. But post-structuralism—along with critiques articulated by some feminists, critical race theorists, and critics of Eurocentrism—calls these values and principles into question.

Applied Anarchisms

The broad critical framework provided by the anarchist critique of authority provides a useful theory or methodology for social critique. In more recent iterations, anarchism has been used to critique gender hierarchies, racial hierarchies, and the like—also including a critique of human domination over nature. Thus anarchism also includes, to name a few varieties: anarcha-feminism or feminist anarchism, queer anarchism or anarchist queer theory, green anarchism or eco-anarchism also associated with anarchist social ecology, and even anarcho-veganism or "veganarchism". In the anarcho-vegan literature we find the following description of a broad and inclusive anarchism:

> "Anarchism is a socio-political theory which opposes all systems of domination

> and oppression such as racism, ableism, sexism, anti-LGBTTQIA, ageism, sizeism, government, competition, capitalism, colonialism, imperialism and punitive justice, and promotes direct democracy, collaboration, interdependence, mutual aid, diversity, peace, transformative justice and equity".

A thorough-going anarchism would thus offer a critique of anything and everything that smacks of hierarchy, domination, centralization, and unjustified authority.

Anarchists who share these various commitments often act upon their critique of authority by engaging in nonconformist practices (free love, nudism, gender disruption, and so on) or by forming intentional communities that live "off the grid" and outside of the norms of mainstream culture. In extreme forms this becomes anarcho-primitivism or anti-civilizational anarchism. Alternative anarchist societies have existed in religious communes in post-Reformation Europe and in the early United States, in Nineteenth Century American utopian communities, the hippy communes of the Twentieth Century, anarchist squats, temporary autonomous zones, and occasional gatherings of like-minded people.

Given this sort of antinomianism and non-conformism it is easy to see that anarchism also often includes a radical critique of traditional ethical norms and principles. Thus radical ethical anarchism can be contrasted with what we might call bourgeois anarchism (with radical anarchism seeking to disrupt traditional social norms and bourgeois anarchism seeking freedom from the state that does not seek such disruption). And although some argue that anarchists are deeply ethical—committed to liberty and solidarity—others will argue that anarchists are moral nihilists who reject morality entirely or who at least reject the idea that there could be a single source of moral authority.

Anarchism in Political Philosophy

Anarchism in political philosophy maintains that there is no legitimate political or governmental authority. In political philosophy anarchy is an important topic for consideration—even for those who are not anarchists—as the a-political background condition against which various forms of political organization are arrayed, compared, and justified. Anarchy is often viewed by non-anarchists as the unhappy or unstable condition in which there is no legitimate authority. Anarchism as a philosophical idea is not necessarily connected to practical activism. There are political anarchists who take action in order to destroy what they see as illegitimate states. The popular imagination often views anarchists as bomb-throwing nihilists. But philosophical anarchism is a theoretical standpoint. In order to decide who (and whether) one should act upon anarchist insight, we require a further theory of political action, obligation, and obedience grounded in further ethical reflection. Simmons explains that philosophical anarchists "do not take the illegitimacy of states to entail a strong moral imperative to oppose or eliminate states". Some anarchists remain obedient to ruling authorities; others revolt or resist in various ways. The question of action depends upon a theory of what sort of political obligation follows from our philosophical, moral, political, religious, and aesthetic commitments.

There is a long history of political anarchism. In the ancient world, anarchism of a sort can be found in the ideas of the Epicureans and Cynics. Although they did not employ the term anarchism, the Epicureans and Cynics avoided political activity, advising retreat from political life in pursuit of tranquility (*ataraxia*) and self-control (*autarkeai*). The Cynics are also known for advocating cosmopolitanism: living without allegiance to any particular state or legal system, while associating with human beings based upon moral principle outside of traditional state structures. Diogenes the Cynic had little respect for political or religious authority. One of his guiding ideas was to "deface the currency". This meant not only devaluing or destroying monetary currency but also a general rejection of the norms of civilized society. Diogenes often mocked political authorities and failed to offer signs of respect. While Diogenes actively disrespected established norms, Epicurus counseled retreat. He advised living unnoticed and avoiding political life (under the phrase *me politeuesthai*—which can be understood as an anti-political admonition).

The assumption that anarchy would be unhappy or unstable leads to justifications of political power. In Hobbes' famous phrase, in the stateless—anarchic—condition of "the state nature" human life would be solitary, poor, nasty, brutish and short. Hobbes' social contract—as well as other versions of the social contract theory as found for example in Locke or Rousseau—are attempts to explain how and why the political state emerges from out of the anarchic state of nature.

Anarchists respond by claiming that the state tends to produce its own sort of unhappiness: as oppressive, violent, corrupt, and inimical to liberty. Discussions about the social contract thus revolve around the question of whether the state is better than anarchy—or whether states and state-like entities naturally and inevitably emerge from out of the original condition of anarchy. One version of this argument about the inevitable emergence of states (by way of something like an "invisible hand") is found in Nozick's influential *Anarchy, State, Utopia*. While Nozick and other political philosophers take anarchy seriously as a starting point, anarchists will argue that invisible hand arguments of this sort ignore the historical actuality of states, which develop out of a long history of domination, inequality, and oppression. Murray Rothbard has argued against Nozick and social contract theory, saying, "no existing state has been immaculately conceived". Different versions of the social contract theory, such as we find in John Rawls's work, view the contract situation as a heuristic device allowing us to consider justice from under "the veil of ignorance". But anarchists will argue that the idea of the original position does not necessarily lead to the justification of the state—especially given background knowledge about the tendency of states to be oppressive. Crispin Sartwell concludes:

> "Even accepting more or less all of the assumptions Rawls packs into the original position, it is not clear that the contractors would not choose anarchy".

An important historical touchstone is William Godwin. Unlike Locke and Hobbes who turned to the social contract to lead us out of the anarchic state of nature, Godwin argued that the resulting governmental power was not necessarily better than anarchy. Locke, of course, allows for revolution when the state becomes despotic. Godwin builds upon that insight. He explained, "we must not hastily conclude that the mischiefs of anarchy are worse than those which government is qualified to produce". He claimed:

> "It is earnestly to be desired that each man should be wise enough to govern himself, without the intervention of any compulsory restraint; and, since government, even in its best state, is an evil, the object principally to be aimed at is that we should have as little of it as the general peace of human society will permit".

Like Rousseau, who praised the noble savage, who was free from social chains until forced into society, Godwin imagined original anarchy developing into the political state, which tended on his view to become despotic. Once the state comes into being, Godwin suggests that despotism is the primary problem since "despotism is as perennial as anarchy is transitory".

Anarchism is often taken to mean that individuals ought to be left alone without any unifying principle or governing power. In some cases anarchism is related to libertarianism (or what is sometimes called "anarcho-capitalism"). But non-rule may also occur when there is unanimity or consensus—and hence no need for external authority or a governing structure of command and obedience. If there were unanimity among individuals, there would be no need for "ruling", authority, or government. The ideas of unanimity and consensus are associated with the positive conception of anarchism as a voluntary association of autonomous human beings, which promotes communal values. One version of the anarchist ideal imagines the devolution of centralized political authority, leaving us with communes whose organizational structure is open-ended and consensual.

Given this emphasis on communal organization it is not surprising that political anarchism has a close historical association with communism, despite the connection mentioned above with free market capitalism. Authors such as Bakunin, Kropotkin, and Goldman developed their anarchism as a response to Marx and Marxism. One of the first authors to explicitly affirm anarchism, Pierre Proudhon, defended a kind of "communism", which he understood as being grounded in decentralized associations, communes, and mutual-aid societies. Proudhon thought that private property created despotism. He argued that liberty required anarchy, concluding:

> "The government of man by man (under whatever name it be disguised) is oppression. Society finds its highest perfection in the union of order with anarchy".

Following Proudhon, Bakunin, Kropotkin, and the other so-called "classical anarchists", anarchism comes to be seen as a focal point for political philosophy and activism.

Let's turn to a conceptual analysis of different arguments made in defense of anarchism.

Absolute, Deontological and a Priori Anarchism

Anarchists often make categorical claims to the effect that no state is legitimate or that there can no such thing as a justifiable political state. As an absolute or *a priori* claim, anarchism holds that all states always and everywhere are illegitimate and unjust. The term "*a priori* anarchism" is found in Simmons 2001; but it is employed already by Kropotkin in his influential 1910 article on anarchism, where he claims that anarchists are not utopians who argue against the state in *a priori* fashion. Despite Kropotkin's claim, some anarchists do offer *a priori* arguments against the state. This sort of claim rests upon an account of the justification of authority that is usually grounded in some form of deontological moral claim about the importance of individual liberty and a logical claim about the nature of state authority.

One typical and well-known example of this argument is found in the work of Robert Paul Wolff. Wolff indicates that legitimate authority rests upon a claim about the right to command obedience. Correlative to this is a duty to obey: one has a duty to obey legitimate authority. As Wolff explains, by appealing to ideas found in Kant and Rousseau, the duty to obey is linked to notions about autonomy, responsibility, and rationality. But for Wolff and other anarchists, the problem is that the state does not have legitimate authority. As Wolff says of the anarchist, "he will never view the commands of the state as legitimate, as having a binding moral force". The categorical nature of this claim indicates a version of absolute anarchism. If the state's commands are never legitimate and create no moral duty of obedience, then there can never be a legitimate state. Wolff imagines that there could be a legitimate state grounded in "unanimous direct democracy"—but he indicates that unanimous direct democracy would be "so restricted in its application that it offers no serious hope of ever being embodied in an actual state". Wolff concludes:

> "If all men have a continuing obligation to achieve the highest degree of autonomy possible, then there would appear to be no state whose subjects have a moral obligation to obey its commands. Hence, the concept of a de jure legitimate state would appear to be vacuous, and philosophical anarchism would seem to be the only reasonable political belief for an enlightened man".

As Wolff puts it here, there appears to be "no state" that is legitimate. This claim is stated in absolute and *a priori* fashion, a point made by Reiman in his critique of Wolff. Wolff does not deny, by the way, that there are de facto legitimate states: governments often do have the approval and support of the people they govern. But this approval and support is merely conventional and not grounded in a moral duty; and approval and support are manufactured and manipulated by the coercive power and propaganda and ideology of the state.

We noted here that Wolff's anarchism is connected to Kant. But Kant is no anarchist: he defended the idea of enlightened republican government in which autonomy would be preserved. Rousseau may be closer to espousing anarchism in some of his remarks—although these are far from systematic. Among classical political philosophers, we might also consider Locke in connection with "libertarian anarchism" or Locke as offering a theory "on the edge of anarchism", as Simmons has put it. But despite his strong defense of individual rights, the stringent way he describes voluntary consent, and his advocacy of revolution, Locke believes that states can be defended based upon the social contract theory.

Leaving the canonical authors of Western political philosophy aside, the most likely place to find deontological and *a priori* anarchism is among the Christian anarchists. Of course, most Christians are not anarchists. But those Christians who espouse anarchism usually do so with the absolute, deontological, and *a priori* claims of the sort made by Tolstoy, Berdyaev, and Ellul—as noted above.

Contingent, Consequentialist and a Posteriori Anarchism

A less stringent form of anarchism will argue that states could be justified in theory—even though, in practice, no state or very few states are actually legitimate. Contingent anarchism will hold that states in the present configuration of things fail to live up to the standards of their own justification. This is an *a posteriori* argument based both in a theoretical account of the justification of the state (for example, the social contract theory of liberal-democratic theory) and in an empirical account of how and why concrete states fail to be justified based upon this theory.

One version of the contingent anarchist argument focuses on the question of the burden of proof for accounts that would justify political authority. This approach has been articulated by Noam Chomsky, who explains:

> "This is what I have always understood to be the essence of anarchism: the conviction that the burden of proof has to be placed on authority, and that it should be dismantled if that burden cannot be met. Sometimes the burden can be met".

Chomsky accepts legitimate authority based in ordinary experience: for example, when a grandfather prevents a child from darting out into the street. But state authority is a much more complicated affair. Political relationships are attenuated; there is the likelihood of corruption and self-interest infecting political reality; there are levels and degrees of mediation, which alienate us from the source of political authority; and the rational autonomy of adults is important and fundamental. By focusing on the burden of proof, Chomsky acknowledges that there may be ways to meet the burden of proof for the justification of the state. But he points out that there is a prima facie argument against the state—which is based in a complex historical and empirical account of the role of power, economics, and historical inertia in creating political institutions. He explains:

> "Such institutions face a heavy burden of proof: it must be shown that under existing conditions, perhaps because of some overriding consideration of deprivation or threat, some form of authority, hierarchy, and domination is justified, despite the prima facie case against it—a burden that can rarely be met".

Chomsky does not deny that the burden of proof could be met. Rather, his point is that there is a prima facie case against the state, since the burden of proof for the justification of the state is rarely met.

Contingent anarchism is based in consequentialist reasoning, focused on details of historical actuality. Consequentialist anarchism will appeal to utilitarian considerations, arguing that states generally fail to deliver in terms of promoting the happiness of the greater number of people—and more strongly that state power tends to produce unhappiness. The actuality of inequality, classism, elitism, racism, sexism, and other forms of oppression can be used to support an anarchist argument, holding that even though a few people benefit from state power, a larger majority suffers under it.

There is a significant difference between anarchism that is offered in pursuit of utilitarianism's greater happiness ideal and anarchism that is offered in defense of the minority against the tyranny of the majority.

Before turning to that conception of anarchism, let's note two classical authors who offer insight into utilitarian anarchism. Godwin articulated a form of anarchism that is connected to a utilitarian concern. Godwin's general moral thought is utilitarian in basic conception, even though he also argues based upon fundamental principles such as the importance of liberty. But Godwin's arguments are *a posteriori*, based upon generalizations from history and with an eye toward the future development of happiness and liberty. He writes:

> "Above all we should not forget, that government is an evil, an usurpation upon the private judgment and individual conscience of mankind; and that, however we may be obliged to admit it as a necessary evil for the present".

This claim is similar to Chomsky's insofar as it recognizes the complicated nature of the historical dialectic. The goal of political development should be in a direction that goes beyond the state (and toward the development of individual reason and morality). But in our present condition, some form of government may be "a necessary evil", which we ought to strive to overcome. The point here is that our judgments about the justification of the state are contingent: they depend upon present circumstances and our current form of development. And while states may be necessary features of the current human world, as human beings develop further, it is possible that the state might outlive its usefulness.

We should note that utilitarian arguments are often used to support state structures in the name of the greater good. Utilitarian anarchists will argue that states fail to do this. But utilitarian conclusions are not usually based upon a fundamental appeal to moral principles such as liberty or the rights of the individual. Thus Bentham described claims about human rights as "anarchical fallacies" because they tended to lead toward anarchy, which he rejected. Bentham described the difference between a moderate utilitarian effort at reform and the anarchist's revolutionary doctrine of human rights, saying that:

> "The anarchist setting up his will and fancy for a law before which all mankind are called upon to bow down at the first word—the anarchist, trampling on truth and decency, denies the validity of the law in question,—denies the existence of it in the character of a law, and calls upon all mankind to rise up in a mass, and resist the execution of it".

More principled deontological anarchism will maintain that states violate fundamental rights and so are not justified. But utilitarian anarchism will not primarily be worried about the violation of a few people's rights (although that is obviously a relevant consideration). Rather, the complaint for a utilitarian anarchist is that state structures tend to produce disadvantages for the greater number of people. Furthermore what Oren Ben-Dor calls "utilitarian-based anarchism" is based upon the idea that there is no *a priori* justification of the state. For the utilitarian, this all depends upon the circumstances and conditions. Ben-Dor calls this anarchism because it rejects any *a priori* notion of state justification. In other words, the utilitarian anarchist does not presume that states are justifiable; rather a utilitarian anarchist will hold that the burden of proof rests upon the defender of states to show that state authority is justifiable on utilitarian grounds, by bringing in historical and empirical data about human nature, human flourishing, and successful social organization.

Individualism, Libertarianism and Socialist Anarchism

Forms of anarchism also differ in terms of the content of the theory, the focal point of the anarchist critique, and the imagined practical impact of anarchism. Socialist forms of anarchism include communist anarchism associated with Kropotkin and communitarian anarchism. The socialist approach focuses on the development of social and communal groups, which are supposed to thrive outside of hierarchical and centralized political structures. Individualist forms of anarchism include some forms of libertarianism or anarcho-capitalism as well as egoistically oriented antinomianism and non-conformism. The individualistic focus rejects group identity and ideas about social/communal good, while remaining firmly rooted in moral claims about the autonomy of the individual.

Individualistic anarchism is historically associated with ideas found in Stirner who said, "every state is a despotism". He argued that there was no duty to obey the state and the law because the law and the state impair self-development and self-will. The state seeks to tame our desires and along with the church it undermines self-enjoyment and the development of unique individuality. Stirner is even critical of social organizations and political parties. While not denying that an individual could affiliate with such organizations, he maintains that the individual retains rights and identity against the party or social organization: he embraces the party; but he ought not allow himself to be "embraced and taken up by the party". Individualist anarchism has often been attributed to a variety of thinkers including Josiah Warren, Benjamin Tucker, and Thoreau.

Individualist anarchism also seems to have something in common with egoism of the sort associated with Ayn Rand. But Rand dismissed anarchism as "a naïve floating abstraction" that could not exist in reality; and she argued that governments properly existed to defend people's rights. A more robust sort of pro-capitalist anarchism has been defended by Murray Rothbard, who rejects "left-wing anarchism" of the sort he associates with communism, while applauding the individualist anarchism of Tucker. Rothbard continues to explain that since anarchism has usually been considered as being primarily a left-wing communist phenomenon, libertarianism should be distinguished from anarchism by calling it "non-archism". A related term has been employed in the literature, "min-archism", which has been used to describe the minimal state that libertarians allow. Libertarians are still individualists, who emphasize the importance of individual liberty, even though they disagree with full-blown anarchists about the degree to which state power can be justified.

In some cases, individualistic anarchism is merely a matter of "lifestyle", which focuses on dress, behavior, and other individualistic choices and preferences. Bookchin and other critics of lifestyle individualism will argue that mere non-conformism does very little to change the status quo and overturn structures of domination and authority. But defenders of lifestyle non-conformism will argue that there is value in opting out of cultural norms and demonstrating contempt for conformity through individual lifestyle choices.

A more robust form of individualist anarchism will focus on key values such as autonomy and self-determination, asserting the primacy of the individual over and against social groups. Individualist anarchists can admit that collective action is important and that voluntary cooperation among individuals can result in beneficial and autonomy preserving community. Remaining disputes will consider whether what results from individual cooperation is a form of capitalism or a form of social sharing or communism. Libertarian anarchists or anarcho-capitalists will defend free market ideas based upon individual choices in trading and producing goods for market.

On the other hand, socialist or communistically oriented anarchism will focus more on a sharing economy. This could be a large form of mutualism or something local and concrete like the sharing of family life or the traditional potlatch. But these ideas remain anarchist to the extent that they want to avoid centralized control and the development of hierarchical structures of domination. Unlike state-centered communism of the sort developed by Marxists, anarchist communism advocates decentralization. The motto of this approach comes from Kropotkin: "all for all". In *The Conquest of Bread* Kropotkin criticizes monopolistic centralization that prevents people from gaining access to socially generated wealth. The solution is "all for all": "What we proclaim is the

Right to Well-Being: Well-Being for All!". The communist idea that all humans should enjoy the fruits of the collective human product shares something with the Marxist idea of "to each according to his need". But Kropotkin argues for the need to evolve beyond centralized communist control—what he criticizes as mere "collectivism"—and toward anarchist communism:

> "Anarchy leads to communism, and communism to anarchy, both alike being expressions of the predominant tendency in modern societies, the pursuit of equality".

Kropotkin argues that the communal impulse already exists and that the advances in social wealth made possible by the development of individualistic capitalism make it likely that we will develop in the direction of communal sharing. He argues that the tendency of history is away from centralized power and toward equality and liberty—and toward the abolition of the state. Kropotkin's communist anarchism is based upon some historical and empirical claims: about whether things can actually be arranged more satisfactorily without state intervention; and about whether states really do personify injustice and oppression. Libertarianism and anarcho-capitalism also think that the free market will work to adequately maximize human well-being and help individuals to realize their own autonomy. But for the socialist and communist anarchists, the question of individual self-realization is less important than the idea of social development. Kropotkin's "all for all" indicates a moral and ontological focus that is different from what we find among the individualists.

Socialist and communally focused forms of anarchism emphasize the importance of social groups. For example, families can be viewed as anarchic structures of social cooperation and solidarity. A social anarchist would be critical of hierarchical and domineering forms of family organization (for example, patriarchal family structure). But social anarchists will emphasize the point that human identity and flourishing occur within extended social structures—so long as it remains a free and self-determining community.

The tension between individualist and socialist anarchism comes to a head when considering the question of the degree to which an individual ought to be subordinated to the community. One problem for so-called "communitarian" theories of social and political life is that they can result in the submergence of individuals into the communal identity. Individualists will want to struggle against this assault upon autonomy and individual identity. Communalists may respond, as Clark does, by claiming that the ideal of a genuine community of autonomous individuals remains a hoped for dream of an "impossible community". On the other hand communally focused theorists will point out that individual human beings cannot exist outside of communal structures: we are social animals who flourish and survive in communities. Thus radical individualism also remains a dream—and as more politically oriented anarchists will point out, individualism undermines the possibility of organized political action, which implies that individualist anarchists will be unable to successfully resist political structures of domination.

Anarchism and Political Activity

Anarchism forces us to re-evaluate political activity. Ancient Greek philosophers such as Aristotle and Plato held that human beings flourished within just political communities and that there was a virtue in serving the polis. Modern political philosophy tended to hold, as well, that political action—including obedience to the law and the ideal of a rule of law—was noble and enlightened. In Hegelian political philosophy, these ideas combine in a way that celebrates citizenship and service to the state. And in contemporary liberal political philosophy, it is often presumed that obedience to the law is required as a *prima facie* duty. Anarchists, of course, call this all into question.

The crucial question for anarchists is thus whether one ought to disengage from political life, whether one ought to submit to political authority and obey the law, or whether one ought to engage in active efforts to actively abolish the state. Those who opt to work actively for the abolition of the state often understand this as a form of "direct action" or "propaganda of the deed". The idea of direct action is often viewed as typical of anarchists, who believe that something ought to be done to actively abolish the state including: graffiti, street theater, organized occupations, boycotts, and even violence. There are disputes among anarchists about what ought to be done, with an important dividing line occurring with regard to the question of violence and criminal behavior.

Before turning to that discussion, let's note one further important theoretical distinction with regard to the question of taking action, connected to the typology offered above: whether action should be justified in consequentialist or non-consequentialist terms. Franks has argued that anarchist direct action ought to exemplify a unity of means and ends. On this view, if liberation and autonomy are what anarchists are pursuing, then the methods used to obtain these goods must be liberationist and celebrate autonomy—and embody this within direct action. Franks argues that the idea that "the end justifies the means" is more typical of state-centered movements, such as Bolshevism—and of right-wing movements. While some may think that anarchists are willing to engage in action "by any means necessary", that phraseology and the crass consequentialism underlying it is more typical of radical movements which are not anarchist. Coercive imposition of the anarchist ideal re-inscribes the problem of domination, hierarchy, centralization, and monopolistic power that the anarchist was originally opposed to.

Nonviolence, Violence and Criminality

One significant philosophical and ethical problem for politically engaged anarchists is the question of how to avoid ongoing cycles of power and violence that are likely to erupt in the absence of centralized political power. One suggestion, is that anarchists will often want to emphasize the unity of means and ends. This idea shows why there is some substantial overlap and conjunction between anarchism and pacifism. Pacifist typically emphasize the unity of means and ends. But not all pacifists are anarchists. However, there is a connection between anarchism and Christian pacifism, as found in Tolstoy, for example. Gandhi was influenced by Tolstoy and the anarchists. Although Gandhi is better known as an anti-colonial activist, Marshall includes Gandhi among the anarchists. It is possible to reconstruct anti-colonial movements and arguments about self-determination and home rule as a kind of anarchism (aimed at destroying colonial power and imperial states). Gandhi noted that there were many anarchists working in India in his time. In saying this, Gandhi uses the term anarchism to characterize bomb-throwing advocates of violence. He says: "I myself am an anarchist, but of another type". Gandhian anarchism, if there is such a thing, embraces nonviolence. In general nonviolent resistance as developed in the Tolstoy-Gandhi-King tradition fits with an approach that turns away from political power and views the state as a purveyor of war and an impediment to equality and human development.

Objecting to this anarcho-pacifist approach are more militant activists who advocate direct action that can include sabotage and other forms of political violence including terrorism. Emma Goldman explains, for example, that anti-capitalist sabotage undermines the idea of private possession. While the legal system considers this to be criminal, Goldman contends it is not. She explains:

> "It is ethical in the best sense, since it helps society to get rid of its worst foe, the most detrimental factor of social life. Sabotage is mainly concerned with obstructing, by every possible method, the regular process of production, thereby demonstrating the determination of the workers to give according to what they receive, and no more".

Goldman struggled with the question of violence through the course of her career. Early on she was a more vocal proponent of revolutionary violence. She began to rethink this later. Nonetheless, like other anarchists of her generation, she attributed violence to the state, which she opposed. She writes:

> "I believe that Anarchism is the only philosophy of peace, the only theory of the social relationship that values human life above everything else. I know that some Anarchists have committed acts of violence, but it is the terrible economic inequality and great political injustice that prompt such acts, not Anarchism. Every institution today rests on violence; our very atmosphere is saturated with it".

Goldman views anarchist violence as merely reactive. In response to state violence, the anarchists often argued that they were merely using violence in self-defense. Another defender of violence is Malatesta who wrote that the revolution against the violence of the ruling class must be violent. He explained:

> "I think that a regime which is born of violence and which continues to exist by

> violence cannot be overthrown except by a corresponding and proportionate violence".

Like Goldman, Malatesta warned against violence becoming an end in itself and giving way to brutality and ferocity for its own sake. He also described anarchists as preachers of love and advocates of peace. He said:

> "What distinguishes the anarchists from all others is in fact their horror of violence, their desire and intention to eliminate physical violence from human relations".

But despite this rejection of violence, Malatesta advocates violence as a necessary evil.

Anarchist violence appears as the violence of an individual against the state. It is easy to see why such violence would be characterized as terroristic and criminal. For an individual to declare war against the state and take action to disrupt the state is criminal. And thus anarchists have also been interested in a critique of crime and criminality—arguing that it is the law and the legal system that creates and produces crime and criminality. This critique was advanced by Kropotkin as early as the 1870s, when he called prisons "schools for crime". Similar ideas are found in Foucault and in more recent criticisms of mass incarceration. Contemporary anarchists will argue that mass incarceration is an example of state power run amok.

Disobedience, Revolution and Reform

The question of violence leads us to a further issue: the question of obedience, disobedience, resistance, and political obligation. Much could be said here about the nature of political obligation and obedience: including whether obedience is merely pragmatic and strategic or based upon notions about loyalty and claims about identification with the nation and its laws. But it is clear that anarchists have no principled reason for political obedience. If the anarchist views the state as illegitimate, then obedience and participation are merely a matter of choice, preference, and pragmatism—and not a matter of loyalty or duty.

Christian anarchists will look, for example, to the case of Jesus and his idea of rendering unto Caesar what is due to Caesar. The anarchist interpretation of this passage claims that this is an indication both of Jesus's disaffection with the state and with his grudging acquiescence to political authority. Christoyannopoulos argues, "Jesus' political subversion is carried out through submission rather than revolt". The crucifixion, on this interpretation, is a subversive event, which "unmasks" political power as "demonic" and illegitimate. Jesus does not recognize the ultimate moral and religious authority of Caesar or Pilate. But he goes along with the political regime. Thus some anarchists may simply be compliant and submissive.

But politically motivated anarchists encourage resistance to state power, including strategic and principled disobedience. Such disobedience could involve symbolic actions—graffiti and the like—or acts of civil resistance, protests, tax resistance and so on—up to, and possibly including, sabotage, property crime, and outright violence. Again, there is overlap with the discussion of violence here, but let's set that question aside and focus on the notion of civil disobedience.

One important example is found in Thoreau, who famously explained his act of disobedience by tax resistance as follows:

> "In fact, I quietly declare war with the State, after my fashion, though I will still make what use and get what advantage of her I can, as is usual in such cases".

Thoreau's disobedience is principled. He recognizes that a declaration of war against the state is a criminal act. He willingly goes to jail. But he also admits that he will cooperate with the state in other cases—since there is something advantageous about cooperation. This indicates the complexity of the question of cooperation, protest, and disobedience. Thoreau's essay, "Civil Disobedience", is often viewed as an anarchist manifesto. Kropotkin discussed him as an anarchist. And Tolstoy admired his act of civil disobedience—as did Gandhi.

Anarchists continue to discuss strategies and tactics of disobedience. One problem throughout this discussion is the degree to which disobedience is effective. If there were to be successful anarchist campaigns of disobedience they would have to be organized and widespread. Whether such campaigns would actually work to disassemble the state apparatus remains an open question.

Until their dreamed-of revolution comes, anarchist must consider the degree to which cooperation with the state involves "selling out" to the political status quo. Perhaps there are reforms and short-term gains that can be obtained through traditional political means: voting, lobbying legislators, etc. But anarchists have often held to an all-or-nothing kind of approach to political participation. We noted above that the Christian anarchist Jacques Ellul has said that he does not vote because anarchy implies conscientious objection. But herein lies a strategic conundrum. If progressively minded anarchists opt out of the political system, this means that less enlightened policies will prevail. By not voting or otherwise engaging in ordinary politics, the anarchist ends up with a system that he or she will be even less happy with than if he or she had actively participated in the system.

This is, really, a problem of revolution versus reform. The revolutionary wants revolution now, believing that it will occur by way of direct action of various sorts. Perhaps the revolutionary is also thinking that the psychological, cultural, and spiritual evolution toward revolutionary consciousness can only occur when direct action is taken: in order for anarchism to emerge, the anarchist may think, one ought to behave and think like an anarchist. But without a concerted and nation-wide revolution, revolutionary action begins to look like mere selfishness, Epicurean opting out, or what Bookchin criticized as "lifestyle anarchism". Meanwhile those reform-minded folks who work within the system of political power and legality can end up supporting a system that they have doubts about. This philosophical problem of reform vs. revolution exists for all radical political agendas. But the problem is especially acute for anarchists, since anarchism is often an all-or-none proposition: if the state is justified then gradualism and reformism make sense; but if no state can be justified, then what is sometimes called "reformist anarchism" is a non-starter.

Utopian Communities and Non-revolutionary Anarchism

Many anarchists are revolutionaries who want change to be created through direct action.The Epicureans and Cynics pointed in this direction. The history of anarchism is replete with efforts to construct anarchist communes that are independent and separated from the rest of state centered political life.

We might pick up the history here with the Christian anarchists and pacifists of the Reformation: the Mennonites, for example; or the Quakers who refused to doff their hats for political authorities and who sought a refuge in Pennsylvania. Indeed, there is an anarchist thread to the colonization of North America, as those who were disgruntled with European political and religious hierarchy left for the "new world" or were forced out by the European authorities. In the Seventeenth Century, Anne Hutchinson was cast out of the Massachusetts Bay Colony and forced to found a new community, when she concluded that the idea of government was flawed. Hutchinson is considered as one of the first anarchists of North America. Separatist communities were founded by the New England abolitionists and transcendentalists, by Josiah Warren, and by others.

Anarchist communes were formed in Europe during the Nineteenth Century and in Spain during the 1930s. There have been ongoing movements and organizations of indigenous peoples and others who inhabit the margins of mainstream political life. In the 1960s and 70s, anarchist separatism was reiterated in the Hippy communes and attempts to live off the grid and get back to nature. Alternative communes, squats, and spontaneous gatherings continue to occur.

Separatist communities have to consider the degree to which they give up on anarchist direct action against dominant political forces, the extent to which they have to accommodate themselves to political reality, and the risk that customary hierarchies will be reinstated within the commune. For the revolutionary anarchist, separatism is a strategy of avoidance that impedes political action. Separatist communes must often obey the rules of the dominant political organization in order to trade and get connected to the rest of the world. Finally, a complaint made about separatist communes is that they can end up being structured by sexist, classist, and other hierarchical organizing principles. One might argue that until the dominant culture is revolutionized, separatism will only be a pale reflection of the anarchist ideal. And yet, on the other hand, advocates of separatism will argue that the best way for anarchist ideals to take hold is to demonstrate that they work and to provide an inspiration and experimental proving ground for anarchism.

If revolutionary activity is taken off the table, then anarchists are left with various forms of gradualism and reformism. One way this might occur is through the creation of "temporary autonomous zones" such as those described by Bey. Along these lines David Graeber provides a description of the cultural and spiritual work that would be required in order to prepare the way for anarchist revolution. Graeber says that this would require "liberation in the imaginary", by which he means that through activism, utopian communities, and the like there can be a gradual change in the way political power is imagined and understood. Revolutionary anarchists will respond to this by arguing that liberation in the imaginary is simply imaginary liberation: without actual change in the status quo, oppression and inequality continue to be a problem.

Objections and Replies

Let's conclude by considering some standard objections to anarchism and typical replies.

Anarchism is Nihilistic and Destructive

Objection: This objection holds that anarchism is merely another name for chaos and for a rejection of order. This objection holds that anarchists are violent and destructive and that they are intent on destroying everything, including morality itself.

Reply: This objection does not seem to recognize that anarchists come in many varieties. Many anarchists are also pacifists—and so do not advocate violent revolution. Many other anarchists are firmly committed to moral principles such as autonomy, liberty, solidarity, and equality. Some anarchists do take their critique of *arché* in a nihilistic direction that denies ethical principles. But one can be committed to anarchism, while advocating for caring communities. Indeed, many of the main authors in the anarchist tradition believed that the state and the other hierarchical and authoritarian structures of contemporary society prevented human flourishing.

Anarchy will always Evolve Back into the State

Objection: This objection holds that anarchism is inherently unstable. Hobbes and other early modern social contract theories maintain that the state emerges as a necessary response to natural anarchy which keeps order and protects our interests. A different theory comes from Nozick, who argues that the "night-watchman state" would emerge out of anarchy by an invisible hand process: as people will exercise their liberty and purchase protection from a protection agency, which would eventually evolve into something like a minimal state.

Reply: Anarchists may argue that the state of nature is simply not a state of war and so that Hobbes's description is false. Some anarcho-primitivists will argue that things were much better for human beings in the original state of nature in small communities living close to the land. Other anarchists might argue that the disadvantages of state organizations—the creation of hierarchies, monopolies, inequalities, and the like—simply outweigh the benefits of state structures; and that rational agents would choose to remain in anarchy rather than allow the state to evolve. Some anarchists may argue that each time a state emerges, it would have to be destroyed. But others will argue that education and human development (including technological development) would prevent the reemergence of the state.

Anarchism is Utopian

Objection: This objection holds that there simply is no way to destroy or deconstruct the state. So exercises in anarchist political theory are fruitless. It would be better, from this point of view to focus on critiques of hierarchy, inequality, and threats to liberty from within liberal or libertarian political theory—and to engage in reforms that occur within the status quo and mainstream political organization.

Reply: Ideal theory is always in opposition to non-ideal theory. But utopian speculation can be useful for clarifying values. Thus philosophical anarchism may be a useful exercise that helps us understand our values and commitment, even though political anarchism has no hope of succeeding. Furthermore, there are examples of successful anarchist communities on a small local scale. These concrete examples can be viewed as experiments in anarchist theory and practice.

Anarchism is Incoherent

Objection: This objection holds that a political theory that abolishes political structures makes no sense. A related concern arises when anarchism is taken to be a critique of authority in every case and in all senses. If anarchists deny then that there can be any *arché* whatsoever, then the claim contradicts itself: we would have a ruling theory that states that there is no ruling theory. This sort of criticism is related to standard criticisms of relativism and nihilism. Related to this is a more concrete and mundane objection that holds that there can be no anarchist movement or collective action, since anarchism is constitutionally opposed to the idea of a movement or collective (since under anarchism there can be no authoritative ruler or set of rules).

Reply: This objection only holds if anarchism is taken to be an all-or-nothing theory of the absolutist variety. Political anarchists do not necessarily agree with the skeptical post-foundationalist critique which holds that there can be no ruling principle or authority whatsoever. Rather, political anarchists hold that there are legitimate authorities but that political power quickly loses its authoritativeness and legitimacy. Furthermore, anarchists tend to advocate for a principle and procedure for organization based upon voluntarism and mutual aid, as well as unanimity and consensus. From this point of view anarchist communities can work very well, provided that they avoid coercive authority. To support this point anarchists will point to historical examples of successful anarchist communes. They will also point to ordinary human relations—in families and civil society relationship—which operate quite well apart form coercive and hierarchical political authority

Reformism

A reformist tries to improve and reform the living conditions for the workers within the capitalist system (tries to make the system more "humane"), while the revolutionary fights for the same reforms as part of the larger struggle to smash capitalism. It is this fear of outright revolution that has forced the ruling class and the state into making concessions to the legitimate demands of workers.

The reformists often sincerely sympathize with the workers, but they do not understand the real cause of the exploitation and misery of the working class. They generally believe that the crimes of capitalism are just a tragic misunderstanding, and if only the bosses could be made to realize the suffering they are causing, things could be better. Some believe that oppression comes just because the capitalists are greedy, and take the burden off the system of capitalism. A reformist struggle is like putting a band-aid on a bullet wound.

Reformists take the capitalist system for granted, believing that the system can be made more human but that changing to a better system is impossible. Because of this outlook they are forced to limit their demands to ones that don't challenge the bosses' rule.

"Of course you need a raise, but if you ask for too much, how is the company going to stay in business?" How many times have the workers been force-fed this line as an excuse for making concessions to the boss?

After exposing in detail the criminal practices of the automotive and other industries, he proposed a mild legislative program to break up the monopolies and bring back a mythical age of small capitalism and fair competition that never existed. There are two reasons legislative reforms similar to Nader's proposals are unworkable. First, capitalism naturally tends towards monopoly and monopolies have dominated the system since before World War I. Second, the monopolies have also dominated the politicians and now dominate them more than ever.

Revolutionaries are the most militant fighters for improvements in the standard of living and for defending the rights of workers, the poor, and the oppressed under capitalism.

Revolutionaries strive to lead the struggle in the trade unions, tenant groups, consumer groups, organizations of welfare recipients and unemployed workers, groups fighting high- er food prices or housing foreclosures.

While reformists are not the class enemy and often win sup- porters because of their legitimate struggle with the bosses, they are unable to consciously lead a struggle against capital- ism because they themselves believe in it. By not showing the workers who their real enemy is, the reformist way of thinking helps capitalism to continue and to oppress the workers even more effectively.

But revolutionaries lead these struggles with a view to enlarging them, deepening them, and with the aim of getting into a still greater struggle to overthrow the whole rotten, oppressive system.

Common Ownership

Common ownership refers to holding the assets of an organization, enterprise or community indivisibly rather than in the names of the individual members or groups of members as common property.

Forms of common ownership exist in every economic system. Common ownership of the means of production is a central goal of communist political movements as it is seen as a necessary democratic mechanism for the creation and continued function of a communist society. Advocates make a distinction between *collective ownership* and *common property* as the former refers to property owned jointly by agreement of a set of colleagues, such as producer cooperatives, whereas the latter refers to assets that are completely open for access, such as a public park freely available to everyone.

While virtually all societies have elements of common ownership, societies have existed where common ownership extended to essentially all possessions. Another term for this arrangement is a "gift economy" or communalism. Many nomadic societies effectively practiced common ownership of land.

Common Ownership in Capitalist Economies

Common ownership is practised by large numbers of voluntary associations and non-profit organizations as well as implicitly by all public bodies. Most co-operatives have some element of common ownership, but some part of their capital may be individually owned.

Marxist Theory

Many socialist movements advocate the common ownership of the means of production by all of society as an eventual goal to be achieved through the development of the productive forces, although many socialists classify socialism as public-ownership of the means of production, reserving common ownership for what Karl Marx termed "upper-stage communism". From a Marxist analysis, a society based on a superabundance of goods and common ownership of the means of production would be devoid of classes based on ownership of productive property.

Common ownership in a hypothetical communist society is distinguished from primitive forms of common property that have existed throughout history, such as Communalism and primitive communism, in that communist common ownership is the outcome of social and technological developments leading to the elimination of material scarcity in society.

From 1918 until 1995 the common ownership of the means of production, distribution and exchange was cited in Clause IV of its constitution as a goal of the British Labour Party and was quoted on the back of its membership cards. The clause read:

> "To secure for the workers by hand or by brain the full fruits of their industry and the most equitable distribution thereof that may be possible upon the basis of the common ownership of the means of production, distribution and exchange, and the best obtainable system of popular administration and control of each industry or service".

Criticism

Neoclassical economic theory analyzes common ownership using contract theory. According to the incomplete contracting approach pioneered by Oliver Hart and his co-authors, ownership matters because the owner of an asset has residual control rights. This means that the owner can decide what to do with the asset in every contingency not covered by a contract. In particular, an owner has stronger incentives to make relationship-specific investments than a non-owner, so ownership can ameliorate the so-called hold-up problem. As a result, ownership is a scarce resource that should not be wasted. In particular, a central result of the property rights approach says that joint ownership is suboptimal. If we start in a situation with joint ownership (where each party has veto power over the use of the asset) and move to a situation in which there is a single owner, the investment incentives of the new owner are improved while the investment incentives of the other parties remain the same. However, in the basic incomplete contracting framework the sub-optimality of joint ownership holds only if the investments are in human capital while joint ownership can be optimal if the investments are in physical capital. Recently, several authors have shown that joint ownership can actually be optimal even if investments are in human capital. In particular, joint ownership can be optimal if the parties are asymmetrically informed, if there is a long-term relationship between the parties, or if the parties have know-how that they may disclose.

Socialist State

A socialist state, socialist republic, or socialist country, sometimes referred to as a workers' state or workers' republic, is a sovereign state constitutionally dedicated to the establishment of socialism. The term communist state is often used interchangeably in the West specifically when referring to one-party socialist states governed by Marxist–Leninist communist parties, despite these countries being officially socialist states in the process of building socialism. These countries never describe themselves as communist nor as having implemented a communist society. Additionally, a number of countries that are multi-party capitalist states make references to socialism in their constitutions, in most cases alluding to the building of a socialist society, naming socialism, claiming to be a socialist state, or including the term socialist republic or people's republic in their country's full name, although this does not necessarily reflect the structure and development paths of these countries' political and economic systems. Currently, these countries include Algeria, Bangladesh, Guyana, India, Nepal, Nicaragua, North Korea, Portugal, Sri Lanka and Tanzania.

The idea of a socialist state stems from the broader notion of state socialism, the political perspective that the working class needs to use state power and government policy to establish a socialist economic system. However, the concept of a socialist state is mainly advocated by Marxist–Leninists and most socialist states have been established by political parties adhering to Marxism–Leninism or some national variation thereof such as Maoism or Titoism. A state, whether socialist or not, is most opposed by anarchists, who reject the idea that the state can be used to establish a socialist society due to its hierarchical and arguably coercive nature, considering a socialist state or state socialism as an oxymoron. The concept of a socialist state is considered unnecessary or counterproductive and rejected also by some classical, libertarian and orthodox Marxists, libertarian socialists and other socialist political thinkers who view the modern state as a byproduct of capitalism which would have no function in a socialist system.

A socialist state is to be distinguished from a multi-party liberal democracy governed by a self-described socialist party, where the state is not constitutionally bound to the construction of socialism. In such cases, the political system and machinery of government is not specifically structured to pursue the development of socialism. Socialist states in the Marxist–Leninist sense are sovereign states under the control of a vanguard party which is organizing the country's economic, political and social development toward the realization of socialism. Economically this involves the development of a state capitalist economy with state-directed capital accumulation with the long-term goal of building up the country's productive forces while simultaneously promoting worldwide socialist revolution.

The first socialist state was the Russian Socialist Federative Soviet Republic, established in 1917. In 1922, it merged with the Byelorussian Soviet Socialist Republic, the

Transcaucasian Soviet Federal Socialist Republic and the Ukrainian Soviet Socialist Republic into a single federal union called the Union of Soviet Socialist Republics (USSR). The Soviet Union proclaimed itself a socialist state and proclaimed its commitment to building a socialist economy in its 1936 constitution and a subsequent 1977 constitution. It was governed by the Communist Party of the Soviet Union as a single-party state ostensibly with a democratic centralism organization, with Marxism–Leninism remaining its official guiding ideology until the Soviet Union's dissolution on 26 December 1991. The political systems of these Marxist–Leninist socialist states revolve around the central role of the party which holds ultimate authority. Internally, the communist party practices a form of democracy called democratic centralism. During the 22nd Congress of the Communist Party of the Soviet Union in 1961, Nikita Khrushchev announced the completion of socialist construction and declared the optimistic goal of achieving communism in twenty years. The Eastern Bloc was a political and economic bloc of Soviet-aligned socialist states in Eastern and Central Europe which adhered to Marxism–Leninism, Soviet-style governance and command economy.

The People's Republic of China was founded on 1 October 1949 and proclaims itself to be a socialist state in its 1982 constitution. The Democratic People's Republic of Korea (North Korea) used to be a Marxist–Leninist state. In 1972, the country adopted a new constitution which changed the official state ideology to *Juche* which is held to be a distinct Korean re-interpretation of the former ideology. Similarly in the Lao People's Democratic Republic, direct references to communism are not included in its founding documents, although it gives direct power to the governing ruling party, the Marxist–Leninist Lao People's Revolutionary Party. The preamble to the constitution of the Socialist Republic of Vietnam states that Vietnam only entered a transition stage between capitalism and socialism after the country was re-unified under the Communist Party of Vietnam in 1976.

The 1992 constitution of the Republic of Cuba states that the role of the Communist Party of Cuba is to "guide the common effort toward the goals and construction of socialism (and the progress toward a communist society)".

Because most existing socialist states operated along Marxist–Leninist principles of governance, the term Marxist–Leninist state or Marxist–Leninist regime is also used by scholars, particularly when focusing on the political systems of these countries. A people's republic is a type of socialist state with a republican constitution. Although the term initially became associated with populist movements in the 19th century such as the German Völkisch movement and the Narodniks in Russia, it is now associated to communist states. A number of the short-lived communist states which formed during World War I and its aftermath called themselves people's republics. Many of these sprang up in the territory of the former Russian Empire following the October Revolution. Additional people's republics emerged following the Allied victory in World War II, mainly within the Eastern Bloc. In Asia, China became a people's republic following the Chinese Communist Revolution and North Korea also became a people's republic. During the 1960s, Romania and Yugoslavia ceased to use the term people's republic in their official name, replacing it with the term socialist republic as a mark of their ongoing political development. Czechoslovakia also added the term socialist republic into its name during this period. It had become a people's republic in 1948, but the country had not used that term in its official name. Albania used both terms in its official name from 1976 to 1991.

The term socialist state is widely used by Marxist–Leninist parties, theorists and governments to mean a state under the control of a vanguard party that is organizing the economic, social and political affairs of said state toward the construction of socialism. States run by communist parties that adhere to Marxism–Leninism, or some national variation thereof, refer to themselves as socialist states or workers and pesants' states. They involve the direction of economic development toward the building up of the productive forces to underpin the establishment of a socialist economy and usually include that at least the commanding heights of the economy are nationalized and under state ownership. This may or may not include the existence of a socialist economy, depending on the specific terminology adopted and level of development in specific countries. For example, the Leninist definition of a socialist state is a state representing the interests of the working class which presides over a state capitalist economy structured upon state-directed accumulation of capital, with the goal of building up the country's productive forces and promoting worldwide socialist revolution, with the realization of a socialist economy as the long-term goal.

In the Western world, particularly in mass media, journalism and politics, these states and countries are often called communist states (although they do not use this term to refer to themselves), despite the fact that these countries never claimed to have achieved communism in their countries—rather, they claim to be building and working toward the establishment of socialism and the development towards communism thereafter in their countries. Terms used by communist states include national-democratic, people's democratic, socialist-oriented and workers and peasants' state.

Constitutional References to Socialism

A number of countries make reference to socialism in their constitutions that are not single-party states embracing Marxism–Leninism and planned economies. In most cases, these are constitutional references to the building of a socialist society and political principles that have little to no bearing on the structure and guidance of these country's machinery of government and economic system. The preamble to the 1976 Constitution of Portugal states that the Portuguese state has as one of its goals opening "the way to socialist society". Algeria, the Congo, India and Sri Lanka have directly used the term socialist in their official constitution and name. Croatia, Hungary and Poland directly denounce "Communism" in their founding documents in reference to their past regimes.

In these cases, the intended meaning of socialism can vary widely and sometimes the constitutional references to socialism are left over from a previous period in the country's history. In the case of many Middle Eastern states, the term socialism was often used in reference to an Arab socialist/nationalist philosophy adopted by specific regimes such as that of Gamal Abdel Nasser and that of the various Ba'ath parties. Examples of countries directly using the term socialist in their names include the Democratic Socialist Republic of Sri Lanka and the Socialist Republic of Vietnam while a number of countries make references to socialism in their constitutions, but not in their names. These include India and Portugal. In addition, countries like Belarus, Colombia, France, Russia and Spain use the varied term social state, leaving a more ambiguous meaning. In the constitutions of Croatia, Hungary and Poland, direct condemnation is made to the respective past socialist regimes. The autonomous region of Rojava which operates under the principles of democratic confederalism has been described as a socialist state.

Other Uses

During the post-war consensus, nationalization of large industries was relatively widespread and it was not uncommon for commentators to describe some European countries as democratic socialist states seeking to move their countries toward a socialist economy. In 1956, leading British Labour Party politician and author Anthony Crosland claimed that capitalism had been abolished in Britain, although others such as Welshman Aneurin Bevan, Minister of Health in the first post-war Labour government and the architect of the National Health Service, disputed the claim that Britain was a socialist state. For Crosland and others who supported his views, Britain was a socialist state. According to Bevan, Britain had a socialist National Health Service which stood in opposition to the hedonism of Britain's capitalist society, arguing:

> "The National Health service and the Welfare State have come to be used as interchangeable terms, and in the mouths of some people as terms of reproach. Why this is so it is not difficult to understand, if you view everything from the angle of a strictly individualistic competitive society. A free health service is pure Socialism and as such it is opposed to the hedonism of capitalist society".

When the British Labour Party or the French Socialist Party were in power during the post-war period, some political commentators claimed that France and the United Kingdom were socialist states and the same is now applied to the Nordic countries and the Nordic model, although as in the rest of Europe the laws of capitalism still operated fully and private enterprise dominated the economy. In the 1980s, the government of President François Mitterrand aimed to expand dirigisme and attempted to nationalize all French banks, but this attempt faced opposition of the European Economic Community because it demanded a free-market capitalist economy among its members. Nevertheless, public ownership in France and the United Kingdom during the height of nationalization in the 1960s and 1970s never accounted for more than 15–20% of capital formation, further dropping to 8% in the 1980s and below 5% in the 1990s after the rise of neoliberalism.

The socialist policies practized by parties such as the Singaporean People's Action Party (PAP) during its first few decades in power were of a pragmatic kind as characterized by its rejection of nationalization. Despite this, the PAP still claimed to be a socialist party, pointing out its regulation of the private sector, state intervention in the economy and social policies as evidence of this. The Singaporean prime minister Lee Kuan Yew also stated that he has been influenced by the democratic socialist British Labour Party.

Political Theories

Marxist Theory of the State

Karl Marx and subsequent thinkers in the Marxist tradition conceive of the state as representing the interests of the ruling class, partially out of material necessity for the smooth operation of the modes of production it presides over. Marxists trace the formation of the contemporary form of the sovereign state to the emergence of capitalism as a dominant mode of production, with its organizational precepts and functions designed specifically to manage and regulate the affairs of a capitalist economy. Because this involves governance and laws passed in the interest of the bourgeoisie as a whole and because government officials either come from the bourgeoisie or are dependent upon their interests, Marx characterized the capitalist state as a dictatorship of the bourgeoisie. Extrapolating from this, Marx described a post-revolutionary government on the part of the working class or proletariat as a dictatorship of the proletariat because the economic interests of the proletariat would have to guide state affairs and policy during a transitional state. Alluding further to the establishment of a socialist and communist economy where social ownership displaces private ownership, and thus class distinctions on the basis of private property ownership are eliminated, the modern state would have no function and would gradually "whither away" or be transformed into a new form of governance.

Influenced by the pre-Marxist utopian socialist philosopher Henri de Saint-Simon, Friedrich Engels theorized the nature of the state would change during the transition to socialism. Both Saint-Simon and Engels described a transformation of the state from an entity primarily concerned with political rule over people (via coercion and law creation) to a scientific "administration of things" that would be concerned with directing processes of production in a socialist society, essentially ceasing to be a state.

Although Marx never referred to a socialist state, he argued that the working class would have to take control of the state apparatus and machinery of government in order to transition out of capitalism and to socialism. The dictatorship of the proletariat would represent this transitional state and would involve working class interests dominating government policy in the same manner that capitalist class interests dominate government policy under capitalism (the dictatorship of the bourgeoisie). Engels argued that as socialism developed, the state would change in form and function. Under socialism, it is not a "government of people, but the administration of things", thereby ceasing to be a state by the traditional definition.

One of the most influential modern visions of a transitional state representing proletarian interests was based on the Paris Commune in which the workers and working poor took control of the city of Paris in 1871 in reaction to the Franco-Prussian War. Marx described the Paris Commune as the prototype for a revolutionary government of the future, "the form at last discovered" for the emancipation of the proletariat. Engels noted that "all officials, high or low, were paid only the wages received by other workers. In this way an effective barrier to place-hunting and careerism was set up". Commenting on the nature of the state, Engels continued: "From the outset the Commune was compelled to recognize that the working class, once come to power, could not manage with the old state machine". In order not to be overthrown once having conquered power, Engels argues that the working class "must, on the one hand, do away with all the old repressive machinery previously used against it itself, and, on the other, safeguard itself against its own deputies and officials, by declaring them all, without exception, subject to recall at any moment". Engels argued such a state would be a temporary affair and suggested a new generation brought up in "new and free social conditions" will be able to "throw the entire lumber of the state on the scrap-heap".

Reform and Revolution

Socialists that embraced reformism, exemplified by Eduard Bernstein, took the view that both socialism and a socialist state will gradually evolve out of political reforms won in the organized socialist political parties and unions. These views are considered a revision of Marxist thought. Bernstein stated: "The socialist movement is everything to me while what people commonly call the goal of Socialism is nothing". Following Marx, revolutionary socialists instead take the view that the working class grows stronger through its battle for reforms (such as in Marx's time the ten-hours bill). In 1848, Marx and Engels wrote:

> "Now and then the workers are victorious, but only for a time. The real fruit of their battles lies, not in the immediate result, but in the ever expanding union of the workers. It ever rises up again, stronger, firmer, mightier. It compels legislative recognition of particular interests of the workers, by taking advantage of the divisions among the bourgeoisie itself. Thus, the ten-hours' bill in England was carried".

According to the orthodox Marxist conception, these battles eventually reach a point where a revolutionary movement arises. A revolutionary movement is required in the view of Marxists to sweep away the capitalist state and the dictatorship of the bourgeoisie which must be abolished and replaced with a dictatorship of the proletariat in order to begin constructing a socialist society. In this view, only through revolution can a socialist state be established as written in *The Communist Manifesto*:

> "In depicting the most general phases of the development of the proletariat, we traced the more or less veiled civil war, raging within existing society, up to the point where that war breaks out into open revolution, and where the violent overthrow of the bourgeoisie lays the foundation for the sway of the proletariat".

Marxist–Leninism Theory

Leninism

Whereas Marx, Engels and classical Marxist thinkers had little to say about the organization of the state in a socialist society, presuming the modern state to be specific to the capitalist mode of production, Vladimir Lenin pioneered the idea of a revolutionary state based on his theory of the revolutionary vanguard party and organizational principles of democratic centralism. Adapted to the conditions of semi-feudal Russia, Lenin's concept of the dictatorship of the proletariat involved a revolutionary vanguard party acting as representatives of the proletariat and its interests. According to Lenin's April Theses, the goal of the revolution and vanguard party is not the introduction of socialism (it could only be established on a worldwide scale), but to bring production and the state under the control of the soviets of workers' deputies. Following the October Revolution in Russia, the Bolsheviks consolidated their power and sought to control and direct the social and economic affairs of the state and broader Russian society in order to safeguard against counterrevolutionary insurrection, foreign invasion and to promote socialist consciousness among the Russian population while simultaneously promoting economic development.

These ideas were adopted by Lenin in 1917 just prior to the October Revolution in Russia and published in *The State and Revolution*. With the failure of the worldwide revolution, or at least European revolution, envisaged by Lenin and Leon Trotsky, the Russian Civil War and finally Lenin's death, war measures that were deemed to be temporary such as forced requisition of food and the lack of democratic control became permanent and a tool to boost Joseph Stalin's power, leading to the emergence of Marxism–Leninism and Stalinism as well as the notion that socialism can be created and exist in a single state.

Lenin argued that as socialism is replaced by communism, the state would "wither away" as strong centralized control progressively reduces as local communities gain more empowerment. As he put succinctly, "so long as the state exists there is no freedom. When there will be freedom, there will be no state".

Trotskyism

Following Stalin's consolidation of power in the Soviet Union and centralization of political power, Trotsky condemned the Soviet government's policies for lacking widespread democratic participation on the part of the population and for suppressing workers' democratic participation in the management of the economy. Because these authoritarian political measures were inconsistent with the organizational precepts of socialism, Trotsky characterized the Soviet Union as a deformed workers' state that would not be able to effectively transition to socialism. Ostensibly socialist states where democracy is lacking, yet the economy is largely in the hands of the state, are termed by orthodox Trotskyist theories as workers' states and not socialist states, using the terms degenerated or deformed workers' states.

Controversy

Anarchism and Marxism

Many democratic and libertarian socialists, including anarchists, mutualists and syndicalists, criticize the concept of socialist state instead of abolishing the bourgeois state apparatus outright. They use the term state socialism in contrast with their own form of socialism which involves either collective ownership (in the form of worker cooperatives) or common ownership of the means of production without centralized state planning. Those libertarian socialists believe there is no need for a state in a socialist system because there would be no class to suppress and no need for an institution based on coercion and therefore regard the state being a remnant of capitalism. Most also hold that statism is itself antithetical to true socialism, the goal of which is the eyes of libertarian socialists such as William Morris, who wrote as follows in a *Commonweal* article: "State Socialism? — I don't agree with it; in fact I think the two words contradict one another, and that it is the business of Socialism to destroy the State and put Free Society in its place".

Classical and orthodox Marxists also view state socialism as an oxymoron, arguing that while an association for managing production and economic affairs would exist in socialism, it would no longer be a state in the Marxist definition which is based on domination by one class. Preceding the Bolshevik-led revolution in Russia, many socialist groups—including reformists, orthodox Marxist currents such as council communism and the Mensheviks as well as anarchists and other libertarian socialists—criticized the idea of using the state to conduct planning and nationalization of the means of production as a way to establish socialism. Lenin himself acknowledged his policies as state capitalism.

Critical of the economy and government of socialist states, left communists such as the Italian Amadeo Bordiga said that their socialism was a form of political opportunism which preserved rather than destroyed capitalism because of the claim that the exchange of commodities would occur under socialism; the use of popular front organisations by the Communist International; and that a political vanguard organized by organic centralism was more effective than a vanguard organized by democratic centralism. The American Marxist Raya Dunayevskaya also dismissed it as a type of state capitalism because state ownership of the means of production is a form of state capitalism; the dictatorship of the proletariat is a form of democracy and single-party rule is undemocratic; and Marxism–Leninism is neither Marxism nor Leninism, but rather a composite ideology which socialist leaders like Joseph Stalin used to expediently determine what is communism and what is not communism among the Eastern Bloc countries.

Leninism

Although most Marxist–Leninists distinguish between socialism and communism, Bordiga, who did consider himself a Leninist and has been described as being "more Leninist than Lenin", did not distinguish between the two in the same way Marxist–Leninists do. Both Lenin and Bordiga did not see socialism as a separate mode of production from communism, but rather just as how communism looks as it emerges out of capitalism before it has "developed on its own foundations".

This is coherent with Marx and Engels, who used the terms socialism and communism interchangeably. Like Lenin, Bordiga used socialism to mean what Marx called the lower-phase communism. For Bordiga, both stages of socialist or communist society—with stages referring to historical materialism—were characterized by the gradual absence of money, the market and so on, the difference between them being that earlier in the first stage a system of rationing would be used to allocate goods to people while in communism this could be abandoned in favour of full free access. This view distinguished Bordiga from Marxist–Leninists, who tended and still tend to telescope the first two stages and so have money and the other exchange categories surviving into socialism, but Bordiga would have none of this. For him, no society in which money, buying and selling and the rest survived could be regarded as either socialist or communist—these exchange categories would die out before the socialist rather than the communist stage was reached. Stalin made the claim that the Soviet Union had reached the lower stage of communism and argued that the law of value still operated within a socialist economy.

Marx himself did not use the term socialism to refer to this development and instead called it a communist society that has not yet reached its higher-stage. The term socialism to mean the lower-state of communism was popularized during the Russian Revolution by Lenin. This view is consistent with and helped to inform early concepts of socialism in which the law of value no longer directs economic activity, namely that monetary relations in the form of exchange-value, profit, interest and wage labour would not operate and apply to Marxist socialism. Unlike Stalin, who first claimed to have achieved socialism with the Soviet Constitution of 1936 and then confirmed it in the *Economic Problems of Socialism in the USSR*, Lenin did not call the Soviet Union a socialist state, nor did he claim that it had achieved socialism. He adopted state capitalist policies, defending them from left-wing criticism, but arguing that they were necessary for the future development of socialism and not socialist in themselves. On seeing the Soviet Union's growing coercive power, Lenin was quoted as saying that Russia had reverted to "a bourgeois tsarist machine barely varnished with socialism".

Libertarian Socialism

A variety of non-state, libertarian communist and socialist positions reject the concept of a socialist state altogether, believing that the modern state is a byproduct of capitalism and cannot be used for the establishment of a socialist system. They reason that a socialist state is antithetical to socialism and that socialism will emerge spontaneously from the grassroots level in an evolutionary manner, developing its own unique political and economic institutions for a highly organized stateless society. Libertarian communists, including anarchists, councillists, leftists and Marxists, also reject the concept of a socialist state for being antithetical to socialism, but they believe that socialism and communism can only be established through revolution and dissolving the existence of the state. Within the socialist movement, there is criticism towards the use of the term socialist states in relation to countries such as China and previously of Soviet Union and Eastern and Central European states before what some term the "collapse of Stalinism" in 1989.

Anti-authoritarian communists and socialists such as anarchists, other democratic and libertarian socialists as well as revolutionary syndicalists and left communists claim that the so-called socialist states actually presided over state capitalist economies and cannot be called socialist. Those socialists who oppose any system of state control whatsoever believe in a more decentralized approach which puts the means of production directly into the hands of the workers rather than indirectly through state bureaucracies—which they claim represent a new elite or class. This leads them to consider state socialism a form of state capitalism (an economy based on centralized management, capital accumulation and wage labor, but with the state owning the means of production) which Engels stated would be the final form of capitalism rather than socialism.

Trotskyism

Some Trotskyists following on from Tony Cliff deny that it even is socialism, calling it instead state capitalism. Other Trotskyists agree that these states could not be described as socialist, but deny that they were state capitalist. They support Leon Trotsky's analysis of pre-restoration Soviet Union as a workers' state that had degenerated into a bureaucratic dictatorship which rested on a largely nationalized industry run according to a production plan and claimed that the former Stalinist states of Central and Eastern Europe were deformed workers' states based on the same relations of production as the Soviet Union.

Socialist Market Economy

The socialist market economy (SME) is the economic system and model of economic development employed in the People's Republic of China. The system is based on the predominance of public ownership and state-owned enterprises within a market economy. The term "socialist market economy" was introduced by Jiang Zemin during the 14th National Congress of the Communist Party of China in 1992 to describe the goal of China's economic reforms. Originating in the Chinese economic reforms initiated in 1978 that integrated China into the global market economy, the socialist market economy represents a preliminary or "primary stage" of developing socialism. Despite this, many Western commentators have described the system as a form of state capitalism.

The economic reform toward a socialist market economy is underpinned by the Marxist framework of historical materialism. In the late 1970s, then-Chairman Deng Xiaoping and the Communist Party leadership rejected the prior Maoist emphasis on culture and political agency as the driving forces behind economic progress and started to place a greater emphasis on advancing the material productive forces as the fundamental and necessary prerequisite for building an advanced socialist society. The adoption of market reforms was seen to be consistent with China's level of development and a necessary step in advancing the productive forces of society. This aligned Chinese policy with a more traditional Marxist perspective where a fully developed socialist planned economy can only come into existence after a market economy has exhausted its historical role and gradually transforms itself into a planned economy, nudged by technological advances that make economic planning possible and therefore market relations less necessary.

The socialist market economy is seen by the Communist Party of China as an early stage in the development of socialism (this stage is variously called the "primary" or "preliminary" stage of socialism), where public ownership coexists alongside a diverse range of non-public forms of ownership. The Communist Party of China maintains that despite the co-existence of private capitalists and entrepreneurs with public and collective enterprise, China is not a capitalist country because the party retains control over the direction of the country, maintaining its course of socialist development. Proponents of this economic model distinguish it from market socialism as market socialists believe that economic planning is unattainable, undesirable or ineffective and thus view the market as an integral part of socialism whereas proponents of the socialist market economy view markets as a temporary phase in development of a fully planned economy.

Cui Zhiyuan traces the theoretical foundations of the socialist market economy to James Meade's model of liberal socialism in which the state acts as a residual claimant on the profits generated by state-owned enterprises that are operated independent of government management.

Proponents initially advocated a socialist market economy as a necessary stage for the development of the economy to a point where a planned socialist economy would become possible. Recent Chinese leaders including Xi Jinping have described the building of the "socialist market economy with Chinese characteristics" as the goal without any reference to a post-market socialist economy.

After the Great Leap Forward and the ousting of the Gang of Four from power in 1976, Chairman Deng Xiaoping refocused China's efforts on economic growth and on finding an economic system compatible with China's specific conditions. However, in doing so he remained committed to the Leninist model of centralized political control and a one-party state.

Jiang Zemin originally introduced the term "socialist market economy" in 1992. He had coined the idea so that China could learn the lessons from advanced capitalist countries without needing to discuss if the reforms are "socialist" or "capitalist." Jiang had asked Deng Xiaoping if he had approved of the term, which he did. The Đổi Mới in the Socialist Republic of Vietnam later adopted the concept. Following its implementation, this economic system has supplemented the centrally planned economy in the People's Republic of China, with high growth-rates in GDP during the past decades having been attributed to it. Within this model, privately owned enterprises have become a major component of the economic system alongside the central state-owned enterprises and the collective/township village enterprises.

The transition to a socialist market economy began in 1978 when Deng Xiaoping introduced his program of socialism with Chinese characteristics. Initial reforms in decollectivising agriculture and opening the economy to foreign investment in the late 1970s and early 1980s later led to large-scale radical reforms, including corporatization of the state sector, partial privatisation of some enterprises, liberalisation of trade and prices and dismantling of the "iron rice bowl" system of job security in the late 1990s. With Deng Xiaoping's reforms, China's GDP rose from some US$150 billion in 1978 to more than $1.6 trillion in 2004, with an annual increase of 9.4 percent.

Analysis

Many commentators and scholars have described China's economic system as a form of state capitalism, particularly after the industrial reforms of the 1980s and 1990s, noting that while the Chinese economy maintains a large state sector, the state-owned enterprises operate like private sector firms and retain all profits without remitting them to the government to benefit the entire population. This makes the rationale for widespread public ownership questionable as well as the applicability of the descriptor "socialist" and has led to concern and debate regarding the distribution of state profits.

However, starting in 2017 as part of its state-owned enterprise reform program the central government began to encourage state-owned enterprises to start paying dividends to the government. Other reforms have transferred state-owned assets to social security funds to help finance pensions and the Shenzhen municipal government has proposed using their state-owned enterprises to finance a social dividend-type of system for its residents.

Chinese economist Cui Zhiyuan argues that James Meade's model of liberal socialism is similar to China's socialist market economy and can be used to make sense of the model. Meade's model of market socialism involved public ownership of firms with independent management where the state acted as a residual claimant to the profits generated by its enterprises, but it did not exercise control rights over management and operations of its firms. The benefits of this model are that the state would have a source of income independent of taxation and debt, enabling a reduction of the tax burden on individual incomes and the private sector while promoting greater equality. Cui points to the Chongqing experience with municipal state-owned enterprises enabling high social expenditure alongside low taxes and extremely high rates of growth as validation of the socialist market economy model. The Chongqing model used state enterprise profits to fund public services including housing, providing the main source of public finance enabling it to lower its corporate tax rate (15% compared to the 33% national corporate tax rate) to attract foreign investment.

Market Socialism versus Capitalism

Julan Du and Chenggang Xu analyzed the Chinese model in a 2005 paper to assess whether it represents a type of market socialism or capitalism. They concluded that China's contemporary economic system represents a form of capitalism rather than market socialism because financial markets exist which permit private share ownership—a feature absent in the economic literature on market socialism—and because state profits are retained by enterprises rather than being distributed among the population in a social dividend or similar scheme, which are central features in most models of market socialism. They concluded that China is not a market socialist economy, but it is an unstable form of capitalism.

Another analysis carried out by the Global Studies Association at the DePaul University in 2006 reports that the Chinese economic system does not constitute a form of socialism when socialism is defined as a planned economy where production for use has replaced production for profit as the driving force behind economic activity, or when socialism is defined as a system where the working class is the dominant class which controls the surplus value produced by the economy. The Chinese economy also does not constitute socialism in the sense of widespread self-management or workplace democracy. The study concluded that as of 2006 capitalism is not the dominant mode of organization either and it is instead partially a pre-capitalist agrarian system with almost 50% of its population engaged in agricultural work.

As of 2015, Curtis J. Milhaupt and Wentong Zheng classify China's economic system as state capitalism because the state directs and guides all major aspects of the Chinese economy—including both the state and private sectors—while not collecting dividends from the ownership of its enterprises. They note that Chinese state-owned enterprises and privately owned enterprises share many similarities with respect to state subsidies, proximity to state power and execution of government policy objectives. Within the state sector, the emphasis is more on government control than on the ownership of assets.

Proponents of the socialist market economy compare it to the New Economic Policy in Soviet Russia that introduced market-oriented reforms while maintaining state-ownership of the commanding heights of the economy. The reforms are justified through the belief that changing conditions necessitate new strategies for socialist development.

According to Li Rongrong in 2003, chairman of the State-Owned Assets Supervision and Administration Commission of the State Council, China's socialist economic system is underpinned by the foundational role of public enterprise:

> "Public ownership, as the foundation of the socialist economic system, is a basic force of the state to guide and promote economic and social development and a major guarantee for realising the fundamental interests and the common prosperity of the majority of the people The state owned economy has taken a dominant place in major trades that have a close bearing on the country's economic lifeline and key areas, and has propped-up, guided and brought along the development of the entire socio-economy. The influence and control capacity of SOEs have further increased. State owned economy has played an irreplaceable role in China's socialist modernisation drive".

Other Marxist analyses point out that because the Chinese economic system is based on commodity production, has a role for private capital and disempowers the working class, it represents a capitalist economy. Classical Marxists believe a socialist commodity economy (or a socialist market economy) is contradictory. Other socialists believe the Chinese have embraced many elements of market capitalism, specifically commodity production and privatisation, resulting in a full-blown capitalist economic system. Although many enterprises are nominally publicly owned, the profits are retained by the enterprises and used to pay managers excessively high salaries rather than being distributed amongst the population.

Characteristics

Enterprise and Ownership Types

Public ownership in the socialist market economy consists of state-owned assets, collectively owned enterprises and the publicly owned shares of mixed enterprises. These various forms of public ownership play a dominant role in the socialist market economy alongside substantial private and foreign enterprises.

There are a few major forms of state-owned enterprises in China today:

- State-owned enterprises: commercial enterprises established by either the central government or a local government, where managers are appointed by the government or public bodies. This category only includes wholly state-funded and managed firms. Most state-owned enterprises are not entities of the central government. Central government state-owned enterprises are subunits of the State-owned Assets Supervision and Administration Commission (SASAC).

- State-holding enterprises: state-holding, or state-controlled enterprises, are publicly listed firms where the state owns a large share or a controlling share within the firms, thereby exerting influence on the management of the firm. These include firms that receive foreign direct investment.
- State joint ownership enterprises.

State Sector

The socialist market economy consists of a wide range of state-owned enterprises (SOE) that represent one form of public ownership. Beginning with the 1978 reforms, in the 1980s during the industrial reforms state enterprises were gradually corporatised and transformed into joint-stock corporations with the state retaining either full or majority ownership of their shares. By the early 2000s, most major SOEs in non-strategic sectors were listed on the Shanghai and Hong Kong stock exchanges and some SOEs adopted mixed ownership structures where the central government and various other state entities—including state banks, other SOEs, provincial and local governments—own varying degrees of the firm's listed shares alongside foreign and private shareholders. The result has been a highly diffuse form of public ownership where state-owned enterprises are owned by various different government entities, agencies and other state-owned enterprises. This makes gauging the true size and scope of the state sector difficult, particularly when SOEs with mixed ownership structures are taken into account. In 2013, the public sector accounted for 30% of the number of firms in China, but 55% of assets, 45% of revenue and 40% of profits.

In 1996, China implemented a comprehensive series of industrial reforms termed "Grasping the large, letting go of the small". These reforms involved closing unprofitable state enterprises, merging smaller enterprises and privatization of other small-to-medium enterprises. Centrally owned SOEs were reformed into joint-stock companies with the aim of delegating more authority to SOE managers. SOEs at all levels shifted their primary focus to profitability and shed their social welfare function of providing social services and benefits to their workers in what was known as the "Iron Rice Bowl" system. The State-owned Assets Supervision and Administration Commission (SASAC) was formed in 2003 to oversee the management of the large centrally owned state enterprises.

Modern SOEs are operationally very different from those in the 1990s. SOEs are much larger in size and fewer in number, with central government-owned SOEs clustered in "strategic sectors" including banking, finance, mining, energy, transportation, telecommunications and public utilities. By comparison, provincial and municipal level SOEs number in the thousands and are involved in almost every industry including information technology and automobiles design and production. State sector reform is an ongoing process in China. As of 2017, the Communist Party of China has rejected the Singapore model of Tamasek-style state investment companies for China's SOEs, where SOEs operate solely to maximize profits on a commercial basis. In particular, China maintains that centrally owned SOEs also pursue national and industrial policy objectives. As a result of recent reforms to increase profitability and unload debt, the government reported the profits of central government-owned SOEs rose by 15.2% in 2017.

Despite becoming increasingly profitable, SOEs in China have not paid dividends to the state, causing some analysts question the rationale for public ownership in the first place. As part of SASAC's ongoing reforms, SOEs will now be encouraged and required to pay a higher portion of their profits as dividends to the state, with some state-owned assets being transferred to social security funds to help finance pensions for China's aging population. This is part of a broader reform effort of restructuring the state sector to become a source of finance for public services. As part of the SOE reform goals outlined in 2015 by SASAC, SOEs are to be classified as either commercial or public service entities, with the former being required to distribute a higher proportion of their profits as dividends. Dividend payments are set to rise from 5–15% to 30% by 2020.

Private Sector

Privately owned enterprises (POEs) are recognized as one of the components of the socialist market economy alongside state, collective and individually owned enterprises. The private sector has played an increasingly large role since the adoption of the 1994 Company Law. Additionally, the boundary between public and private enterprises have blurred in China as many publicly listed firms are under mixed ownership by various state and non-state entities. Additionally, private sector firms that operate in industries targeted for growth often receive favorable loans and preferential government treatment while SOEs in non-strategic sectors might be exempt from subsidies. As an example, ZTE Corporation is a majority state-owned enterprise that was forced to rely on equity markets whereas its employee-owned private sector competitor Huawei is viewed as a "national champion" and therefore received major state funding from state banks. Like their state-owned counterparts POEs are expected to follow state policies and are subject to party control, suggesting that the distinction between public and private ownership is not a meaningful distinction to make for understanding China's economic model. As of 2015, state control and state-directed development (in both public and private sectors) is the overriding feature of the Chinese economic system that plays a more substantial role than the public ownership of assets.

While the private sector has been accorded a role in the socialist market economy and has greatly increased in size and scope since the 1990s, the private sector does not dominate the Chinese economy. The exact size of the private sector is difficult determine in part because private enterprises may have a minority of their stock owned by state entities and because of different classification standards used for classifying enterprises. For example, in the first quarter of 2016 the National Bureau of Statistics of China reported fixed investment by private firms at 35% by wholly state-owned SOEs at 27%, with the bulk of the remainder belonging to non-wholly state funded limited liability corporations.

Economic Planning

By the early 1990s, Soviet-type economic planning had been replaced with market relations and markets became the fundamental driving force in the socialist market economy, with the State Planning Commission being reformed into the National Development and Reform Commission in 2003. Indicative planning and industrial policies have substituted material balance planning and play a substantial role in guiding the market economy for both the state and private sectors. The planning system consists of three layers, with each layer using a different planning mechanism.

Compulsory planning is limited to state-owned enterprises operating in strategic sectors, including research, education and infrastructure development plans. Compulsory planning outlines targeted outcomes and the supply of raw materials and financial resources needed. Contractual planning sets objectives and the overall means of achieving these goals and then negotiates with enterprises and local governments to establish detailed objectives and how resources are to be allocated to the targeted sectors. Indicative planning operates at the lowest level of the planning system, where the government outlines industrial targets and then uses market instruments (tax exemptions, subsidies and favorable bank loans) to induce firms in the targeted industry to meet these targets.

Production for Use

Production for use is a phrase referring to the principle of economic organization and production taken as a defining criterion for a socialist economy. It is held in contrast to production for profit. This criterion is used to distinguish socialism from capitalism, and was one of the fundamental defining characteristics of socialism initially shared by Marxian socialists, evolutionary socialists, social anarchists and Christian socialists.

This principle is broad and can refer to an array of different configurations that vary based on the underlying theory of economics employed. In its classic definition, production for use implied an economic system whereby the law of value and law of accumulation no longer directed economic activity, whereby a direct measure of utility and value is used in place of the abstractions of the price system, money, and capital. Alternative conceptions of socialism that don't utilize the profit system such as the Lange model involve the use of a price system and monetary calculation.

The central critique of the capitalist profits system by socialists is that the accumulation of capital ("making money") becomes increasingly detached from the process of producing economic value, leading to waste, inefficiency, and social issues. Essentially, it is a distortion of proper accounting based on the assertion of the law of value instead of the "real" costs of the factors of production, objectively determined outside of social relations.

Proponents of socialism argue that production for profit (i.e., capitalism) does not always satisfy the economic needs of people, especially the working-class, because capital only invests in production when it is profitable. This fails to satisfy demand, that is the needs of people who lack basic necessities but have insufficient purchasing power to acquire these needs in a manner that would be profitable for businesses. This results in a number of inefficiencies: unsold items are rarely given away to people who need but can't afford them, unemployed workers are not utilized to produce such services, and resources are expended on occupations that serve no other purpose than to support the accumulation of profit instead of being utilized to provide useful goods and services. For example, the United States housing bubble resulted in an overproduction of housing units that could not be sold at a profit, despite there being sufficient demand and need for housing units.

Production for use in some form was the historically dominant modality until the initial primitive accumulation of capital.

Economic planning is not synonymous with production for use. Planning is essential in modern globalised production both within enterprises and within nation states. Planning to maximize profitability (i.e., within industries and private corporations) or to improve the efficiency of capital accumulation in the capitalist macro-economy (i.e. monetary policy, fiscal policy and industrial policy) does not change the fundamental criteria and need to generate a financial profit to be reinvested into the economy, lest it go into a crisis. A more recent critique of production for profit is that it fails spectacularly to address issues such as externalities which the board and management of a for profit enterprise are often under a fiduciary responsibility to ignore if they harm or conflict with the shareholders' profit motives.

Criticisms of Production for Profit

Some socialists suggest a number of irrational outcomes occur from capitalism and the need to accumulate capital when capitalist economies reach a point in development whereby investment accumulates at a greater rate than growth of profitable investment opportunities. The central socialist critique of the profits system is that the accumulation of capital becomes further detached from the process of producing economic value, leading to waste, inefficiency and underlying social issues.

Advertisement and planned obsolescence are strategies used by businesses to generate demand for the continual consumption required for capitalism to sustain itself, so that instead of satisfying social and individual needs, capitalism first and foremost serves the artificial need for the accumulation of capital.

The creation of industries, projects and services comes about for no other purpose than generating profit, economic growth or maintaining employment. The drive to create such industries arises from the need to absorb the savings in the economy, and thus, to maintain the accumulation of capital. This can take the form of corporatization and commercialization of public services, i.e., transforming them into profit-generating industries to absorb investment, or the creation and expansion of sectors of the economy that do not produce any economic value by themselves because they deal only with exchange-related activities, sectors such as financial services. This can contribute to the formation of economic bubbles, crises and recessions.

For socialists, the solution to these problems entails a reorientation of the economic system from production for profit and the need to accumulate capital to a system where production is adjusted to meet individual and social demands directly.

Criticisms of Central Planning

Socialist and non-socialist opponents of the Soviet model of economic planning have criticized the Soviet centralized model of a planned economy on similar grounds to the critique leveled against capitalism as production was often undertaken in order to fulfill plan targets as opposed to being produced for use.

Contrasted with State Capitalism

As an objective criterion for socialism, production for use can be used to evaluate the socialistic content of the composition of former and existing economic systems. For example, an economic system that is dominated by nationalized firms organized around the production of profit, whether this profit is retained by the firm or paid to the government as a dividend payment, would be a state capitalist economy. In such a system, the organizational structure of the firm remains similar to a private-sector firm; non-financial costs are externalized because profitability is the criterion for production, so that the majority of the economy remains essentially capitalist despite the formal title of public ownership. This has led many socialists to categorize the current Chinese economic system as a capitalist or state-capitalist economy.

The economy of the Soviet Union was based upon capital accumulation for reinvestment and production for profit; the difference between it and Western capitalism was that the Soviet Union achieved this through nationalized industry and state-directed investment, with the eventual goal of building a socialist society based upon production for use and self-management. Vladimir Lenin described the Soviet economy as "state-monopoly capitalism" and did not consider it to be socialism. During the 1965 Liberman Reforms, the Soviet Union re-introduced profitability as a criterion for industrial enterprises. Other views argue the Soviet Union evolved into a non-capitalist and non-socialist system characterized by control and subordination of society by party and government officials who coordinated the economy; this can be called bureaucratic collectivism.

Contrary Socialist Theories

The concept of production for use has been rejected by some socialists, most notably proponents of market socialism, who argue that socially held enterprises can compete with each other and generate profit in a market economy, with or without addressing the issue of distribution of this profit. Neoclassical economists argue that, under conditions of Pareto optimality, the pursuit of profit leads to a satisfaction of economic demands (the provision of use-values) and that market socialism would be able to achieve this outcome while retaining profitability as the operational criteria for socialist enterprises. In particular, some market socialists justify their position by claiming that society as a whole would control the surplus product (the profit generated by publicly owned firms), which could be used to finance public goods or public investment as opposed to accumulating in the hands of capitalists and shareholders.

Many social democrats currently reject this concept altogether and wish to retain the capitalist economic system by promoting a welfare state and economic interventions in order to make capitalism more "equitable" without questioning the legitimacy of the profits system.

Production for use refers to an arrangement whereby the production of goods and services is carried out *ex ante* (directly) for their utility (also called "use-value"). The implication is that the value of economic output would be based on use-value or a direct measure of utility as opposed to exchange-value; because economic activity would be undertaken to directly satisfy economic demands and human needs, the productive apparatus would directly serve individual and social needs. This is contrasted with production for exchange of the produced good or service in order to profit, where production is subjected to the perpetual accumulation of capital, a condition where production is only undertaken if it generates profit, implying an *ex post* or indirect means of satisfying economic demand. The profits system is oriented toward generating a profit to be reinvested into the economy (and the constant continuation of this process), the result being that society is structured around the need for a perpetual accumulation of capital. In contrast, production for use means that the accumulation of capital is not a compulsory driving force in the economy, and by extension, the core process which society and culture revolves around. Production for profit, in contrast, is the dominant mode of production in the modern world system, equivocates "profitability" and "productivity" and presumes that the former always equates to the latter.

Some thinkers, including the Austrian philosopher and political economist Otto Neurath, have used the phrase "socialization" to refer to the same concept of "production for use". In Neurath's phraseology, "total socialization" involves calculation in kind in place of financial calculation and a system of planning in place of market-based allocation of economic goods. Alternative conceptions exist in the form of market socialism.

Usage

- Karl Marx referred to the "production of use-values" as a feature of any economic mode of production, but characterized capitalism as a mode of production that subjugated the production of use-value for the self-expansion of capital (i.e., capital accumulation or production for profit). In contrast, socialism was vaguely defined as a system based on the direct production of use-value free of the process of continuous capital accumulation.
- Eugene V. Debs popularly used the phrase when running for president of the United States in 1912, stating that capitalism is founded upon production for profit, and in contrast, socialism is postulated upon production for use.
- Norman Thomas, a presidential candidate in the United States for the Socialist Party of America in the six elections from 1928 to 1948, contrasted socialism with capitalism by stating that socialism is based on production for use and an end to the profit system.
- Friedrich Hayek defined socialism as "the common ownership of the means of production and their 'employment for use, not for profit'", associating the rise of the welfare state by social democrats in post-World War II Europe as a rejection of socialism in the technical sense.

Social Production and Peer-to-peer Processes

Michel Bauwens identifies the emergence of the open software movement and peer-to-peer production as an emergent alternative mode of production to the capitalist economy that is based on collaborative self-management, common ownership of resources, and the (direct) production of use-values through the free cooperation of producers who have access to distributed capital.

Commons-based peer production generally involves developers who produce goods and services with no aim to profit directly, but freely contribute to a project relying upon an open common pool of resources and software code. In both cases, production is carried out directly for use - software is produced solely for their use-value.

Valuation and Calculation

Multiple forms of valuation have been proposed to govern production in a socialist economy, to serve as a unit of account and to quantify the usefulness of an object in socialism. These include valuations based on labor-time, the expenditure of energy in production, or disaggregated units of physical quantities.

Physical Quantities

The classic formulation of socialism involved replacing the criteria of value from money (exchange-value) to physical utility (use-value), to be quantified in terms of physical quantities (Calculation in kind and Input-Output analysis) or some natural unit of accounting, such as energy accounting.

Input-output model analysis is based upon directly determining the physical quantities of goods and services to be produced and allocating economic inputs accordingly; thus production targets are pre-planned. Soviet economic planning was overwhelmingly focused on material balances - balancing the supply of economic inputs with planned output targets.

Marginal Cost

Oskar Lange formulated a mechanism for the direct allocation of capital goods in a socialist economy that was based on the marginal cost of production. Under a capitalist economy, managers of firms are ordered and legally required to base production around profitability, and in theory, competitive pressure creates a downward pressure on profits and forces private businesses to be responsive to demands of consumers, indirectly approximating production for use. In the Lange Model, the firms would be publicly owned and the managers would be tasked with setting the price of output to its marginal cost, thereby achieving pareto efficiency through direct allocation.

Cybernetics

Cybernetics, the use of computers to coordinate production in an optimal fashion, has been suggested for socialist economies. Oskar Lange, rejecting his earlier proposals for market socialism, argued that the computer is more efficient than the market process at solving the multitude of simultaneous equations required for allocating economic inputs efficiently (either in terms of physical quantities or monetary prices).

Salvador Allende's socialist-led government developed Project Cybersyn, a form of decentralized economic planning though the experimental computer-led viable system model of computed organisational structure of autonomous operative units though an algedonic feedback setting and bottom-up participative decision-making by the Cyberfolk component. The project was disbanded after the 1973 Chilean coup d'état.

Free Market

Based on the perspective that the law of value would continue to operate in a socialist economy, it is argued that a market economy purged of parasitical and wasteful elements in the form of private ownership of the means of production and the distortions that arise from the concentration of power and wealth in a class of capitalists would enable the market to operate efficiently without distortions. Simply replacing the antagonistic interests between capitalists and workers in enterprises would alter the orientation of the economy from private profit to meeting the demands of the community as firms would seek to maximize the benefits to the member-workers, who would as a whole comprise society. Cooperative economist Jaroslav Vanek suggests that worker self-management and cooperative ownership of enterprises operating in a free-market would allow for a genuine free-market economy free of the market-distorting, monopolistic tendencies and antagonistic interests that emerge from private ownership over production.

Social Ownership

Social ownership is any of various forms of ownership for the means of production in socialist economic systems, encompassing public ownership, employee ownership, cooperative ownership, citizen ownership of equity, common ownership and collective ownership. Historically social ownership implied that capital and factor markets would cease to exist under the assumption that market exchanges within the production process would be made redundant if capital goods were owned by a single entity or network of entities representing society, but the articulation of models of market socialism where factor markets are utilized for allocating capital goods between socially owned enterprises broadened the definition to include autonomous entities within a market economy. Social ownership of the means of production is the common defining characteristic of all the various forms of socialism.

The two major forms of social ownership are society-wide public ownership and cooperative ownership. The distinction between these two forms lies in the distribution of the surplus product. With society-wide public ownership, the surplus is distributed to all members of the public through a social dividend, whereas with co-operative ownership the economic surplus of an enterprise is controlled by all the worker-members of that specific enterprise.

The goal of social ownership is to eliminate the distinction between the class of private owners who are the recipients of passive property income and workers who are the recipients of labor income (wages, salaries and commissions), so that the surplus product (or economic profits in the case of market socialism) belong either to society as a whole or to the members of a given enterprise. Social ownership would enable productivity gains from labor automation to progressively reduce the average length of the working day instead of creating job insecurity and unemployment. Reduction of necessary work time is central to the Marxist concept of human freedom and overcoming alienation, a concept widely shared by Marxist and non-Marxist socialists alike.

The term "socialization" refers to the process of restructuring the economic framework, organizational structure and institutions of an economy on a socialist basis. The comprehensive notion of socialization and the public ownership form of social ownership implies an end to the operation of the laws of capitalism, capital accumulation and the use of money and financial valuation in the production process, along with a restructuring of workplace-level organization.

Objectives

Social ownership is variously advocated to end the Marxian concept of exploitation, to ensure that income distribution reflects individual contributions to the social product, to eliminate unemployment arising from technological change, to ensure a more egalitarian distribution of the economy's surplus, or to create the foundations for a non-market socialist economy.

In Karl Marx's analysis of capitalism, social ownership of the means of production emerges in response to the contradictions between socialized production and private appropriation of surplus value in capitalism. Marx argued that productivity gains arising from the substitution of variable capital (labor inputs) for constant capital (capital inputs) would cause labor displacement to outstrip the demand for labor. This process would lead to stagnant wages and rising unemployment for the working class alongside rising property income for the capitalist class, further leading to an over-accumulation of capital. Marx argued that this dynamic would reach a point where social ownership of the highly automated means of production would be necessitated to resolve this contradiction and resulting social strife. Thus the Marxist case for social ownership and socialism is not based on any moral critique of the distribution of property income (wealth) in capitalism, but rather the Marxist case for socialism is based on a systematic analysis of the development and limits of the dynamic of capital accumulation.

For Marx, social ownership would lay the foundations for the transcendence of the capitalist law of value and the accumulation of capital, thereby creating the foundation for socialist planning. The ultimate goal of social ownership of productive property for Marx was to expand the "realm of freedom" by shortening average work hours so that individuals would have progressively larger portion of their time to pursue their genuine and creative interests. Thus the end goal of social ownership is the transcendence of the Marxist concept of alienation.

The economist David McMullen identifies five major benefits of social ownership, where he defines it as society-wide ownership of productive property: first, workers would be more productive and have greater motivation since they would directly benefit from increased productivity, secondly this ownership stake would enable greater accountability on the part of individuals and organizations, thirdly social ownership would eliminate unemployment, fourth it would enable the better flow of information within the economy, and finally it would eliminate wasteful activities associated with "wheeling and dealing" and wasteful government activities intended to curb such behavior and deal with unemployment.

From a non-Marxist, market socialist perspective, the clearest benefit of social ownership is an equalization of the distribution of property income, eliminating the vast disparities in wealth that arise from private ownership under capitalism. Property income (profit, interest and rent) is distinguished from labor income (wages and salaries) which in a socialist system would continue to be unequal based on one's marginal product of labor – social ownership would only equalize passive property income.

Notable non-Marxist and Marxist socialist theorists alike have argued that the most significant argument for social ownership of the means of production is to enable productivity gains to ease the work burden for all individuals in society, resulting in progressively shorter hours of work with increasing automation and thus a greater amount of free time for individuals to engage in creative pursuits and leisure.

Criticism of Private Ownership

Social ownership is contrasted with the concept of private ownership of the means of production, promoted as a solution to what its proponents see as being inherent issues to private ownership. Market socialists and non-market socialists therefore have slightly different conceptions of social ownership. The former believe that private ownership and private appropriation of property income is the fundamental issue with capitalism, and thus believe that the process of capital accumulation and profit-maximizing enterprise can be retained, with their profits being used to benefit society in the form of a social dividend. By contrast, non-market socialists argue that the major problems with capitalism arise from its contradictory economic laws that make it unsustainable and historically limited. Therefore, social ownership is seen as a component of the establishment of non-market coordination and alternative "socialist laws of motion" that overcome the systemic issues of capital accumulation.

The socialist critique of private ownership is heavily influenced by the Marxian analysis of capitalist property forms as part of its broader critique of alienation and exploitation in capitalism. Although there is considerable disagreement among socialists about the validity of certain aspects of Marxian analysis, the majority of socialists are sympathetic to Marx's views on exploitation and alienation. Socialists critique the private appropriation of property income on the grounds that because such income does not correspond to a return on any productive activity and is generated by the working class, it represents exploitation. The property-owning (capitalist) class lives off passive property income produced by the working population by virtue of their claim to ownership in the form of stock, bonds or private equity. This exploitative arrangement is perpetuated due to the structure of capitalist society. From this perspective, capitalism is regarded as class system akin to historical class systems like slavery and feudalism.

Private ownership has also been criticized on ethical grounds by the economist James Yunker. Yunker argues that because passive property income requires no mental or physical exertion on the part of the recipient and because its appropriation by a small group of private owners is the source of the vast inequalities in contemporary capitalism, this establishes the ethical case for social ownership and socialist transformation.

Socialization as a Process

Socialization is conceived as a process that transforms the economic processes and, by extension, the social relations within an economy. As such, it is distinct from the process of "nationalization" which does not necessarily imply a transformation of the organizational structure of organizations or the transformation of the economic framework under which economic organizations operate.

Marxists envision socialization as a restructuring of social relations to overcome alienation, replacing hierarchical social relations within the workplace with an association of members.

Socialization Debates

During the 1920s, socialists in Austria and Germany were engaged in a comprehensive dialogue about the nature of socialization and how a program of socialization could be effectively carried out. Austrian scientific thinkers whose ideas were based on Ernst Mach's empiricist notion of energy and technological optimism, including Josef Popper-Lynkeus and Carl Ballod, proposed plans for rational allocation of exhaustible energy and materials through statistical empirical methods. This conception of non-capitalist calculation involved the use of energy and time units, the latter being viewed as the standard cardinal unity of measurement for socialist calculation. These thinkers belonged to a technical school of thought called "scientific utopianism", which is an approach to social engineering that explores possible forms of social organization.

The most notable thinker belonging to this school of thought was the Viennese philosopher and economist Otto Neurath, whose conception of socialism as a natural, non-monetary economic system became widespread within the socialist movement following the end of World War I. Neurath's position was held in contrast to other socialists in this period, including the revisionist perspective stemming from Eduard Bernstein, the orthodox social democratic perspective of Karl Kautsky, the Austro-Marxism models of labor-time calculation from Otto Bauer and the emerging school of neoclassical market socialism. Neurath's position opposed all models of market socialism because it rejected the use of money, but was also held in contrast with the more orthodox Marxist conception of socialism held by Karl Kautsky, where socialism only entails the elimination of money as capital along with super-session of the process of capital accumulation.

Otto Neurath conceptualized a comprehensive view of socialization during the socialization debates. "Total socialization" involved not only a form of ownership but also the establishment of economic planning based on calculation in kind, and was contrasted with "partial socialization". "Partial socialization" involved the use of in-kind calculation and planning within a single organization, which externally operated within the framework of a monetary market economy. Neurath's conception of socialism was the initial point of criticism of Ludwig Von Mises in the socialist calculation debate.

In the subsequent socialist calculation debates, a dichotomy between socialists emerged between those who argued that socialization entailed the end of monetary valuation and capital markets, and those who argued that monetary prices could be used within a socialized economy. A further distinction arose between market socialists who argued that social ownership can be achieved within the context of a market economy, where worker-owned or publicly owned enterprises maximized profit and those who argued that socially owned enterprises operate according to other criteria, like marginal cost pricing.

Typology

Social ownership and socialization is categorically distinct from the process of nationalization. In most cases, "socialization" is understood to be a deeper process of transforming the social relations of production within economic organizations as opposed to simply changing titles of ownership. In this sense, "socialization" often involves both a change in ownership and a change in organizational management, including self-management or some form of workplace democracy in place of a strict hierarchical form of control. More fundamentally, social ownership implies that the surplus product (or economic profits) generated by publicly owned enterprise accrues to all of society – state ownership does not necessarily imply this.

Fundamentally, there are two major forms of "social ownership". The first is society-wide public ownership by an entity or network of entities representing society. The second major form of social ownership is employee-owned cooperative enterprise, with the members of each individual enterprise being co-owners of their organization. These possibilities give rise to a socialization dilemma, faced by advocates of public ownership: if social ownership is entrusted exclusively to state agents, then it is liable to bureaucratization; if it is entrusted exclusively to workers, then it is liable to monopoly power and abuse of market position.

Additionally, there are two major forms of management or "social control" for socially owned organizations, both of which can exist alongside the two major modes of social ownership. The first variant of control is public management, where enterprises are run by management held accountable to an agency representing the public either at the level of national, regional or local government. The second form of social control is worker self-management, where managers are elected by the member-workers of each individual enterprise or enterprises are run according to self-directed work processes.

The exact forms of social ownership vary depending on whether or not they are conceptualized as part of a market economy or as part of a non-market planned economy.

Public Ownership

Public ownership can exist both within the framework of a market economy and within the framework of a non-market planned economy. In market socialist proposals, public ownership takes the form of state-owned enterprises that acquire capital goods in capital markets and operate to maximize profits, which are then distributed among the entire population in the form of a social dividend. In non-market models of socialism, public ownership takes the form of a single entity or a network of public entities coordinated by economic planning. A contemporary approach to socialism involves linking together production and distribution units by modern computers to achieve rapid feedback in the allocation of capital inputs to achieve efficient economic planning.

The economist Alec Nove defines social ownership as a form of autonomous public ownership, drawing a distinction between state-owned and directed enterprises. Nove advocates for the existence of both forms of enterprise in his model of feasible socialism.

Public ownership was advocated by neoclassical socialist economists during the interwar socialist calculation debate, most notable Oskar Lange, Fred M. Taylor, Abba P. Lerner and Maurice Dobb.

Neoclassical market socialist economists in the latter half of the 20th century who advocated public ownership highlighted the distinction between "control" and "ownership". John Roemer and Pranab Bardhan argued that public ownership, meaning a relatively egalitarian distribution of enterprise profits, does not require state control – Publicly owned enterprises can be controlled by agents who don't represent the state.

David McMullen's concept of decentralized non-market socialism advocates social ownership of the means of production, believing it to be far more efficient than private ownership. In his proposal, property titles would be replaced by "usership" rights and the exchange of capital goods would no longer be possible. Market exchange in capital goods would be replaced by internal transfers of resources, but an internal and decentralized price system would be fundamental to this systems' operation.

However, by itself public ownership is not socialist as it can exist under a wide variety of different political and economic systems. State ownership by itself does not imply social ownership where income rights belong to society as a whole. As such, state ownership is only one possible expression of public ownership, which itself is one variation of the broader concept of social ownership.

Social Ownership of Equity

The social ownership of capital and corporate stock has been proposed in the context of a market socialist system, where social ownership is achieved either by having a public body or employee-owned pension funds that own corporate stock.

The American economist John Roemer developed a model of market socialism that features a form of public ownership where individuals receive a non-transferable coupon entitling them to a share of the profits generated by autonomous non-governmental publicly owned enterprises. In this model, "social ownership" refers to citizen ownership of equity in a market economy.

James Yunker argues that public ownership of the means of production can be achieved in the same way private ownership is achieved in modern capitalism, using the shareholder system that effectively separates management from ownership. Yunker posits that social ownership can be achieved by having a public body, designated the Bureau of Public Ownership (BPO), own the shares of publicly listed firms without affecting market-based allocation of capital inputs. Yunker termed this model *Pragmatic market socialism* and argued that it would be at least as efficient as modern-day capitalism while providing superior social outcomes as public ownership would enable profits to be distributed among the entire population rather than going largely to a class of inheriting rentiers.

An alternative form of social ownership of equity is ownership of corporate stock through wage earner funds and pension funds. The underlying concept was first expounded upon in 1976 by the management theorist Peter Drucker, who argued that pension funds could reconcile employees' need for financial security with capital's need to be mobile and diversified, referring to this development as "pension fund socialism". In Sweden during the late 1970s, the Meidner program was advanced by the Swedish Social Democratic Party as a way to socialize enterprises through employee wage earners' funds, which would be used to purchase corporate stock. Rudolf Meidner's original plan was to require Swedish companies over a certain size to issue shares equal to 20 percent of profits, which would be owned by wage-earner funds controlled by employees through their trade unions. This plan was rejected and a watered-down proposal was adopted in 1984, which left corporate decision making just as it was and limited the scope of employee ownership to less than 3.5% of listed company shares in 1990.

Cooperative Ownership

Cooperative ownership is the organization of economic units into enterprises owned by their workforce (workers cooperative) or by customers who use the products of the enterprise (this latter concept is called a consumer cooperative). Cooperatives are often organized around some form of self-management, either in the form of elected managers held accountable to the workforce, or in the form of direct management of work processes by the workers themselves. Cooperatives are often proposed by proponents of market socialism, most notably by the economists Branko Horvat, Jaroslav Vanek and Richard Wolff.

Cooperative ownership comes in various forms, ranging from direct workers' ownership, employee stock ownership plans through pension funds, to the weakest version involving profit sharing. Profit-sharing and varying degrees of self-management or "Holacracy" is practiced in many of the high-technology companies of Silicon Valley.

The earliest model of cooperative socialism is mutualism, proposed by the French anarchist philosopher Pierre-Joseph Proudhon. In this system, the state would be abolished and economic enterprises would be owned and operated as producer cooperatives, with worker-members compensated in labor vouchers.

The model of market socialism promoted in the former Socialist Federal Republic of Yugoslavia was based on what was officially called "social ownership", involving an arrangement where workers of each firm each became members and joint-owners and managed their own affairs in a system of workers' self-management.

Contemporary proponents of cooperative ownership cite higher motivation and performance in existing cooperatives. Critics argue that cooperative ownership by itself does not resolve the structural issues of capitalism like economic crises and the business cycle, and that cooperatives have an incentive to limit employment in order to boost the income of existing members.

Commons and Peer-to-peer

In the context of non-market proposals, social ownership can include holding the means of producing wealth in common (common ownership), with the concept of "usership" replacing the concept of ownership. Commons-based peer production involves the distribution of a critical mass of inputs and all outputs through information networks as free goods rather than commodities to be sold for profit by capitalist firms.

The economist Pat Devine defines social ownership as "ownership by those who are affected by – who have an interest in – the use of the assets involved", distinguishing it from other forms of ownership. Devine argues that this variant of social ownership will be more efficient than the other types of ownership because "it enables the tacit knowledge of all those affected to be drawn upon in the process of negotiating what should be done to further the social interest in any particular context".

The phrases "social production" and "social peer-to-peer" production have been used to classify the type of workplace relationships and ownership structures found in the open-source software movement and Commons-based peer production processes, which operate, value and allocate value without private property and market exchange.

Ownership in Soviet-type Economies

In Soviet-type economies, the means of production and natural resources were almost entirely owned by the state and collective enterprises. State enterprises were integrated into a national planning system, where factor inputs were allocated to them by the Ministry for Technical Supply (Gossnab).

According to *The Great Soviet Encyclopedia*, "socialist ownership" is a form of social ownership that forms the basis for the socialist system, involving the collective appropriation of material wealth by working people. Social ownership arises out of the course of capitalist development, creating the objective conditions for further socialist transformation and for the emergence of a planned economy with the aim of raising the living standards for everyone in society.

Misuse of the Term

Particularly in the United States, the term "socialization" has been mistakenly used to refer to any state or government-operated industry or service (the proper term for such being either nationalization or municipalization). It has also been incorrectly used to mean any tax-funded programs, whether privately run or government run.

Lange Model

The Lange model (or Lange–Lerner theorem) is a neoclassical economic model for a hypothetical socialist economy based on public ownership of the means of production and a trial-and-error approach to determining output targets and achieving economic equilibrium and Pareto efficiency. In this model, the state owns non-labor factors of production, and markets allocate final goods and consumer goods. The Lange model states that if all production is performed by a public body such as the state, and there is a functioning price mechanism, this economy will be Pareto-efficient, like a hypothetical market economy under perfect competition. Unlike models of capitalism, the Lange model is based on direct allocation, by directing enterprise managers to set price equal to marginal cost in order to achieve Pareto efficiency. By contrast, in a capitalist economy managers are instructed to maximize profits for private owners, while competitive pressures are relied on to indirectly lower the price to equal marginal cost.

This model was first proposed by Oskar R. Lange in 1936 during the socialist calculation debate, and was expanded by economists like H. D. Dickinson and Abba P. Lerner. Although Lange and Lerner called it "market socialism", the Lange model is a form of planned economy where a central planning board allocates investment and capital goods, while markets allocate labor and consumer goods. The planning board simulates a market in capital goods by a trial-and-error process first elaborated by Vilfredo Pareto and Léon Walras.

The Lange model has never been implemented anywhere, not even in Oskar Lange's home country, Poland, where Soviet-type economic planning was imposed after World War II, precluding experimentation with Lange-style economy. Some parallels might be drawn with the New Economic Mechanism or so-called Goulash Communism in Hungary under Kádár, although this was not a pure Lange-model system.

The model is sometimes called the "Lange–Lerner" model. Abba Lerner wrote a series of articles that greatly influenced Lange's thinking. For example, Lerner caused Lange to re-write his 1936 and 1937 articles on market socialism, before they were re-published as chapters in a 1938 book. Lerner influenced Lange's thinking on social dividend payments. Lerner also argued that investment in the Lange model would inevitably be politicized.

The Lange model was developed in response to Ludwig von Mises and Friedrich Hayek's criticisms of socialism during the socialist calculation debate. The critics argued that any body that owns and consolidates a society's means of production cannot acquire the information needed to calculate general equilibrium prices, and that market-determined prices were essential for the rational allocation of producer goods. The Lange model contains principles proposed by neoclassical economists Vilfredo Pareto and Léon Walras. Lange's theory emphasizes the idea of Pareto efficiency: a situation is Pareto-efficient if there is no way to rearrange things to make any individual better off without making anyone worse off. To achieve Pareto efficiency, a set of conditions must be formulated in stages. This idea of deriving conditions to ensure that consumer preferences are in balance with the maximum amount of goods and services produced is emphasized by Walras. The theorem indicates that a socialist economy based on public ownership could achieve one of the principal economic benefits of capitalism - a rational price system - and was an important theoretical force behind the development of the concept of market socialism.

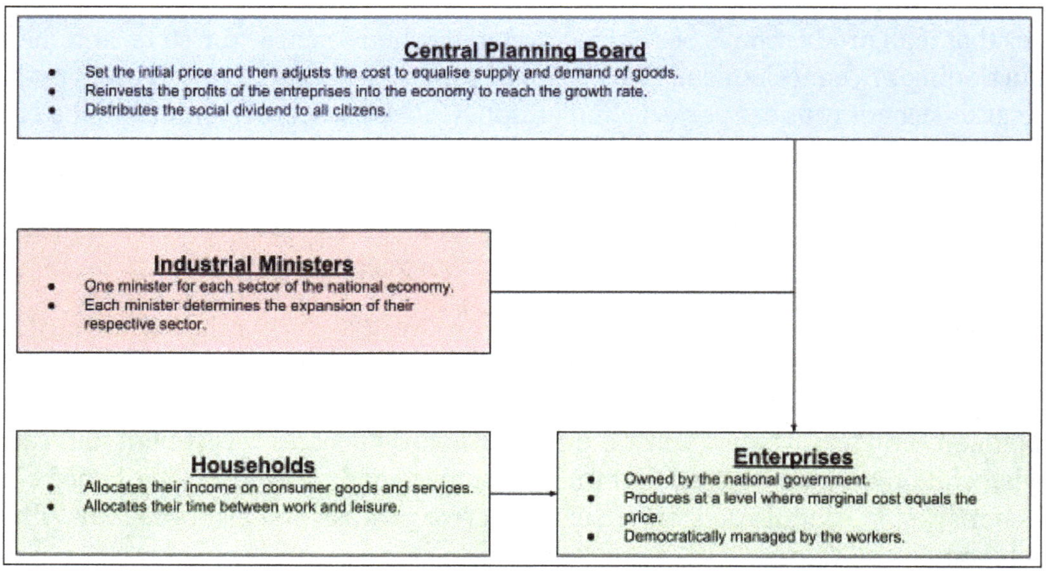

A chart to show how the model would hypothetically function.

The Lange model suggests three levels of decision-making. The lowest level contains firms and households, the intermediate level contains industrial ministries, and the highest level is the central planning board. The board sets the initial price of consumer goods arbitrarily and informs the producing firms of these prices. The state-owned firms then produce at the level of output where marginal cost equals price, P = MC, so as to minimize the cost of production. At the intermediate level, industrial ministries determine the sectoral expansion of industry. Households decide how to allocate income and how much labor to supply by choosing between work and leisure.

Institutions

The key institutions of the Lange model include the central planning board (CPB), industrial ministries for each economic sector, and state enterprises managed democratically by their employees.

Trial-and-error Price Adjustments

Because prices are set by the central planning board "artificially" aiming to achieve planned growth objectives, it is unlikely that supply and demand will be in equilibrium at first. To produce the correct amount of goods and services, the Lange model suggests a trial-and-error method. If there is a surplus of a particular good, the central planning board lowers the price of that good. Conversely, if there is a shortage of a good, the board raises the price. This process of price adjustments takes place until equilibrium between supply and demand is achieved.

Central Planning Board

The central planning board (CPB) has three major functions in the Lange model: First it instructs firms to set price to equal marginal cost, secondly it adjusts prices to attain market-clearing prices for goods and services, and finally, it reinvests the economic profit derived from state enterprises into the economy based on a target rate of growth. The central planning board also distributes social dividends to the population.

Social Dividend

Apart from setting prices, the central planning board allocates social dividends. Because all non-labor factors of production are publicly owned, the rents and profits of these resources belong to the public. The profits would be used to finance a social dividend scheme based on the individuals' share in the income derived from the socially owned capital and natural resources, providing a complementary source of income for workers alongside their salaries and wages.

Advantages

The Lange economic model has a number of theoretical advantages. One advantage is public control over investment. The rate of economic growth would be largely state-determined and a major determinant would be investment ratio.

Another advantage argued by Lange was that externalities could be better accounted for, thanks to the state's ability to manipulate resource prices. Because the state controls all firms, they could easily factor the cost of an externality into the price of a certain resource. Because decisions are made at higher rather than lower levels, it is argued that these decisions are less likely to have undesirable environmental consequences.

Furthermore, because the state uses marginal cost pricing and determines entry, Langean socialism can avoid monopolies and the accompanying lack of allocative efficiency and x-efficiency.

The model claims to solve another main criticism of capitalism. Lange believed that his model would reduce cyclical instability because the state would control savings and investment, consequently eliminating a major source of inefficiency, inequality and social instability that arises from violent cyclical shifts under capitalism.

Criticisms

Milton Friedman criticized the Lange model on methodological grounds. According to Friedman, the model rested on "models of imaginary worlds" rather than "generalizations about the real world", making the claims of the model immune to falsification. He also criticized the model on logical grounds by pointing out that any system which posits state ownership of enterprise requires the continuous intervention by force from the state as any time an individual started a private enterprise the state must either shut it down or seize it, or use force to deter individuals from starting private enterprises in the first place.

Socialist Economics

Socialist economics comprises the economic theories, practices and norms of hypothetical and existing socialist economic systems.

A socialist economic system is characterized by social ownership and operation of the means of production that may take the form of autonomous cooperatives or direct public ownership wherein production is carried out directly for use. Socialist systems that utilize markets for allocating inputs and capital goods among economic units are designated market socialism. When planning is utilized, the economic system is designated as a socialist planned economy. Non-market forms of socialism usually include a system of accounting based on calculation-in-kind to value resources and goods.

Socialist economics has been associated with different schools of economic thought. Marxian economics provided a foundation for socialism based on analysis of capitalism, while neoclassical economics and evolutionary economics provided comprehensive models of socialism. During the 20th century, proposals and models for both planned economies and market socialism were based heavily on neoclassical economics or a synthesis of neoclassical economics with Marxian or institutional economics.

As a term, socialist economics may also be applied to the analysis of former and existing economic systems that were implemented in socialist states, such as in the works of Hungarian economist János Kornai.

Karl Marx and Friedrich Engels believed that hunter-gatherer societies and some primitive agricultural societies were communal, and called this primitive communism. Engels wrote about this at length in the book The Origin of the Family, Private Property and the State, which was based on the unpublished notes of Marx on the work of Lewis Henry Morgan.

Values of socialism have roots in pre-capitalist institutions such as the religious communes, reciprocal obligations, and communal charity of Mediaeval Europe, the development of its economic theory primarily reflects and responds to the monumental changes brought about by the dissolution of feudalism and the emergence of specifically capitalist social relations. As such it is commonly regarded as a movement belonging to the modern era. Many socialists have considered their advocacy as the preservation and extension of the radical humanist ideas expressed in Enlightenment doctrine such as Jean-Jacques Rousseau's Discourse on Inequality, Wilhelm von Humboldt's Limits of State Action, or Immanuel Kant's insistent defense of the French Revolution.

Capitalism appeared in mature form as a result of the problems raised when an industrial factory system requiring long-term investment and entailing corresponding risks was introduced into an internationalized commercial (mercantilist) framework. Historically speaking, the most pressing needs of this new system were an assured supply of the elements of industry (land, elaborate machinery, and labour) and these imperatives led to the commodification of these elements.

According to influential socialist economic historian Karl Polanyi's classic account, the forceful transformation of land, money and especially labour into commodities to be allocated by an autonomous market mechanism was an alien and inhuman rupture of the pre-existing social fabric. Marx had viewed the process in a similar light, referring to it as part of the process of "primitive accumulation" whereby enough initial capital is amassed to begin capitalist production. The dislocation that Polyani and others describe, triggered natural counter-movements in efforts to re-embed the economy in society. These counter-movements, that included, for example, the Luddite rebellions, are the incipient socialist movements. Over time such movements gave birth to or acquired an array of intellectual defenders who attempted to develop their ideas in theory.

As Polanyi noted, these counter-movements were mostly reactive and therefore not full-fledged socialist movements. Some demands went no further than a wish to mitigate the capitalist market's worst effects. Later, a full socialist program developed, arguing for systemic transformation. Its theorists believed that even if markets and private property could be tamed so as not to be excessively "exploitative", or crises could be effectively mitigated, capitalist social relations would remain significantly unjust and anti-democratic, suppressing universal human needs for fulfilling, empowering and creative work, diversity and solidarity.

Within this context socialism has undergone four periods: the first in the 19th century was a period of utopian visions; then occurred the rise of revolutionary socialist and Communist movements in the 19th century as the primary opposition to the rise of corporations and industrialization; the polarisation of socialism around the question of the Soviet Union, and adoption of socialist or social democratic policies in response; and the response of socialism in the neo-liberal era. As socialism developed, so did the socialist system of economics.

Socialism and Classical Political Economy

The first organized theories of socialist economics were significantly impacted by classical economic theory, including elements in Adam Smith, Robert Malthus and David Ricardo. In Smith there is a conception of a common good not provided by the market, a class analysis, a concern for the dehumanizing aspects of the factory system, and the concept of rent as being unproductive. Ricardo argued that the renting class was parasitic. This, and the possibility of a "general glut", an over accumulation of capital to produce goods for sale rather than for use, became the foundation of a rising critique of the concept that free markets with competition would be sufficient to prevent disastrous downturns in the economy, and whether the need for expansion would inevitably lead to war.

Socialist Political Economy before Marx

A key early socialist theorist of political economy was Pierre-Joseph Proudhon. He was the most well-known of nineteenth century mutualist theorists and the first thinker to refer to himself as an anarchist. Others were: Technocrats like Henri de Saint-Simon, agrarian radicals like Thomas Spence, William Ogilvie and William Cobbett; anti-capitalists like Thomas Hodgskin; communitarian and utopian socialists like Robert Owen, William Thompson and Charles Fourier; anti-market socialists like John Gray and John Francis Bray; the Christian mutualist William Batchelder Greene; as well as the theorists of the Chartist movement and early proponents of syndicalism.

The first advocates of socialism promoted social leveling in order to create a meritocratic or technocratic society based upon individual talent. Count Henri de Saint-Simon was the first individual to coin the term "socialism". Saint-Simon was fascinated by the enormous potential of science and technology, which led him to advocate a socialist society that would eliminate the disorderly aspects of capitalism and which would be based upon equal opportunities. Saint-Simon advocated a society in which each person was ranked according to his or her capacities and rewarded according to his or her work. This was accompanied by a desire to implement a rationally organized economy based on planning and geared towards large-scale scientific and material progress, which embodied a desire for a semi-planned economy.

Other early socialist thinkers were influenced by the classical economists. The Ricardian socialists, such as Thomas Hodgskin and Charles Hall, were based on the work of David Ricardo and reasoned that the equilibrium value of commodities approximated producer prices when those commodities were in elastic supply, and that these producer prices corresponded to the embodied labor. The Ricardian socialists viewed profit, interest and rent as deductions from this exchange-value.

Karl Marx and Das Kapital

Karl Marx employed systematic analysis in an attempt to elucidate capitalism's contradictory laws of motion, as well as to expose the specific mechanisms by which it exploits and alienates. He radically modified classical political economic theories. Marx transformed the labor theory of value, which had been worked upon by Adam Smith and David Ricardo, into his "law of value", and used it for the purpose of revealing how commodity fetishism obscures the reality of capitalist society.

His approach, which Friedrich Engels would call "scientific socialism", would stand as the branching point in economic theory. In one direction went those who rejected the capitalist system as fundamentally anti-social, arguing that it could never be harnessed to effectively realize the fullest development of human potentialities wherein "the free development of each is the condition for the free development of all.".

Marx's *Das Kapital* is an incomplete work of economic theory; he had planned four volumes but completed two and left his collaborator Engels to complete the third. In many ways, the work is modelled on Smith's *Wealth of Nations*, seeking to be a comprehensive logical description of production, consumption, and finance in relation to morality and the state. The work of philosophy, anthropology, sociology, and economics includes the following topics:

- Law of value: Capitalist production is the production of "an immense multitude of commodities" or generalised commodity production. A commodity has two essential qualities firstly, they are useful, they satisfy some human want, "the nature of such wants, whether, for instance, they spring from the stomach or from fancy, makes no difference" and secondly they are sold on a market or exchanged. Critically the exchange value of a commodity "is independent of the amount of labour required to appropriate its useful qualities". However, rather depends on the amount of socially necessary labour required to produce it. All commodities are sold at their value, so the origin of the capitalist profit is not in cheating or theft, but in the fact that the cost of reproduction of labour power, or the worker's wage, is less than the value created during their time at work, enabling the capitalists to yield a surplus value or profit on their investments.

- Historical property relations: Historical capitalism represents a process of momentous social upheaval where rural masses were separated from the land and ownership of the means of production by force, deprivation, and legal manipulation, creating an urban proletariat based on the institution of wage-labour. Moreover, capitalist property relations aggravated the artificial separation between city and country, which is a key factor in accounting for the metabolic rift between human beings in capitalism and their natural environment, which is at the root of our current ecological dilemmas.
- Commodity fetishism: Marx adapted previous value-theory to show that in capitalism phenomena involved with the price system (markets, competition, supply and demand) constitute a powerful ideology that obscures the underlying social relations of capitalist society. "Commodity fetishism" refers to this distortion of appearance. The underlying social reality is one of economic exploitation.
- Economic exploitation: Workers are the fundamental creative source of new value. Property relations affording the right of usufruct and despotic control of the workplace to capitalists are the devices by which the surplus value created by workers is appropriated by the capitalists.
- Capital accumulation: Inherent to capitalism is the incessant drive to accumulate as a response to the competitive forces acting upon all capitalists. In such a context the accumulated wealth which is the source of the capitalist's social power derives itself from being able to repeat the circuit of Money→Commodity→Money, where the capitalist receives an increment or "surplus value" higher than their initial investment, as rapidly and efficiently as possible. Moreover, this driving imperative leads capitalism to its expansion on a worldwide scale.
- Crises: Marx identified natural and historically specific (i.e. structural) barriers to accumulation that were interrelated and interpenetrated one another in times of crises. Different types of crises, such as realization crises and overproduction crises, are expressions of capitalism's inability to constructively overcome such barriers. Moreover, the upshot of crises is increased centralization, the expropriation of the many capitalists by the few.
- Centralization: The interacting forces of competition, endemic crises, intensive and extensive expansion of the scale of production, and a growing interdependency with the state apparatus, all promote a strong developmental tendency towards the centralization of capital.
- Material development: as a result of its constant drive to optimize profitability

by increasing the productivity of labour, typically by revolutionizing technology and production techniques, capitalism develops so as to progressively reduce the objective need for work, suggesting the potential for a new era of creative forms of work and expanded scope for leisure.

- Socialization and the pre-conditions for social revolution: By socializing the labour process, concentrating workers into urban settings in large-scale production processes and linking them in a worldwide market, the agents of a potential revolutionary change are created. Thus Marx felt that in the course of its development capitalism was at the same time developing the preconditions for its own negation. However, although the objective conditions for change are generated by the capitalist system itself, the subjective conditions for social revolution can only come about through the apprehension of the objective circumstances by the agents themselves and the transformation of such understanding into an effective revolutionary program.

Anarchist Economics

Anarchist economics is the set of theories and practices of economics and economic activity within the political philosophy of anarchism.

PIERRE KROPOTKINE

LA

CONQUÊTE DU PAIN

PRÉFACE

PAR

ÉLISÉE RECLUS

DEUXIÈME ÉDITION

PARIS

TRESSE & STOCK, ÉDITEURS

PALAIS-ROYAL

The Conquest of Bread by Peter Kropotkin, influential work which presents the economic vision of anarcho-communism.

Pierre Joseph Proudhon was involved with the Lyons mutualists and later adopted the name to describe his own teachings. Mutualism is an anarchist school of thought that originates in the writings of Pierre-Joseph Proudhon, who envisioned a society where each person might possess a means of production, either individually or collectively, with trade representing equivalent amounts of labor in the free market. Integral to the scheme was the establishment of a mutual-credit bank that would lend to producers at a minimal interest rate, just high enough to cover administration. Mutualism is based on a labor theory of value that holds that when labor or its product is sold, in exchange, it ought to receive goods or services embodying "the amount of labor necessary to produce an article of exactly similar and equal utility". Receiving anything less would be considered exploitation, theft of labor, or usury.

Collectivist anarchism is a revolutionary doctrine that advocates the abolition of the state and private ownership of the means of production. Instead, it envisions the means of production being owned collectively and controlled and managed by the producers themselves. Once collectivization takes place, workers' salaries would be determined in democratic organizations based on the amount of time they contributed to production. These salaries would be used to purchase goods in a communal market. Collectivist anarchism is most commonly associated with Mikhail Bakunin, the anti-authoritarian sections of the First International, and the early Spanish anarchist movement.

Anarcho-communism is a theory of anarchism which advocates the abolition of the state, private property, and capitalism in favor of common ownership of the means of production, direct democracy and a horizontal network of voluntary associations, and workers' councils with production and consumption based on the guiding principle: "from each according to ability, to each according to need". Unlike mutualism, collectivist anarchism and Marxism, anarcho-communism as defended by Peter Kropotkin and Errico Malatesta rejected the labor theory of value altogether, instead advocating a gift economy and to base distribution on need. As a coherent, modern economic-political philosophy, anarcho-communism was first formulated in the Italian section of the First International by Carlo Cafiero, Emilio Covelli, Errico Malatesta, Andrea Costa, and other ex-Mazzinian Republicans. Out of respect for Mikhail Bakunin, they did not make their differences with collectivist anarchism explicit until after Bakunin's death. By the early 1880s, most of the European anarchist movement had adopted an anarcho-communist position, advocating the abolition of wage labour and distribution according to need. Ironically, the "collectivist" label then became more commonly associated with Marxist state socialists who advocated the retention of some sort of wage system during the transition to full communism.

Left-wing market anarchism strongly affirm the classical liberal ideas of self-ownership and free markets, while maintaining that, taken to their logical conclusions, these ideas support strongly anti-corporatist, anti-hierarchical, pro-labor positions and anti-capitalism in economics and anti-imperialism in foreign policy.

After Marx

Non-revolutionary socialists were inspired by the writings of John Stuart Mill, and later John Maynard Keynes and the Keynesians, who provided theoretical justification for state involvement in existing market economies. According to the Keynesians, if business cycles could be smoothed out by national ownership of key industries and state direction of their investment, class antagonism would be effectively tamed.They argue that a compact would form between labour and the capitalist class and that there would be no need for revolution. Joan Robinson and Michael Kalecki formed the basis of a critical post-Keynesian economics that at times went well beyond liberal reformism.

Marxist economists developed different tendencies based on conflicting interpretations of Marx's ideas, such as the 'Law of Value' and crisis theory. The monopoly capitalist school saw Paul A. Baran and Paul Sweezy attempt to modify Marx's theory of capitalist development—which was based upon the assumption of price competition—to reflect evolution to a stage where both economy and state were subject to the dominating influence of giant corporations.

World-systems analysis restated Marx's ideas about the worldwide division of labour and the drive to accumulate from the holistic perspective of capitalism's historical development as a global system. Immanuel Wallerstein, wrote in 1979:

> "There are today no socialist systems in the world-economy any more than there are feudal systems because there is only *one* world-system. It is a world-economy and it is by definition capitalist in form. Socialism involves the creation of a new kind of world-system, neither a redistributive world-empire nor a capitalist world-economy but a socialist world-government. I don't see this projection as being in the least utopian but I also don't feel its institution is imminent. It will be the outcome of a long social struggle in forms that may be familiar and perhaps in very few forms, that will take place in *all* the areas of the world-economy".

Piero Sraffa attempted to construct a value theory that was an explanation of the normal distribution of prices in an economy, as well that of income and economic growth. He found that the net product or surplus in the sphere of production was determined by the balance of bargaining power between workers and capitalists, which was subject to the influence of non-economic, presumably social and political, factors.

The mutualist tendency associated with Pierre-Joseph Proudhon also continued, influencing the development of libertarian socialism, anarchist communism, syndicalism and distributivism.

Characteristics

A socialist economy is a system of production where goods and services are produced directly for use, in contrast to a capitalist economic system, where goods and services are produced to generate profit (and therefore indirectly for use). "Production under socialism would be directly and solely for use. With the natural and technical resources of the world held in common and controlled democratically, the sole object of production would be to meet human needs." Goods and services would be produced for their usefulness, or for their use-value, eliminating the need for market-induced needs to ensure a sufficient amount of demand for products to be sold at a profit. Production in a socialist economy is therefore "planned" or "coordinated", and does not suffer from the business cycle inherent to capitalism. In most socialist theories, economic planning only applies to the factors of production and not to the allocation of goods and services produced for consumption, which would be distributed through a market. Karl Marx stated that "lower-stage communism" would consist of compensation based on the amount of labor one contributes to the social product.

The ownership of the means of production varies in different socialist theories. It can either be based on public ownership by a state apparatus; direct ownership by the users of the productive property through worker cooperative; or commonly owned by all of society with management and control delegated to those who operate/use the means of production.

Management and control over the activities of enterprises is based on self-management and self-governance, with equal power-relations in the workplace to maximize occupational autonomy. A socialist form of organization would eliminate controlling hierarchies so that only a hierarchy based on technical knowledge in the workplace remains. Every member would have decision-making power in the firm and would be able to participate in establishing its overall policy objectives. The policies/goals would be carried out by the technical specialists that form the coordinating hierarchy of the firm, who would establish plans or directives for the work community to accomplish these goals.

However, the economies of the former Socialist states, excluding Yugoslavia, were based on bureaucratic, top-down administration of economic directives and micromanagement of the worker in the workplace inspired by capitalist models of scientific management. As a result, some socialist movements have argued that said economies were not socialist due to the lack of equal power-relations in the workplace, the presence of a new "elite", and because of the commodity production that took place in these economies. These economic and social systems have been classified as being either "bureaucratic collectivist", "state capitalist" or "deformed workers' states" by its critics. The exact nature of the USSR *et al* remains unresolved within said socialist movements. However, other socialist movements defend the systems that were in place in Eastern Europe and the Soviet Union, remembering, as said above, that public ownership of the means of production can signify many variants. In the case of the Soviet Union and its satellites, it was the State which controlled and managed almost all of the economy as a big huge enterprise. Furthermore, the products that were manufactured in Soviet-type economies were produced directly for use, given the fact that all of them were sold to the public at below-market prices (i.e. they were sold in deficit to satisfy the needs of the population).

> "I am convinced there is only one way to eliminate (the) grave evils (of capitalism), namely through the establishment of a socialist economy, accompanied by

an educational system which would be oriented toward social goals. In such an economy, the means of production are owned by society itself and are utilized in a planned fashion. A planned economy, which adjusts production to the needs of the community, would distribute the work to be done among all those able to work and would guarantee a livelihood to every man, woman, and child. The education of the individual, in addition to promoting his own innate abilities, would attempt to develop in him a sense of responsibility for his fellow-men in place of the glorification of power and success in our present society".

Economic Planning

Economic planning is a mechanism for the allocation of economic inputs and decision-making based on direct allocation, in contrast to the market mechanism, which is based on indirect allocation. An economy based on economic planning appropriates its resources as needed, so that allocation comes in the form of internal transfers rather than market transactions involving the purchasing of assets by one government agency or firm by another. Decision-making is carried out by workers and consumers on the enterprise-level.

Economic planning is not synonymous with the concept of a *command economy*, which existed in the Soviet Union, and was based on a highly bureaucratic administration of the entire economy in accordance to a comprehensive plan formulated by a central planning agency, which specified output requirements for productive units and tried to micromanage the decisions and policies of enterprises. The command economy is based on the organizational model of a capitalist firm, but applies it to the entire economy.

Various advocates of economic planning have been staunch critics of command economies and centralized planning. For example, Leon Trotsky believed that central planners, regardless of their intellectual capacity, operated without the input and participation of the millions of people who participate in the economy and understand the local conditions and rapid changes in the economy. Therefore, central planners would be unable to effectively coordinate all economic activity because they lacked this informal information.

Economic planning in socialism takes a different form than economic planning in capitalist mixed economies (such as dirigisme, central banking and indicative planning); in the former case planning refers to production of use-value directly (planning of production), while in the latter case planning refers to the planning of capital accumulation in order to stabilize or increase the efficiency of this process.

Anti-capitalism

The goal of socialist economics is to neutralize capital (or, in the case of market socialism, to subject investment and capital to social planning), to coordinate the production of goods and services to directly satisfy demand (as opposed to market-induced needs), and to eliminate the business cycle and crises of overproduction that occur as a result of an economy based on capital accumulation and private property in the means of production.

Socialists generally aim to achieve greater equality in decision-making and economic affairs, grant workers greater control of the means of production and their workplace, and to eliminate exploitation by directing the surplus value to employees. Free access to the means of subsistence is a requisite for liberty, because it ensures that all work is voluntary and no class or individual has the power to coerce others into performing alienating work.

The ultimate goal for Marxist socialists is the emancipation of labor from alienating work, and therefore freedom from having to perform such labor to receive access to the material necessities for life. It is argued that freedom from necessity would maximize individual liberty, as individuals would be able to pursue their own interests and develop their own talents without being coerced into performing labor for others (the power-elite or ruling class in this case) via mechanisms of social control, such as the labor market and the state. The stage of economic development in which this is possible is contingent upon advances in the productive capabilities of society. This advanced stage of social relations and economic organization is called *pure communism*.

Economic Value Theories

Socialist economic theories base the value of a good or service on its use value, rather than its cost of production (labor theory of value) or its exchange value (marginal utility). Other socialist theories, such as mutualism and market socialism, attempt to apply the labor theory of value to socialism, so that the price of a good or service is adjusted to equal the amount of labor time expended in its production. The labor-time expended by each worker would correspond to labor credits, which would be used as a currency to acquire goods and services. Market socialists that base their models on neoclassical economics, and thus marginal utility, such as Oskar Lange and Abba Lerner, have proposed that publicly owned enterprises set their price to equal marginal cost, thereby achieving pareto efficiency. Anarcho-communism as defended by Peter Kropotkin and Errico Malatesta rejected the labor theory of value and exchange value itself, advocated a gift economy and to base distribution on need.

Economic Models and Systems

Robin Hahnel and Michael Albert identify five different economic models within socialist economics:

- Public enterprise centrally planned economy in which all property is owned by the State and all key economic decisions are made centrally by the State, e.g. the former Soviet Union.

- Public enterprise state-managed market economy, one form of market socialism which attempts to use the price mechanism to increase economic efficiency, while all decisive productive assets remain in the ownership of the state, e.g. socialist market economy in China after reform.
- A mixed economy, also a capitalist economy where public and private ownership are mixed, and where industrial planning is ultimately subordinate to market allocation, the model generally adopted by social democrats e.g. in twentieth century Sweden. Many different proposals for socialist economic systems call for a type of mixed economy, where multiple forms of ownership over the means of production co-exist with one another.
- Public enterprise employee managed market economies, another form of market socialism in which publicly owned, employee-managed production units engage in free market exchange of goods and services with one another as well as with final consumers, e.g. mid twentieth century Yugoslavia, Two more theoretical models are Prabhat Ranjan Sarkar's Progressive Utilization Theory and Economic democracy.
- Public enterprise participatory planning, an economy featuring social ownership of the means of production with allocation based on an integration of decentralized democratic planning, e.g. stateless communism, libertarian socialism. An incipient historical forebear is that of Catalonia during the Spanish Revolution. More developed theoretical models include those of Karl Polanyi, Participatory Economics, Inclusive Democracy and the negotiated coordination model of Pat Devine, as well as in Cornelius Castoriadis's pamphlet "Workers' Councils and the Economics of a Self-Managed Society".

János Kornai identifies five distinct types of socialism:

- Classical/Marxist conception, where socialism is a stage of economic development in which wage labour, private property in the means of production and monetary relations have been made redundant through the development of the productive forces, so that capital accumulation has been superseded by economic planning. Economic planning in this definition means conscious allocation of economic inputs and the means of production by the associated producers to directly maximise use-values as opposed to exchange-values, in contrast to the "anarchy of production" of capitalism.
- Walrasian/Market Socialist which defines socialism as public-ownership or co-operative-enterprises in a market economy, with prices for producer goods set through a trial-and-error method by a central planning board. In this view, socialism is defined in terms of de jure public property rights over major enterprises.
- Leninist conception, which includes a form of political organisation based on control of the means of production and government by a single political party

apparatus that claims to act in the interest of the working class, and an ideology hostile toward markets and political dissent, with coordination of economic activity through centralised economic planning (a "command economy").

- Social democratic concept, based on the capitalist mode of production, which defines socialism as a set of values rather than a specific type of social and economic organisation. It includes unconditional support for parliamentary democracy, gradual and reformist attempts to establish socialism and support for socially progressive causes. Social democrats are not opposed to the market or private property; instead they try to ameliorate the effects of capitalism through a welfare state, which relies on the market as the fundamental coordinating entity in the economy and a degree of public ownership/public provision of public goods in an economy otherwise dominated by private enterprise.
- East Asian model, or socialist market economy, based on a largely free-market, capital accumulation for profit and substantial private ownership along with state-ownership of strategic industries monopolised by a single political party. János Kornai ultimately leaves the classification of this model (as either socialist or capitalist) to the reader.

Socialism can be divided into market socialism and planned socialism based on their dominant mechanism of resource allocation. Another distinction can be made between the type of property structures of different socialist systems (public, cooperative or common) and on the dominant form of economic management within the economy (hierarchical or self-managed).

Economic Democracy

Economic democracy is a model of market socialism primarily developed by the American economist David Schweickart. In Schweickart's model, enterprises and natural resources are owned by society in the form of public banking, and management is elected by the workers within each firm. Profits would be distributed among the workers of the respective enterprise.

Lange–Lerner Model

The Lange–Lerner model involves public ownership of the means of production and the utilization of a trial-and-error approach to achieving equilibrium prices by a central planning board. The Central Planning Board would be responsible for setting prices through a trial-and-error approach to establish equilibrium prices, effectively acting as the abstract *Walrasian auctioneer* in Walrasian economics. Managers of the state-owned firms would be instructed to set prices to equal marginal cost (P=MC), so that economic equilibrium and Pareto efficiency would be achieved. The Lange model was expanded upon by the American economist Abba Lerner and became known as the

Lange–Lerner theorem, particularly the role of the social dividend. Forerunners of the Lange model include the neoclassical economists Enrico Barone and Fred M. Taylor.

Self-managed Economy

The self-managed economy is a form of socialism where enterprises are owned and managed by their employees, effectively negating the employer-employee (or wage labor) dynamic of capitalism and emphasizing the opposition to alienation, self-managing and cooperative aspect of socialism. Members of cooperative firms are relatively free to manage their own affairs and work schedules. This model was developed most extensively by the Yugoslav economists Branko Horvat, Jaroslav Vanek and the American economist Benjamin Ward.

Worker Self-directed Enterprise

Worker self-directed enterprise is a recent proposal advocated by the American Marxian economist Richard D. Wolff. This model shares many similarities with the model of socialist self-management in that employees own and direct their enterprises, but places a greater role on democratically elected management within a market economy.

Democratic Planned Socialism

Democratic planned socialism is a form of decentralized planned economy.

Feasible Socialism

Feasible socialism was the name Alec Nove gave his outline for socialism in his work *The Economics of Feasible Socialism*. According to Nove, this model of socialism is "feasible" because it can be realized within the lifetime of anyone living today. It involves a combination of publicly owned and centrally directed enterprises for large-scale industries, autonomous publicly owned enterprises, consumer and worker-owned cooperatives for the majority of the economy, and private ownership for small businesses. It is a market-based mixed economy that includes a substantial role for macroeconomic interventionism and indicative economic planning.

Pragmatic Market Socialism

The American economist James Yunker detailed a model where social ownership of the means of production is achieved the same way private ownership is achieved in modern capitalism through the shareholder system that separates management functions from ownership. Yunker posits that social ownership can be achieved by having a public body, designated the Bureau of Public Ownership (BPO), owning the shares of publicly listed firms without affecting market-based allocation of capital inputs. Yunker termed this model pragmatic market socialism because it does not require massive changes to society and would leave the existing management system intact, and would be at least as efficient as modern-day capitalism while providing superior social outcomes as public ownership of large and established enterprises would enable profits to be distributed among the entire population in a social dividend rather than going largely to a class of inheriting rentiers.

Participatory Economy

Participatory economics utilizes participatory decision making as an economic mechanism to guide the production, consumption and allocation of resources in a given society.

Computer-managed Allocation

Proposals for utilizing computer-based coordination and information technology for the coordination and optimization of resource allocation (also known as cybernetics) within an economy have been outlined by various socialists, economists and computer scientists, including Oskar Lange, the Soviet engineer Viktor Glushkov, and more recently Paul Cockshott and Allin Cottrell.

Peer-to-peer Economy and Open Source

The "networked information age" has enabled the development and emergence of new forms of organizing the production of value in non-market arrangements that have been termed commons-based peer production along with the negation of ownership and the concept of property in the development of software in the form of open source and open design.

Negotiated Coordination

Economist Pat Devine has created a model of coordination called "negotiated coordination", which is based upon social ownership by those affected by the use of the assets involved, with decisions made by those at the most localised level of production.

Elements of Socialism in Practice

Although a number of economic systems have existed with various socialist attributes, or have been deemed socialist by their proponents, almost all of the economic systems listed below have largely retained elements of capitalism such as wage labor, the accumulation of capital, and commodity production. Nonetheless, various elements of a socialist economy have been implemented or experimented with in various economies throughout history.

Various forms of socialist organizational attributes have existed as minor modes of production within the context of a capitalist economy throughout history—examples of this include cooperative enterprises in a capitalist economy, and the emerging free-software movement based on social peer-to-peer production.

Centrally Planned Economies

A centrally planned economy combines public ownership of the means of production with centralized state planning. This model is usually associated with the Soviet-style command economy. In a centrally planned economy, decisions regarding the quantity of goods and services to be produced are planned in advance by a planning agency. In the early years of Soviet central planning, the planning process was based upon a selected number of physical flows with inputs mobilized to meet explicit production targets measured in natural or technical units. This material balances method of achieving plan coherence was later complemented and replaced by value planning, with money provided to enterprises so that they could recruit labour and procure materials and intermediate production goods and services. The Soviet economy was brought to balance by the interlocking of three sets of calculation, namely the setting up of a model incorporating balances of production, manpower and finance. The exercise was undertaken annually and involved a process of iteration (the "method of successive approximation"). Although nominally a "centrally planned" economy, in reality formulation of the plan took place on a more local level of the production process as information was relayed from enterprises to planning ministries. Aside from the USSR and Eastern bloc economies, this economic model was also utilized by the People's Republic of China, Socialist Republic of Vietnam, Republic of Cuba and North Korea.

Soviet Union

The Soviet Union and some of its European satellites aimed for a fully centrally planned economy. They dispensed almost entirely with private ownership over the means of production. However, workers were still effectively paid a wage for their labour. Some believe that according to Marxist theory this should have been a step towards a genuine workers' state. However, some Marxists consider this a misunderstanding of Marx's views of historical materialism and his views of the process of socialization.

The characteristics of this model of economy were:

- Production quotas for every productive unit. A farm, mine or factory was judged on the basis of whether its production met the quota. It would be provided with a quota of the inputs it needed to start production, and then its quota of output would be taken away and given to downstream production units or distributed to consumers.
- Allocation through political control. In contrast with systems where prices *determined* allocation of resources, in the Soviet Union, allocation, particularly of

means of production was determined by the bureaucracy. The prices that were constructed were done so *after* the formulation of the economy plan, and such prices did not factor into choices about what was produced and how it was produced in the first place.

- Full employment. Every worker was ensured employment. However workers were generally not directed to jobs. The central planning administration adjusted relative wages rates to influence job choice in accordance with the outlines of the current plan.
- Clearing goods by planning: if a surplus of a product was accumulated, then the central planning authority would either reduce the quota for its production or increase the quota for its use.
- Five-year plans for the long-term development of key industries.

The planning system in the Soviet Union was introduced under Stalin between 1928 and 1934. Following the Second World War, in the seven countries with communist governments in Central and Eastern Europe, central planning with five- (or six-) year plans on the Soviet model had been introduced by 1951. The common features were the nationalization of industry, transport and trade, compulsory procurement in farming (but not collectivization) and a monopoly on foreign trade. Prices were largely determined on the basis of the costs of inputs, a method derived from the labour theory of value. Prices did not therefore incentivize production enterprises whose inputs were instead purposely rationed by the central plan. This "taut planning" began around 1930 in the Soviet Union and was only attenuated after the economic reforms in 1966–1968 when enterprises were encouraged to make profits.

The stated purpose of planning according to the communist party was to enable the people through the party and state institutions to undertake activities that would have been frustrated by a market economy (for example, the rapid expansion of universal education and health care, urban development with mass good quality housing and industrial development of all regions of the country). Nevertheless, markets continued to exist in socialist planned economies. Even after the collectivization of agriculture in the Soviet Union in the 1930s, members of the collective farm and anyone with a private garden plot were free to sell their own produce (farm workers were often paid in kind). Licensed markets operated in every town and city borough where non-state-owned enterprises (such as cooperatives and collective farms) were able to offer their products and services. From 1956/59 onwards all wartime controls over manpower were removed and people could apply and quit jobs freely in the Soviet Union. The use of market mechanisms went furthest in Yugoslavia, Czechoslovakia and Hungary. From 1975 Soviet citizens had the right to engage in private handicraft and in 1981 collective farmers could raise and sell livestock privately. It should also be noted that households were free to dispose of their income as they chose and incomes were lightly taxed.

Dispute that the Soviet Model is Socialism

Various scholars and political economists have criticized the claim that the centrally planned economy, and specifically, the Soviet model of economic development, constitutes a form of socialism. They argue that the Soviet economy was structured upon the accumulation of capital and the extraction of surplus value from the working class by the planning agency in order to reinvest this surplus into the economy—and to distribute to managers and senior officials, indicating the Soviet Union (and other Soviet-style economies) were state capitalist economies. More fundamentally, these economies are still structured around the dynamic of capitalism: the accumulation of capital and production for profit (as opposed to being based on production for use—the defining criterion for socialism), and have not yet transcended the system of capitalism but are in fact a variation of capitalism based on a process of state-directed accumulation.

On the other side of the argument are those who contend that no surplus value was generated from labour activity or from commodity markets in the socialist planned economies and therefore claim that there was no exploiting class, even if inequalities existed. Since prices were controlled and set below market clearing levels there was no element of 'value added' at the point of sale as occurs in capitalist market economies. Prices were built up from the average cost of inputs, including wages, taxes, interest on stocks and working capital, and allowances to cover the recoupment of investment and for depreciation, so there was no 'profit margin' in the price charged to customers. Wages did not reflect the purchase price of labour since labour was not a commodity traded in a market and the employing organizations did not own the means of production. Wages were set at a level that permitted a decent standard of living and rewarded specialist skills and educational qualifications. In macroeconomic terms, the plan allocated the whole national product to workers in the form of wages for the workers' own use, with a fraction withheld for investment and imports from abroad. The difference between the average value of wages and the value of national output per worker did not imply the existence of surplus value since it was part of a consciously formulated plan for the development of society. Furthermore, the presence of inequality in the socialist planned economies did not imply that an exploiting class existed. In the USSR communist party members were able to buy scarce goods in special shops and the leadership elite took advantage of state property to live in more spacious accommodation and sometimes luxury. Although they received privileges not commonly available and thus some additional income in kind there was no difference in their official remuneration in comparison to their non-party peers. Enterprise managers and workers received only the wages and bonuses related to the production targets that had been set by the planning authorities. Outside of the cooperative sector, which enjoyed greater economic freedoms and whose profits were shared among all members of the cooperative, there was no profit-taking class.

Other socialist critics point to the lack of socialist social relations in these economies—specifically the lack of self-management, a bureaucratic elite based on hierarchical and centralized powers of authority, and the lack of genuine worker control over the means of production—leading them to conclude that they were not socialist but either bureaucratic collectivism or state capitalism. Trotskyists argue they are neither socialist nor capitalist—but are deformed workers' states.

This analysis is consistent with Lenin's April Theses, which stated that the goal of the Bolshevik revolution was *not* the introduction of socialism, which could only be established on a worldwide scale, but was intended to bring production and the state under the control of the Soviets of Workers' Deputies. Furthermore, these "Communist states" often do not claim to have achieved socialism in their countries; on the contrary, they claim to be *building* and working toward the establishment of socialism in their countries. For example, the preamble to the Socialist Republic of Vietnam's constitution states that Vietnam only entered a transition stage between capitalism and socialism after the country was re-unified under the Communist party in 1976, and the 1992 Constitution of the Republic of Cuba states that the role of the Communist Party is to "guide the common effort toward the goals and construction of socialism".

This view is challenged by Stalinists and their followers, who claim that socialism was established in the Soviet Union after Joseph Stalin came to power and instituted the system of five year plans. The 1936 Constitution of the USSR, known as the Fundamental Law of Victorious Socialism, embodied the claim that the foundations for socialism had been laid. Joseph Stalin introduced the theory of socialism in one country, which argued that socialism can be built in a single country, despite existing in a global capitalist economic system. Nevertheless, it was recognized that the stage during which developed socialism would be built would be a lengthy one and would not be achieved by the USSR on its own. According to the official textbooks, the first stage of the transition period from capitalism to socialism had been completed by the 1970s in the European socialist countries (except Poland and Yugoslavia), and in Mongolia and Cuba. The next stage of developed socialism would not be reached until "the economic integration of the socialist states becomes a major factor of their economic progress" and social relations had been reconstructed on "collectivist principles". Communist writers accepted that during these earlier stages in constructing socialism, the exchange of commodities on the basis of the average socially necessary labour embodied within them occurred and involved the mediation of money. Socialist planned economies were systems of commodity production but this was directed in a conscious way towards meeting the needs of the people and not left to the "anarchy of the market". At the stage of developed socialism, "the state of dictatorship of the proletariat changes into a state of all people reflecting the increasing homogeneity of society" and the "evening out of economic development levels" within and between socialist countries. It would provide the foundations for a further stage of perfected socialist society, where an abundance of goods permitted their distribution according to need. Only then could the world socialist system progress towards the higher phase of communism.

References

- Anarchism: plato.stanford.edu, Retrieved 01 May, 2020
- Busky, Donald F. (20 July 2000). Democratic Socialism: A Global Survey. Praeger. p. 2. ISBN 978-0275968861
- Reformism: workers.org, Retrieved 08 February, 2020
- Schmitz, Patrick W. (2008). "Joint ownership and the hold-up problem under asymmetric information". Economics Letters. 99 (3): 577–580. doi:10.1016/j.econlet.2007.10.008
- Socialist-Realism, art: britannica.com, Retrieved 14 January, 2020
- Bockman, Johanna (2011). Markets in the name of Socialism: The Left-Wing origins of Neoliberalism. Stanford University Press. p. 20. ISBN 978-0-8047-7566-3

Socialist Calculation 5

- **Socialist Calculation Debate**
- **Calculation in Kind**
- **Decentralized Planning**
- **Labor-time Calculation**

The debate of socialist calculation revolves around the question of how the socialist economy would evaluate economic calculation in the absence of values, money, financial assets and private ownership. A few of the elements within it are decentralized planning, labor-time calculation, participatory economics, etc. All the concepts related to socialist calculation have been carefully analyzed in this chapter.

Without some such central control of the means of production, planning in the sense in which we have used the term ceases to be a problem. It becomes unthinkable. This would probably be agreed by the majority of economists of all camps, although most other people who believe in planning still think of it as something that could be rationally attempted inside the framework of a society based on private property.

In fact, however, if by "planning" is meant the actual direction of productive activity by authoritative prescription of either the quantities to be produced, the methods of production to be used, or the prices to be fixed, it can be easily shown not that such a thing is impossible, but that any isolated measure of this sort will cause reactions that will defeat its own end, and that any attempt to act consistently will necessitate further and further measures of control until all economic activity is brought under one central authority.

It is impossible within the scope of this discussion of socialism to enter further into this separate problem of state intervention in a capitalistic society. It is mentioned here only to say explicitly that it is excluded from our considerations. Well-accepted analysis shows that it does not provide an alternative that can be rationally chosen or that can be expected to provide a stable or satisfactory solution of any of the problems to which it is applied.

But here, again, it is necessary to guard against misunderstanding. To say that partial planning of the kind we are alluding to is irrational is, however, not equivalent to saying that the only form of capitalism that can be rationally advocated is that of complete laissez-faire in the old sense. There is no reason to assume that the historically given legal institutions are necessarily the most "natural" in any sense.

The recognition of the principle of private property does not by any means necessarily imply that the particular delimitation of the contents of this right as determined by the existing laws are the most appropriate. The question as to which is the most appropriate permanent framework that will secure the smoothest and most efficient working of competition is of the greatest importance and one that, it must be admitted, has been sadly neglected by economists.

But, on the other hand, to admit the possibility of changes in the legal framework is not to admit the possibility of a further type of planning in the sense in which we have used the word so far. There is an essential distinction here that must not be overlooked: the distinction between a permanent legal framework so devised as to provide all the necessary incentives to private initiative to bring about the adaptations required by any change and a system where such adaptations are brought about by central direction. It is this, and not the question of the maintenance of the existing order versus the introduction of new institutions, which is the real issue.

In a sense both systems can be described as being the product of rational planning. But in the one case this planning is concerned only with the permanent framework of institutions and may be dispensed with if one is willing to accept the institutions that have grown in a slow historical process, while in the other it has to deal with day-to-day changes of every sort.

There can be no doubt that planning of this sort involves changes of a type and magnitude hitherto unknown in human history. It is sometimes urged that the changes now in progress are merely a return to the social forms of the pre-industrial era. But this is a misapprehension. Even when the medieval guild system was at its height, and when restrictions to commerce were most extensive, they were not used as a means actually to direct individual activity. They were certainly not the most rational permanent framework for individual activity that could have been devised, but they were essentially only a permanent framework inside which current activity by individual initiative had free play.

With our attempts to use the old apparatus of restrictionism as an instrument of almost day-to-day adjustment to change, we have already gone much further in the direction of central planning of current activity than has ever been attempted before. If we follow the path on which we have started, if we try to act consistently and to combat the self-frustrating tendencies of any isolated act of planning, we shall certainly embark upon an experiment that until recently had no parallel in history. But even at this stage we have gone very far.

If we are to judge the potentialities aright, it is necessary to realize that the system under which we live, choked up with attempts at partial planning and restrictionism, is almost as far from any system of capitalism that could be rationally advocated as it is different from any consistent system of planning. It is important to realize in any investigation of the possibilities of planning that it is a fallacy to suppose capitalism as it exists today is the alternative. We are certainly as far from capitalism in its pure form as we are from any system of central planning. The world of today is just interventionist chaos.

Classical political economy broke down mainly because it failed to base its explanation of the fundamental phenomenon of value on the same analysis of the springs of economic activity that it had so successfully applied to the analysis of the more complex phenomena of competition. The labor theory of value was the product of a search after some illusory substance of value rather than an analysis of the behavior of the economic subject.

The decisive step in the progress of economics was taken when economists began to ask what exactly were the circumstances that made individuals behave toward goods in a particular way. To ask the question in this form led immediately to the recognition that to attach a definite significance or value to the units of different goods was a necessary step in the solution of the general problem that arises everywhere when a multiplicity of ends compete for a limited quantity of means.

The omnipresence of this problem of value wherever there is rational action was the basic fact from which a systematic exploration of the forms, under which it would make its appearance under different organizations of economic life, could proceed. Up to a certain point, from the very beginning, the problems of a centrally directed economy found a prominent place in the expositions of modern economics. It was obviously so much simpler to discuss the fundamental problems on the assumption of the existence of a *single* scale of values consistently followed than on the assumption of a multiplicity of individuals following their personal scales that in the early chapters of the new systems the assumption of a Communist state was frequently used — and used with considerable advantage — as an expository device.

But it was used only to demonstrate that any solution would necessarily give rise to essentially the same value phenomena — rent, wages, interest, etc. — that we actually observe in a competitive society, and the authors then generally proceeded to show how the interaction of independent activities of the individuals produced these phenomena spontaneously, without inquiring further whether they could be produced in a complex modern society by any other means.

The mere absence of an agreed common scale of values seemed to deprive that problem of any practical importance. It is true that some of the earlier writers of the new school not only thought that they had actually solved the problem of socialism but also believed that their utility calculus provided a means that made it possible to combine individual utility scale into a scale of ends objectively valid for society as a whole. But it is now generally recognized that this latter belief was just an illusion and that there are no scientific criteria that would enable us to compare or assess the relative importance of needs of different persons, although conclusions implying such illegitimate interpersonal comparisons of utilities can still be found in discussions of special problems.

But it is evident that, as the progress of the analysis of the competitive system revealed the complexity of the problems that it solved spontaneously, economists became more and more skeptical about the possibility of solving the same problems by deliberate decision.

It is perhaps worth noting that as early as 1854 the most famous among the predecessors of the modern "marginal utility" school, the German Herman Heinrich Gossen, had come to the conclusion that the central economic authority projected by the Communists would soon find that it had set itself a task that far exceeded the powers of individual men. Among the later economists of the modern school, the point in which Gossen had already based his objection, the difficulty of rational calculation when there is no private property, was frequently hinted at.

It was particularly clearly put by Professor Edwin Cannan, who stressed the fact that the aims of socialists and Communists could only be achieved by "abolishing both the institution of private property and the practice of exchange, without which value, in any reasonable sense of the word, cannot exist." But, beyond general statements of this sort, critical examination of the possibilities of a socialist economic policy made little headway, for the simple reason that no concrete socialist proposal of how these problems would be overcome existed to be examined.

It was only early in the present century that at last a general statement of the kind we have just examined, concerning the impracticability of socialism by the eminent Dutch economist, N.G. Pierson, provoked Karl Kautsky, then the leading theoretician of Marxian socialism, to break the traditional silence about the actual working of the future socialist state and to give in a lecture, still somewhat hesitantly and with many apologies, a description of what would happen on the morrow of the Revolution. But Kautsky only showed that he was not even really aware of the problem that the economists had seen.

He thus gave Pierson the opportunity to demonstrate in detail that a socialist state would have its problems of value just as any other economic system and that the task socialists had to solve was to show how in the absence of a pricing system the value of different goods was to be determined.

It is particularly valuable for its discussion of the problems arising out of the international trade between several socialist communities. The economic problems of socialism that appeared before the first World War confined themselves more or less to the demonstration that the main categories of prices, as wages, rent, and interest, would have to figure at least in the calculations of the planning authority in the same way in which they appear today and would be determined by essentially the same factors. The modern development of the theory of interest played a particularly important role in this connection. After Böhm-Bawerk, it was particularly Professor Gustav Cassel who showed convincingly that interest would have to form an important element in the rational calculation of economic activity.

But none of these authors even attempted to show how these essential magnitudes could be arrived at in practice. The one author who at least approached the problem was the Italian economist Enrico Barone, who in 1908, in an article on the "Ministry of Production in the Collectivist State," developed certain suggestions of Pareto's.

When, with the end of the war of 1914–1918, socialist parties came into power in most of the states of central and eastern Europe, the discussion on all these problems necessarily entered a new and decisive phase. The victorious socialist parties had now to think of a definite program of action, and the socialist literature of the years immediately following World War I was for the first time largely concerned with the practical question of how to organize production on socialist lines.

These discussions were very much under the influence of the experience of the war years when the states had set up food and raw material administrations to deal with the serious shortage of the most essential commodities. It was generally assumed that this had shown that not only was central direction of economic activity practicable and even superior to a system of competition but also that the special technique of planning developed to cope with the problems of war economics might be equally applied to the permanent administration of a socialist economy.

Apart from Russia, where the rapidity of change in the years immediately following the revolution left little time for quiet reflection, it was mainly in Germany and even more so in Austria that these questions were most seriously debated. Particularly in the latter country whose socialists had long played a leading role in the intellectual development of socialism, and where a strong and undivided socialist party had probably exercised a greater influence on its economic policy than in any other country outside Russia, the problems of socialism had assumed enormous practical importance.

It may perhaps be mentioned in passing that it is rather curious how little serious study has been devoted to the economic experiences of that country in the decade after the First World War, although they are probably more relevant to the problems of a socialist policy in the Western world than anything that has happened in Russia. But, whatever one may think about the importance of the actual experiments made in Austria, there can be little doubt that the theoretical contributions made there to the understanding of the problems will prove to be a considerable force in the intellectual history of our time.

Among these early socialist contributions to the discussions, in many ways the most interesting and in any case the most characteristic for the still very limited recognition of the nature of the economic problems involved, is a book by Otto Neurath that appeared in 1919, in which the author tried to show that war experiences had revealed that it was possible to dispense with any considerations of value in the administration of the supply of commodities and that all the calculations of the central planning authorities should and could be carried out *in natura*, i.e., that the calculations need not be carried through in terms of some common unit of value but that they could be made in kind.

Neurath was quite oblivious of the insuperable difficulties that the absence of value calculations would put in the way of any rational economic use of the resources and even seemed to consider it as an advantage. Similar strictures apply to the works published about the same time by one of the leading spirits of the Austrian Social Democratic Party, Otto Bauer. It is impossible here to give any detailed account of the argument of these and a number of other related publications of that time. They have to be mentioned, however, because they are important as representative expression of socialist thought just before the impact of the new criticism and because much of this criticism is naturally directed or implicitly concerned with these works.

In Germany discussion centered round the proposals of the "socialization commission" set up to discuss the possibilities of the transfer of individual industries to the ownership and control of the state. It was this commission or in connection with its deliberations that economists like Emil Lederer and Eduard Heimann and the ill-fated Walther Rathenau developed plans for socialization that became the main topic of discussion among economists.

For our purpose, however, these proposals are less interesting than their Austrian counterparts, because they did not contemplate a completely socialized system but were mainly concerned with the problem of the organization of individual socialized industries in an otherwise competitive system. For this reason their authors did not have to face the main problems of a really socialist system. They are important, nevertheless, as symptoms of the state of public opinion at the time when and in the nation in which the more scientific examination of these problems began.

One of the projects of this period deserves perhaps special mention not only because its authors are the inventors of the now fashionable term *planned economy* but also because it so closely resembles the proposals for planning now so prevalent in Great Britain. This is the plan developed in 1919 by the economics and labor minister, Rudolf Wissel, and his undersecretary of state, W. von Moellendorf. But interesting as their proposals of organization of individual industries are and relevant to many of the problems discussed in England at the present moment as is the discussion to which they gave rise, they cannot be regarded as socialist proposals of the kind discussed here but belong to the halfway house between capitalism and socialism, discussion of which for reasons mentioned above has been deliberately excluded from the present essay.

The distinction of having first formulated the central problem of socialist economics in such a form as to make it impossible that it should ever again disappear from the discussion belongs to the Austrian economist Ludwig von Mises. In an article on "Economic Calculation in a Socialist Community," which appeared in the spring of 1920, he demonstrated that the possibility of rational calculation in our present economic system was based on the fact that prices expressed in money provided the essential condition that made such reckoning possible. The essential point on which Professor Mises went far beyond anything done by his predecessors was the detailed demonstration that an economic use of the available resources was only possible if this pricing was applied not only to the final product but also to all the intermediate products and factors of production, and that no other process was conceivable that would in the same way take account of all the relevant facts as did the pricing process of the competitive market.

Together with the larger work, Professor Mises's study represents the starting point from which all the discussions of the economic problems of socialism, whether constructive or critical, which aspire to be taken seriously must necessarily proceed.

While Professor Mises's writings contain beyond doubt the most complete and successful exposition of what from then onward became the central problem, and while they had by far the greatest influence on all further discussions, it is an interesting coincidence that about the same time two other distinguished authors arrived independently at very similar conclusions.

"Professor Mises's study represents the starting point from which all the discussions of the economic problems of socialism, whether constructive or critical, which aspire to be taken seriously must necessarily proceed."

The first was the great German sociologist Max Weber, who in his posthumous magnum opus, *Wirtschaft und Gesellschaft*, which appeared in 1921, dealt expressly with the conditions that in a complex economic system made rational decisions possible. Like Mises (whose article he quotes as having come to his notice only when his own discussion was already set up in print), he insisted that the *in natura* calculations proposed by the leading advocates of a planned economy could not provide a rational solution of the problems that the authorities in such a system would have to solve.

He emphasized in particular that the rational use and the preservation of capital could be secured only in a system based on exchange and the use of money, and that the wastes due to the impossibility of rational calculation in a completely socialized system might be serious enough to make it impossible to maintain alive the present populations of the more densely inhabited countries.

The assumption that some system of accounting would in time be found or invented if one only tried seriously to tackle the problem of a moneyless economy does not help here: the problem is the fundamental problem of any complete socialization and it is certainly impossible to talk of a *rationally* "planned economy" while in so far as the all-decisive point is concerned no means for the construction of a "plan" is known.

A practically simultaneous development of the same ideas is to be found in Russia. Here, in the summer of 1920, in the short interval after the first military successes of the new system, when it had for once become possible to utter criticisms in public, Boris Brutzkus, a distinguished economist mainly known for his studies in the agricultural problems of Russia, subjected to a searching criticism, in a series of lectures, the doctrines governing the action of the Communist rulers.

These lectures, which appeared under the title "The Problems of Social Economy under Socialism" in a Russian journal and were only many years later made accessible to a wider public in a German translation, show in their main conclusion a remarkable resemblance to the doctrines of Mises and Max Weber, although they arose out of the study of the concrete problems that Russia had to face at that time and although they were written at a time when their author, cut off from all communication with the outside world, could not have known of the similar efforts of the Austrian and German scholars. Like Professor Mises and Max Weber, his criticism centers round the impossibility of a rational calculation in a centrally directed economy from which prices are necessarily absent.

Although to some extent Max Weber and Professor Brutzkus share the credit of having pointed out independently the central problem of the economics of socialism, it was the more complete and systematic exposition of Professor Mises, particularly in his larger work on *Die Gemeinwirtschaft*, that has mainly influenced the trend of further discussion on the Continent. In the years immediately succeeding its publication a number of attempts were made to meet his challenge directly and to show that he was wrong in his main thesis and that even in a strictly centrally directed economic system values could be exactly determined without any serious difficulties. But, although the discussion on this point dragged on for several years, in the course of which Mises twice replied to his critics, it became more and more clear that, in so far as a strictly centrally directed planned system of the type originally proposed by most socialists was concerned, his central thesis could not be refuted.

Much of the objections made at first were really more a quibbling about words caused by the fact that Mises had occasionally used the somewhat loose statement that socialism was "impossible," while what he meant was that socialism made rational calculation impossible. Of course any proposed course of action, if the proposal has any meaning at all, is possible in the strict sense of the word, i.e., it may be tried. The question can only be whether it will lead to the expected results, that is, whether the proposed course of action is consistent with the aims that it is intended to serve.

Insofar as it had been hoped to achieve by means of central direction of all economic activity *at one and the same time* a distribution of income independent of private property in the means of production and a volume of output that was at least approximately the same or even greater than that procured under free competition, it was more and more generally admitted that this was not a practicable way to achieve these ends.

But it was only natural that, even where Professor Mises's main thesis was conceded, this did not mean an abandonment of the search for a way to realize the socialist ideals. Its main effect was to divert attention from what had so far been universally considered as the most practicable forms of socialist organization to the exploration of alternative schemes.

It is possible to distinguish two main types of reaction among those who conceded his central argument. In the first place, there were those who thought that the loss of efficiency, the decline in general wealth that will be the effect of the absence of a means of rational calculation, would not be too high a price for the realization of a more just distribution of this wealth. Of course, if this attitude is based on a clear realization of what this choice implies, there is no more to be said about it, except that it seems doubtful whether those who maintain it would find many who would agree with their idea.

The real difficulty here is, of course, that for most people the decision on this point will depend on the extent to which the impossibility of rational calculation would lead to a reduction of output in a centrally directed economy compared with that of a competitive system. Although in the opinion of the present writer it seems that careful study can leave no doubt about the enormous magnitude of that difference, it must be admitted that there is no simple way to prove how great that difference would be. The answer here cannot be derived from general considerations but will have to be based on a careful comparative study of the working of the two alternative systems and presupposes a much greater knowledge of the problems involved than can possibly be acquired in any other way but by a systematic study of economics.

Socialist Calculation Debate

The socialist calculation debate, sometimes known as the economic calculation debate, was a discourse on the subject of how a socialist economy would perform economic calculation given the absence of the law of value, money, financial prices for capital goods and private ownership of the means of production. More specifically, the debate was centered on the application of economic planning for the allocation of the means of production as a substitute for capital markets and whether or not such an arrangement would be superior to capitalism in terms of efficiency and productivity.

A central aspect of the debate concerned the role and scope of the law of value in a socialist economy. Although contributions to the question of economic coordination and calculation under socialism existed within the socialist movement prior to the 20th century, the phrase socialist calculation debate emerged in the 1920s beginning with Ludwig von Mises' critique of socialism. The historical debate was cast between the Austrian School represented by Mises and Friedrich Hayek, who argued against the feasibility of socialism; and between neoclassical and Marxian economists, most notably Cläre Tisch (as a forerunner), Oskar R. Lange, Abba P. Lerner, Fred M. Taylor, Henry Douglas Dickinson and Maurice Dobb, who took the position that socialism was both feasible and superior to capitalism. The debate was popularly viewed as a debate between proponents of capitalism and proponents of socialism, but in reality a significant portion of the debate was between socialists who held differing views regarding the utilization of markets and money in a socialist system and to what degree the law of value would continue to operate in a hypothetical socialist economy. Socialists generally held one of three major positions regarding the unit of calculation, including the view that money would continue to be the unit of calculation under socialism; that labor-time would be a unit of calculation; or that socialism would be based on calculation in natura or calculation performed in-kind.

Debate among socialists has existed since the emergence of the broader socialist movement between those advocating market socialism, centrally planned economies and decentralized planning. Recent contributions to the debate in the late 20th century and early 21st century involve proposals for market socialism and the use of information technology and distributed networking as a basis for decentralized economic planning.

Karl Marx and Friedrich Engels held a broad characterization of socialism, characterized by some form of public or common ownership of the means of production and worker self-management within economic enterprises and where production of economic value for profit would be replaced by an *ex ante* production directly for use which implied some form of economic planning and planned growth in place of the dynamic of capital accumulation and therefore the substitution of commodity-based production and market-based allocation of the factors of production with conscious planning.

Although Marx and Engels never elaborated on the specific institutions that would exist in socialism or on processes for conducting planning in a socialist system, their broad characterizations laid the foundation for the general conception of socialism as an economic system devoid of the law of value and law of accumulation and principally where the category of value was replaced by calculation in terms of natural or physical units so that resource allocation, production and distribution would be considered technical affairs to be undertaken by engineers and technical specialists.

An alternative view of socialism prefiguring the neoclassical models of market socialism consisted of conceptions of market socialism based on classical economic theory and Ricardian socialism, where markets were utilized to allocate capital goods among worker-owned cooperatives in a free-market economy. The key characteristics of this system involved direct worker ownership of the means of production through producer and consumer cooperatives and the achievement of genuinely free markets by removing the distorting effects of private property, inequality arising from private appropriation of profits and interest to a rentier class, regulatory capture and economic exploitation. This view was expounded by mutualism and was severely criticized by Marxists for failing to address the fundamental issues of capitalism involving instability arising from the operation of the law of value, crises caused by over-accumulation of capital and lack of conscious control over the surplus product. As a result, this perspective played little to no role during the socialist calculation debate in the early 20th century.

Early arguments against the utilization of central economic planning for a socialist economy were brought up by proponents of decentralized economic planning or market socialism, including Pierre-Joseph Proudhon, Peter Kropotkin and Leon Trotsky. In general, it was argued that centralized forms of economic planning that excluded participation by the workers involved in the industries would not be sufficient at capturing adequate amounts of information to coordinate an economy effectively while also undermining socialism and the concept of worker's self-management and democratic decision-making central to socialism. However, no detailed outlines for decentralized economic planning were proposed by these thinkers at this time.

In the early 20th century, Enrico Barone provided a comprehensive theoretical framework for a planned socialist economy. In his model, assuming perfect computation techniques, simultaneous equations relating inputs and outputs to ratios of equivalence would provide appropriate valuations in order to balance supply and demand.

Proposed Units for Accounting and Calculation

Debate on the use of Money

In contrast to Neurath, Karl Kautsky argued that money would have to be utilized in a socialist economy. Kautsky states the fundamental difference between socialism and capitalism is not the absence of money in the former; rather, the important difference is in the ability for money to become capital under capitalism. In a socialist economy, there would be no incentive to use money as financial capital, therefore money would have a slightly different role in socialism.

Labor-time Calculation

Jan Appel drafted a contribution to the Socialist calculation debate which then went through a discussion process before being published as *Foundations of Communist Production and Distribution* by the General Workers' Union of Germany in 1930. An English translation by Mike Baker was published in 1990.

Interwar Debate

Economic Calculation Problem

Ludwig von Mises believed that private ownership of the means of production was essential for a functional economy, arguing:

> "Every step that takes us away from private ownership of the means of production and from the use of money also takes us away from rational economics".

His argument against socialism was in response to Otto Neurath arguing for the feasibility of central planning. Mises argued that money and market-determined prices for the means of production were essential in order to make rational decisions regarding their allocation and use.

Criticism of the Calculation Problem

Bryan Caplan, an anarcho-capitalist economist, has criticized the version of the calculation problem advanced by Mises arguing that the lack of economic calculation makes socialism impossible and not merely inefficient. Caplan argues that socialism makes economic calculation impossible, yet that problem may not be severe enough to make socialism impossible "beyond the realm of possibility". For instance, he points out that the fall of the Soviet Union does not prove that calculation was the main issue there. He suggests that more likely the problems resulted from bad incentives arising out of the one-party political system and degree of power granted to the party-elite.

Knowledge Problem

> "If a universal mind existed, of the kind that projected itself into the scientific fancy of Laplace – a mind that could register simultaneously all the processes of nature and society, that could measure the dynamics of their motion, that could forecast the results of their inter-reactions – such a mind, of course, could a priori draw up a faultless and exhaustive economic plan, beginning with the number of acres of wheat down to the last button for a vest. The bureaucracy often imagines that just such a mind is at its disposal; that is why it so easily frees itself from the control of the market and of Soviet democracy. But, in reality, the bureaucracy errs frightfully in its estimate of its spiritual resources. The innumerable living participants in the economy, state and private, collective and individual, must serve notice of their needs and of their relative strength not only through the statistical determinations of plan commissions but by the direct pressure of supply and demand".

Proponents of decentralized economic planning have also criticized central economic planning. For example, Leon Trotsky believed that central planners, regardless of their intellectual capacity, operated without the input and participation of the millions of people who participate in the economy and so they would be unable to respond to local conditions quickly enough to effectively coordinate all economic activity.

Lange Model

Oskar Lange responded to Mises' assertion that socialism and social ownership of the means of production implied that rational calculation was impossible by outlining a model of socialism based on neoclassical economics. Lange conceded that calculations would have to be done in value terms rather than using purely natural or engineering criteria, but he asserted that these values could be attained without capital markets and private ownership of the means of production. In Lange's view, this model qualified as socialist because the means of production would be publicly owned with returns to the public enterprises accruing to society as a whole in a social dividend while worker's self-management could be introduced in the public enterprises.

This model came to be referred to as the Lange model. In this model, a Central Planning Board (CPB) would be responsible for setting prices through a trial-and-error approach to establish equilibrium prices, effectively running a Walrasian auction. Managers of the state-owned firms would be instructed to set prices to equal marginal cost (P=MC) so that economic equilibrium and Pareto efficiency would be achieved. The Lange model was expanded upon by Abba Lerner and became known as the Lange–Lerner theorem.

Paul Auerbach and Dimitris Sotiropoulos have criticized the Lange model for degrading the definition of socialism to a form of "capitalism without capital markets" attempting to replicate capitalism's efficiency achievements through economic planning. Auerbach and Sotiropoulos argue that Friedrich Hayek provided an analysis of the dynamics of capitalism that is more consistent with Marxian analysis because Hayek viewed finance as a fundamental aspect of capitalism and any move through collective ownership or policy reform to undermine the role of capital markets would threaten the integrity of the capitalist system. According to Auerbach and Sotiropoulos, Hayek gives an unexpected endorsement to socialism that is more sophisticated than Lange's superficial defense of socialism.

Contemporary Contributions

Networked Digital Feedback

Peter Joseph argues for a transition from fragmented economic data relay to fully integrated, sensor-based digital systems. Using an internet of sensory instruments to measure, track and feed back information, this can unify numerous disparate elements and systems, greatly advancing awareness and efficiency potentials.

In an economic context, this approach could relay and connect data regarding how best to manage resources, production processes, distribution, consumption, recycling, waste disposal behavior, consumer demand and so on. Such a process of networked economic feedback would work on the same principle as modern systems of inventory and distribution found in major commercial warehouses. Many companies today use a range of sensors and sophisticated tracking means to understand rates of demands, exactly what they have, where it is or where it may be moving and when it is gone. It is ultimately an issue of detail and scalability to extend this kind of awareness to all sectors of the economy, macro and micro.

Not only is price no longer needed to gain critical economic feedback, but the information price communicates is long delayed and incomplete in terms of economic measures required to dramatically increase efficiency. Mechanisms related networked digital feedback systems make it possible to efficiently monitor shifting consumer preference, demand, supply and labor value, virtually in real time. Moreover, it can also be used to observe other technical processes price cannot, such as shifts in production protocols, allocation, recycling means, and so on. As of February 2018, it is now possible to track trillions of economic interactions related to the supply chain and consumer behavior by way of sensors and digital relay as seen with the advent of Amazon Go.

Cybernetic Coordination

Paul Cockshott, Allin Cottrell, and Andy Pollack have proposed new forms of coordination based on modern information technology for non-market socialism. They argue that economic planning in terms of physical units without any reference to money or prices is computationally tractable given the high-performance computers available for particle physics and weather forecasting. Cybernetic planning would involve an *a priori* simulation of the equilibration process that idealized markets are intended to achieve.

Participatory Economics

Proposals for decentralized economic planning emerged in the late 20th century in the form of participatory economics and negotiated coordination.

Decentralized Pricing without Markets

David McMullen argues that social ownership of the means of production and the absence of markets for them is fully compatible with a decentralized price system. In a post-capitalist society, transactions between enterprises would entail transfers of social property between custodians rather than an exchange of ownership. Individuals would be motivated by the satisfaction from work and the desire to contribute to good economic outcomes rather than material reward. Bids and offer prices would aim to minimize costs and ensure that output is guided by expected final demand for private and collective consumption. Enterprises and startups would receive their investment funding from project assessment agencies. The required change in human behavior would take a number generations and would have to overcome considerable resistance. However, McMullen believes that economic and cultural development increasingly favors the transition.

Market Socialism

James Yunker argues that public ownership of the means of production can be achieved the same way private ownership is achieved in modern capitalism through the shareholder system that separates management from ownership. Yunker posits that social ownership can be achieved by having a public body, designated the Bureau of Public Ownership (BPO), owning the shares of publicly listed firms without affecting market-based allocation of capital inputs. Yunker termed this model pragmatic market socialism and argued that it would be at least as efficient as modern-day capitalism while providing superior social outcomes as public ownership of large and established enterprises would enable profits to be distributed among the entire population rather than going largely to a class of inheriting rentiers.

Mechanism Design

Beginning in the 1970s, new insights into the socialist calculation debate emerged from mechanism design theory. According to mechanism design theorists, the debate between Hayek and Lange became a stalemate that lasted for forty years because neither side was speaking the same language as the other, partially because the appropriate language for discussing socialist calculation had not yet been invented. According to these theorists, what was needed was a better understanding of the informational problems that prevent coordination between people. By fusing game theory with information economics, mechanism design provided the language and framework in which both socialists and advocates of capitalism could compare the merits of their arguments. As Palda writes in his summary of the contributions of mechanism design to the socialist calculation debate, "it seemed that socialism and capitalism were good at different things. Socialism suffered from cheating, or 'moral hazard', more than capitalism because it did not allow company managers to own shares in their own companies. The flip side of the cheating problem in socialism is the lying or 'adverse selection' problem in capitalism. If potential firm managers are either good or bad, but telling them apart is difficult, bad prospects will lie to become a part of the firm".

Relation to Neoclassical Economics

In his book Whither Socialism?, Joseph Stiglitz criticized models of market socialism from the era of the socialist calculation debate in the 1930s as part of a more general criticism of neoclassical general equilibrium theory, proposing that market models be augmented with insights from information economics. Alec Nove and Janos Kornai held similar positions regarding economic equilibrium. Both Nove and Kornai argued that because perfect equilibrium does not exist, a comprehensive economic plan for production cannot be formulated, making planning ineffective just as real-world market economies do not conform to the hypothetical state of perfect competition. In his book *The Economics of Feasible Socialism*, Nove also outlined a solution involving a socialist economy consisting of a mixture of macro-economic planning with market-based coordination for enterprises where large industries would be publicly owned and small- to medium-sized concerns would be organized as cooperatively owned enterprises.

Calculation in Kind

Calculation in kind or calculation in-natura is a way of valuating resources and a system of accounting that uses disaggregated physical magnitudes as opposed to a common unit of calculation. As the basis for a socialist economy it was proposed to replace money and financial calculation. Calculation in kind would value each commodity based only on its use value, for purposes of economic accounting. By contrast, in money-based economies, a commodity's value includes an exchange value.

Calculation in kind would quantify the utility of an object *directly* without recourse to a general unit of calculation. This differs from other proposed methods of socialist calculation, such as simultaneous equations, Taylor-Lange accounting prices, and the use of labor time as a measure of cost.

Calculation in kind was strongly advocated by the positivist philosopher and political economist Otto Neurath when employed by the Bavarian Soviet Republic. This led to a discussion in the early 1920s, in which much of the discussion about socialism centered on whether economic planning should be based on physical quantities or monetary accounting. Neurath was the most forceful advocate of *physical planning* (economic planning using calculation-in-kind) in contrast to market socialist neoclassical economists who advocated use of notional prices computed by solving simultaneous equations. Austrian school critics of socialism, particularly Ludwig von Mises, based his critique of socialism on the calculation problem.

Proponents of in-kind calculation argue that the use of a common medium like money distorts information about the utility of an object. Socialists in favor of calculation in kind argued that, in a system of in-kind calculation, waste associated with the monetary system would be eliminated, and in particular objects would no longer be desired for functionally useless purposes like resale and speculation - they would only be desired for their use-value.

Decentralized Planning

A decentralized-planned economy or decentrally-planned economy (occasionally called horizontally-planned economy due to its horizontalism) is a type of planned economy in which the investment and allocation of consumer and capital goods is explicated accordingly to an economy-wide plan built and operatively coordinated through a distributed network of disparate economic agents or even production units itself. Decentralized planning is usually held in contrast to centralized planning, in particular the Soviet Union's command economy, where economic information is aggregated and used to formulate a plan for production, investment and resource allocation by a single central authority. Decentralized planning can take shape both in the context of a mixed economy as well as in a post-capitalist economic system.

This form of economic planning implies some process of democratic and participatory decision-making within the economy and within firms itself in the form of industrial democracy. Computer-based forms of democratic economic planning and coordination between economic enterprises have also been proposed by various computer scientists and radical economists. Proponents present decentralized and participatory economic planning as an alternative to market socialism for a post-capitalist society.

Decentralized-planning has been proposed as a basis for socialism and has been variously advocated by democratic socialists, council communists and anarchists who advocate a non-market form of socialism, in total rejection of Soviet-type central economic planning. Some writers such as Robin Cox have argued that decentralized planning allows for a spontaneously self-regulating system of stock control (relying solely on calculation in kind) to come about and that in turn decisively overcomes the objections raised by the economic calculation argument that any large scale economy must necessarily resort to a system of market prices.

Models

Cybernetics

The use of computers to coordinate production in an optimal fashion has been variously proposed for socialist economies. The Polish economist Oskar Lange argued that the computer is more efficient than the market process at solving the multitude of simultaneous equations required for allocating economic inputs efficiently (either in terms of physical quantities or monetary prices).

The 1970 Chilean distributed decision support system Project Cybersyn was pioneered by Salvador Allende's socialist government in an attempt to move towards a decentralised planned economy with the experimental viable system model of computed organisational structure of autonomous operative units though an algedonic feedbacwwk setting and bottom-up participative decision-making by the Cyberfolk component.

Negotiated Coordination

Economist Pat Devine has created a model of decentralized economic planning called "negotiated coordination" which is based upon social ownership of the means of production by those affected by the use of the assets involved, with the allocation of consumer and capital goods made through a participatory form of decision-making by those at the most localized level of production. Moreover, organizations that utilize modularity in their production processes may distribute problem solving and decision making .

Participatory Planning

The planning structure of a decentralized planned economy is generally based on a consumers council and producer council (or jointly, a distributive cooperative) which is sometimes called a consumers' cooperative. Producers and consumers, or their representatives, negotiate the quality and quantity of what is to be produced. This structure is central to participatory economics, guild socialism and economic theories related to anarchism.

Political Advocacy

Decentralized planning has been a feature of socialist and anarchist economics. Variations of decentralized planning include participatory economics, economic democracy and industrial democracy and have been promoted by various political groups, most notably libertarian socialists, guild socialists, libertarian Marxists, Trotskyists, anarchists and democratic socialists.

During the Spanish Revolution, some areas where anarchist and libertarian socialist influence through the CNT and UGT was extensive, particularly rural regions, were run on the basis of decentralized planning resembling the principles laid out by anarcho-syndicalist Diego Abad de Santillan in the book *After the Revolution*.

Labor-time Calculation

Labor-time calculation is a method of economic calculation that uses labor time as the basic unit of accounting and valuation. This method of calculation was advocated by the economists Otto Bauer, Helene Bauer and Otto Leichter de as an alternative to calculation in kind for a socialist economy. Otto Leichter criticized in-kind calculation on the basis that rational accounting required a general unit for comparing costs of heterogeneous goods.

The basis for labor-time calculation is found in Karl Marx's analysis of value in capitalism. However, Marx was vehemently opposed to any proposal for using labor-time as the basis for socialist calculation because his concept of socially necessary labor time was a conceptual framework for understanding and analyzing value in capitalism. In Marx's view socialism would operate according to its own economic "laws of motion" distinct from those of capitalism.

Labour Voucher

Labour vouchers (also known as labour cheques, labour certificates and personal credit) are a device proposed to govern demand for goods in some models of socialism and to replace some of the tasks performed by currency under capitalism.

Unlike money, vouchers cannot circulate and are not transferable between people. They are also not exchangeable for any means of production, hence they are not transmutable into capital. Once a purchase is made, the labour vouchers are either destroyed or must be re-earned through labour. With such a system in place, monetary theft would become impossible.

Such a system is proposed by many as a replacement for traditional money while retaining a system of remuneration for work done. It is also a way of ensuring that there is no way to make money out of money as in a capitalist market economy. Additionally, the only kind of market that could exist in an economy operating through the use of labour vouchers would be an artificial market (market) for mostly non-productive goods and services. As with the dissolution of money, capital markets could no longer exist and labour markets would also likely cease to exist with the abolition of wage labor which would by necessity occur with the adoption of vouchers.

Author and activist Michael Albert and economist Robin Hahnel have proposed a similar system of remuneration in their economic system of participatory economics (parecon). A difference is that in parecon credits are generally awarded based on both the time spent working and the amount of effort and sacrifice spent during labour, rather than simple contribution. Some later advocates of participism and parecon have also proposed awarding more based on job difficulty or danger. In contrast to the physical note or cheque format used for labour vouchers in the past, parecon credits are proposed as being entirely digital in keeping with advances with technology and are stored in electronic accounts and usable through cards similar to current day debit cards.

Labour vouchers were first proposed in the 1820s by Josiah Warren and Robert Owen. Two early attempts at implementing labour vouchers (called labour notes at the time by their proponents) were made by both following their experiences attempting to establish a utopian community at New Harmony, Indiana in which currency was prohibited.

In 1827, Warren established the Cincinnati Time Store where goods could be purchased with labor vouchers representing an agreement to perform labor. However, he folded the store in 1830 in order to devote his effort to establishing communities that implemented his principles of labour-based prices.

Beginning in 1832, Owen and his followers attempted to implement labour notes in London and Glasgow by establishing marketplaces and banks that accepted them.

The followers of Owen stood for a society of co-operative communities. Each community would own its own means of production and each member of a community would work to produce what had been agreed was needed and in return would be issued with a labour voucher certifying for how many hours he or she had worked. A person could then use this labour voucher to obtain from the community's stock of consumer goods any product or products which had taken the same number of hours to produce.

Owen believed that this co-operative commonwealth could begin to be introduced under capitalism and in the first half of the 1830s some of his followers established labour bazaars on a similar principle in which workers brought the products of their labour to the bazaar and received in exchange a labour voucher that entitled them to take from the bazaar any item or items which had taken the same time to produce after taking into account the costs of the raw materials. These bazaars were ultimately failures, but the idea of labour vouchers appeared in substantially similar forms in France in the writings of Pierre-Joseph Proudhon.

Although he disagreed with the manner in which they were implemented by Owen, they were later advocated by Karl Marx as a way of dealing with immediate and temporary shortages upon the establishment of socialism. Marx explained that this would be necessary since socialism emerges from capitalism and would be "stamped with its birthmarks". In Marx's proposal, an early socialist society would reward its citizens according to the amount of labour they contribute to society. In the *Critique of the Gotha Programme*, Marx said:

> "The individual producer receives back from society—after the deductions have been made—exactly what he gives to it. What he has given to it is his individual quantum of labour. For example, the social working day consists of the sum of the individual hours of work; the individual labour time of the individual producer is the part of the social working day contributed by him, his share in it. He receives a certificate from society that he has furnished such-and-such an amount of labour (after deducting his labour for the common funds); and with this certificate, he draws from the social stock of means of consumption as much as the same amount of labour cost. The same amount of labor which he has given to society in one form, he receives back in another".

However, Marx essentially refused the idea in the *Poverty of Philosophy*, especially within the capitalism. Marx stated that the time in itself separated from other people's time is not suitable to measure the value of work. The value "is constituted, not by the time needed to produce it by itself, but in relation to the quota of each and every other product which can be created at the same time". Marx opinion was that the introduction of labour voucher would create a lazy society and economy because there will not be concurrency between the employers and employees, so nobody could tell what is the optimal (minimal) time which needs to produce something. Generally, any working time doesn't equal to any other working time. Moreover what if "Peter" works 12 hours per day, meanwhile "Paul" works only 6 hours. This means that "Peter" worked 6 unnecessary hours and his labour vouchers worth for nothing as regards this +6 hours, not to mention other factors of the work. To summarize Marx's opinion in the *Poverty of Philosophy*, the labour voucher is not suitable to create a new socialist society. The theory of Proudhon and other's is nothing more than a utopian apology of the existing capitalist system. By Friedrich Engels, Proudhon himself tried to introduce the labour voucher system in 1849, but his attempt collapsed soon. Marx was adamant in saying that labour vouchers were not a form of money as they cannot circulate—a problem he pointed out with Owen's system of labour-time notes.

After the October Revolution, the Bolsheviks were forced to let the direct production-exchange and gave valueless vouchers to the peasantry for the grain and the foodstuff which were confiscated by brutal force, but this method led to local rebellions and after all to the civil war. Vladimir Lenin never suggested introducing the labour voucher system in the industrial areas. No other socialist countries used later the labour voucher system.

During the Great Depression, European communities implemented local currencies with varying success. The aptly-named economist Sir Leo Chiozza Money advocated for a similar monetary scheme in his 1934 book *Product Money* (Methuen) with notes or certificates being issued for productive work and destroyed once exchanged for consumption goods. In Nazi Germany, Adolf Hitler (Hjalmar Schacht finance-minister and banker) applied a kind of labour-voucher named MEFO-bond, whose aim was to hide the rearmament program's expenditures before the Western world as the big trusts did not pay by money-transfer to each other, but bought MEFO bonds from the state and changed these bonds in closed circuit. More modern implementations as time-based currencies were implemented in the United States starting in the 1970s.

Systems that Advocate Labour Vouchers

The following political and economic systems propose the adoption of labour vouchers (in some form or another) either permanently or as a temporary means of remuneration during a transitional stage between a monetary economy and a completely moneyless economy based on free association.

- Owenism.
- Mutualism.
- Collectivist anarchism.
- DeLeonism.
- Participism.
- Inclusive Democracy.

Inclusive Democracy is unique in proposing two kinds of vouchers. Basic vouchers issued to each citizen according to need are used for essential goods and services such as health care while non-basic vouchers awarded to each worker for labor contributed are used to pay for non-essential commercial goods and services.

Criticisms

Capitalists—whether statist, minarchist, or anarcho-capitalist—generally oppose labour vouchers as they are not money and thus claim an economy using them could not set prices according to marginal utility and would theoretically have to rely on the labour theory of value, which adherents of the subjective theory of value generally see as inflexible and restricting economic freedom of choice for the consumer. Some proposed systems which advocate labour vouchers, namely participism, reject the labour theory of value.

The system has also been criticized by many libertarian socialists, particularly anarcho-communists, who propose abolishing all remuneration and prices and advocate instead a gift economy with the value determined by calculation in kind. In criticizing collectivist anarchism's retaining of labour vouchers and cheques, Peter Kropotkin said:

> "For after having proclaimed the abolition of private property, and the possession in common of all means of production, how can they uphold the wages system in any form? It is, nevertheless, what collectivists are doing when they recommend labour-cheques".

The World Socialist Movement has argued against using labour vouchers as either a permanent or a temporary system while transitioning to their desired anarcho-communist economy based on free access. They claim that seeing as most of the occupations that currently exist under capitalism will no longer exist, scarcity would no longer be an issue. They also state:

> "Labour vouchers would tend to maintain the idea that our human worth is determined by how much or how many goods we can own (or produce). Labour vouchers imply that a very huge administrative organisation must police who takes the goods produced by society. In other words, there must be people who spend their time ensuring that other people do not take things without paying for them. That is normal in a profit-oriented society, but a waste of human labour in socialism".

References

- Socialist-calculation: mises.org, Retrieved 24 August, 2020
- Huerta de Soto, Jesús (2010). Socialism, Economic Calculation and Entrepreneurship. Edward Elgar Publishing. pp. 103–104. ISBN 978-1-84980-065-5
- Medina, Eden (2006). "Designing Freedom, Regulating a Nation: Socialist Cybernetics in Allende's Chile". J. Lat. Am. Stud. Cambridge University Press (38): 571–606. doi:10.1017/S0022216X06001179
- Howell, Jerry; Chmielewski, Tom (December 1, 2009). The Complete Idiot's Guide to Barter and Trade Exchanges: Get the Things Your Business Needs Without Spending a Dime (Kindle ed.). p. 46. ISBN 9781101152010

PERMISSIONS

All chapters in this book are published with permission under the Creative Commons Attribution Share Alike License or equivalent. Every chapter published in this book has been scrutinized by our experts. Their significance has been extensively debated. The topics covered herein carry significant information for a comprehensive understanding. They may even be implemented as practical applications or may be referred to as a beginning point for further studies.

We would like to thank the editorial team for lending their expertise to make the book truly unique. They have played a crucial role in the development of this book. Without their invaluable contributions this book wouldn't have been possible. They have made vital efforts to compile up to date information on the varied aspects of this subject to make this book a valuable addition to the collection of many professionals and students.

This book was conceptualized with the vision of imparting up-to-date and integrated information in this field. To ensure the same, a matchless editorial board was set up. Every individual on the board went through rigorous rounds of assessment to prove their worth. After which they invested a large part of their time researching and compiling the most relevant data for our readers.

The editorial board has been involved in producing this book since its inception. They have spent rigorous hours researching and exploring the diverse topics which have resulted in the successful publishing of this book. They have passed on their knowledge of decades through this book. To expedite this challenging task, the publisher supported the team at every step. A small team of assistant editors was also appointed to further simplify the editing procedure and attain best results for the readers.

Apart from the editorial board, the designing team has also invested a significant amount of their time in understanding the subject and creating the most relevant covers. They scrutinized every image to scout for the most suitable representation of the subject and create an appropriate cover for the book.

The publishing team has been an ardent support to the editorial, designing and production team. Their endless efforts to recruit the best for this project, has resulted in the accomplishment of this book. They are a veteran in the field of academics and their pool of knowledge is as vast as their experience in printing. Their expertise and guidance has proved useful at every step. Their uncompromising quality standards have made this book an exceptional effort. Their encouragement from time to time has been an inspiration for everyone.

The publisher and the editorial board hope that this book will prove to be a valuable piece of knowledge for students, practitioners and scholars across the globe.

INDEX

CPSIA information can be obtained
at www.ICGtesting.com
Printed in the USA
LVHW061114030222
710136LV00005B/125

9 781639 875580